Conversations
before the end of time

Suzi Gablik

Conversations

before the end of time

T&H THAMES AND HUDSON

First published in the United States of America in hardcover in 1995 by Thames and Hudson Inc., 500 Fifth Avenue, New York, New York, 10110

First published in Great Britain in 1995 by Thames and Hudson Ltd, London

Library of Congress Catalog Card Number 95-60205

British Library Cataloguing-in-Publication Data
A catalogue record for this book is available
from the British Library

ISBN 0-500-01673-9

Designed by Beth Tondreau Design

Printed and bound in the United States of America

The assertion that technological society is something higher than what came before, and that it is bound to bring us a better world, has lately fallen open to grave doubts. The Industrial Revolution is about a century old, and we have had ample time to draw a few conclusions about how it is going. It is not too soon to observe that this revolution may not be living up to its advertising . . . [and is] creating terrible and possibly catastrophic impacts on the earth.

> Jerry Mander
> *In the Absence of the Sacred*

Has the catastrophe already happened? For certain animal and vegetable species it is by now too late, and the fatal deterioration of certain areas is already irreversible.

Beyond partial measures, justified though they may be, a genuine ecological recovery can succeed only through a break with the general trends. . . . To restore the environment means working at a loss, at least in terms of the market. It means rejecting the law of profit. . . . It would mean rejecting the "general line" of modernity-world for the sake of the long-term general interests of the human race. Are we ready for this major break?

Jean Chesneaux
Brave Modern World

We've been very alienated from our resources, but our time of grace is over. The idea that technology is able to buy us out of our problems is an illusion. We are going to have to make vast changes in our consciousness and behavioral patterns, because if we don't, we won't be here.

Newton Harrison
Art Journal

Civilizations, and the paradigms they were based on, are disintegrating all over the earth, all at once. And the very technology we cling to increases the disintegration, so it's another vicious circle, nothing can stop it. . . .

Collectively, we're sharing the experience of the end of Western civilization—a great and tragic moment. It's tragic not because Western civilization is better than other civilizations, but because there's a ground note of tragedy when anything passes from the world forever.

Michael Ventura
We've Had a Hundred Years of Psychotherapy—And the World's Getting Worse

There have, of course, always been shifts and discontinuities in history. . . . This generation . . . may be living in civilization's terminal culture. . . . The regime of technological culture is terminal in that it is lethal to the ecology on which it depends. . . . Our culture disseminates a view that life without industrial economy is virtually impossible. . . . To claim there is another way, to claim that another way is *required,* assaults some of the core beliefs that define, for good or ill, who we are as a people.

> Christopher Manes
> *Green Rage*

What is it about human beings in Western culture that permits us to pursue activities that threaten our very survival? What is it that is so important to us that we are apparently willing to destroy the planet—and ultimately ourselves—to get it? Why do we persist in these practices even after we realize their self-defeating futility? What does this tell us about our society and our own nature? What is our true nature? What matters most deeply to us? Is our society in accord with our true nature and deepest values?

> William Keepin
> *ReVision Magazine*

This devil's dance is dedicated to
Fern and Laurie

Contents

Introduction • 15

What Is Art For? • 37
ELLEN DISSANAYAKE

Doin' Dirt Time • 56
RACHEL DUTTON AND ROB OLDS

Making Art About Centipedes • 84
CHRISTOPHER MANES

No Art in the Lifeboats • 106
HILTON KRAMER

Ten Thousand Artists,
Not One Master • 133
SATISH KUMAR

Creating the Space for a Miracle • 155
DAVID PLANTE

When You're Healed,
Send Me a Postcard • 176
JAMES HILLMAN

You Don't Have to Have a Penis
to Be a Genius • 202
GUERRILLA GIRLS

Viewing the World as Process • 226
CAROLYN MERCHANT

Breaking Out of the White Cube • 247
RICHARD SHUSTERMAN

Searching For the Essence of Art • 266
ARTHUR C. DANTO

Removing the Frame • 290
MARY JANE JACOB

*Two Undiscovered Aborigines Dancing
on the Wound of History* • 312
COCO FUSCO

A Few Beautifully Made Things • 334
THEODORE ROSZAK

Our Students Need the City • 355
CAROL BECKER

The Liminal Zones of Soul • 381
THOMAS MOORE

The Aesthetics of Everyday Life • 410
BARBARA KIRSHENBLATT-GIMBLETT

*Adrift on the Fickle Seas
of the Art World* • 434
LAURIE ZUCKERMAN

A Farewell to Modernism • 453
LEO CASTELLI

Selected Bibliography • 473

Introduction

I never really intended to write this book. It wasn't
something premeditated that ripened like a Stilton
cheese in the mind for a necessary period of time. Rather,
it was a case of seeing synchronicity everywhere, so that
the conversations included here, done over several years,
are actually a record of my own life, and in many ways are
the continuation of a learning process that took root in my
previous book, *The Reenchantment of Art*.

Many people over the years have asked me what caused my thinking to change—how I came to abandon the obligatory modernist culture and principles of art in which I had been schooled. What had given me the right to challenge so much cultural authority?

First, let me say that the very act of writing a book has always been, for me, a way of testing my values, principles and beliefs; and following where the energy takes me can also be a process involving my own transformation. My sense of art was radically changed, for instance, by writing *The Reenchantment of Art,* an undertaking that led me to question the very roots of modern aesthetic structure: its vision-centered concepts, its passive, spectatorial orientation, and the critical discourse that goes with it. That book represented my own epistemological "break" with the paradigm of vision and the disembodied eye as the axiomatic basis for artistic practice. It also represented my own search for alternatives to viewing the self as autonomous. Like James Hillman, that "renegade warrior of archetypal psychology," I entertain "some severe doubts" about the individualistic ontology that is the silent faith of both psychotherapy and art.

As my sense of art slowly transformed from a visual language of forms into something more interactive and dialectical in nature, I began to see how the model of the lone genius struggling against society, which has been the philosophical basis for Western culture, has deprived art of its astonishing potential to build community through empathic social interaction. Embedded in modernism is a subtle and far-reaching message concerning the loneliness and isolation of the self, whereas the participatory and dialogical practices I had been writing about predispose one to step outside that frame of reference and invite others into the process. This line of thinking caused me to move away from romanticism and modernism, and to consider instead the possibility of a "connective" aesthetics, based in vigorously active and impassioned engagement that would restore art's connectedness with the world after a century of vision-oriented, purist ideals. Once the roar of individualistic preoccupation with self began to subside in my own consciousness, however, the irresistible question was posed: wasn't there some way to embody these principles in my own work? Couldn't writing itself happen in such a way that it would be participatory and interactive, and find itself in the relationship between self and other?

There is no question that *The Reenchantment of Art* had an active agenda: it was a call to arms on behalf of a socially and environmentally engaged artistic practice. But the people who just wanted to make or enjoy art, unencumbered by that kind of intense moral purpose, felt undermined, because it tampered with the way they see their task—and they became resistant. Had I been naive, then, to think that I was merely articulating a process which was at that point about to emerge, and putting a template on events that were already beginning to happen? In sensing the changes in the atmosphere and identifying the issues and conflicts, was I not just being a witness to the end of modernism and its idea of history, and mapping out possibilities for an alternative agenda in a way that would be meaningful for others? What *is* the function of the critic, I wondered? To frame a philosophy, have a vision, become morally engaged and be an influential force for change? Or is the critic's role merely to report on what's already out there? Much later, when I knew I would be talking with the critic Arthur C. Danto for this book, I was eager to probe him on this question of critics having an agenda. But Danto, it turns out, is someone who plainly doesn't have one, and doesn't want to have one. I couldn't help wondering if that saved a lot of anguish and made life easier. I also talked with Richard Shusterman, another philosopher-critic and a colleague of Danto's, who claims that criticism has a moral responsibility in the establishment of new cultural paradigms, and who finds Danto's work deficient because of his reticence to engage in this task. Meanwhile, for me, the issue had taken on the dimensions of a personal koan: how to maintain a vigorous point of view without negating the existence of others, or becoming so identified with that position that one invited in the dogs. Active agendas cause a lot of teeth-gnashing because they cross the fatal line into advocacy. But I knew I was not called, myself, to just stroll around and look at things, revealing after long contemplation the more elusive aspects of what I had seen. Was it possible to have an embodied stance, then, and not be exclusionary?

The question haunted me. It was like a riddle I couldn't answer, a code I couldn't crack—at least, not with the tools I already had in place. I knew that if I could somehow solve it, the resolution would reduce the pain and confusion I now felt over my role. I wondered how I could step directly into the paradox and dance with it, so that it might become a catalyst for creativity and growth.

They say that when the student is ready, the teacher will appear. Mine showed up in the form of a book called *The Leader as Martial Artist,* by Arnold Mindell, a process-oriented therapist who lectures internationally on conflict resolution. But I was not prepared for the directness of the answer that came—as if a voice were speaking to me live from its pages—which said: "Your position, albeit a minority one, is a disturbing one for others. It expresses the suffering in the whole field, and you should understand that many will not be able to listen. . . . You are not alone in your feelings, so taking too much of the conflict personally will not be useful for you or the group." What Mindell helped me to understand was that once you upset and threaten belief systems or goals, and disturb the web of which you are a part, you are likely to be challenged, opposed or attacked. According to Mindell, the attacks should not be seen as personal attacks that make you bleed; rather they are the voice of history asking you to expand yourself to include others. One position, one voice, lacks dialectical resonance. When you collaborate, you are not permanently identified with one position. When you practice taking all the positions and listening to all the sides, you help the field to balance its global parts: the new parts, the older ones they are trying to replace, and the interaction between the old and the new. By helping the field to process its edges and incongruities, you mediate between the various parts and enable others to do the same.

Although I did not yet fully grasp the profound implications of Mindell's philosophy for my own future work, I was beginning to understand how the shared experience of dialogue allows one to have and maintain one's own point of view, while at the same time trying to understand and include another's. I began to see that what was needed was not a monologue—my voice making contemporary art debates intelligible to a broad audience—but a dialogue in which I did not necessarily have a program of my own, but would simply create an empty space for whatever specific process was trying to happen.

Meanwhile, I kept finding myself thrown together on the lecture circuit with many unusual and interesting people, one of whom was James Hillman. When his book *We've Had a Hundred Years of Psychotherapy—And the World's Getting Worse* came out, it was in the form of a series of face-to-face conversations with Los Angeles journalist Michael Ventura. In animated exchanges, the two men rake the current practice of psychotherapy over the coals for its narcissistic concern with individual souls and destinies at a time when the world soul, as Hillman says, "is sinking like an overloaded garbage barge." Hillman claims that therapy has contributed to the devastating plight of the world by focusing only upon inner life and pointing always "away from the world and toward the recesses of the chest." Individual pain is magnified, while the overwhelming reality of politics and the environment —the suffering of oceans and rivers, of cities and forests —is ignored. "If the fish turn belly up," Hillman declares, "that is far more important to what is happening to my soul than what my mother did to me when I was four."

For me, their book was a model of relatedness and

interdependence, a true interpenetration of souls. Rather than being streamlined arguments, their discussions were intimate and provocative commentaries on the fate of our society and its collective future that managed to avoid falling into the cold, impersonal and left-brained kind of intellectualism associated with more theoretical forms of discourse. "How do you live in a time of decline," Hillman asks Ventura in the book, "and what role does therapy have in a time of decline?" Hardly realizing it, in my mind I was already turning the question around: how do you live in a time of decline, and what role does art have in such a time?

Just at that moment, my old friend Ellen Dissanayake came to visit me, in the summer of 1992. Still caught up in the spirit of Hillman and Ventura, and wanting to try my hand, I suggested to her that we tape a conversation together about the ideas in her book *Homo Aestheticus,* which had recently been published. My thought then was to experiment a bit with the conversational form, and maybe to publish the result somewhere in lieu of a review. But like someone making a painting whose colors run off the canvas, I did not anticipate that what I was really signing up for was to write another book.

"There are many ways to allow processes to unfold," Mindell writes, "but perhaps the most essential way is to *stay with the edge,* with awareness of the group's forbidden communication. . . . Be willing to sit with the emerging difficulties as the differing sides connect and communicate." Although I did not approach the individuals who converse with me here with a specific agenda or story in mind, the truth is that, deep down, I *was* tracking the forbidden edge of something—an almost unspeakable topic that surfaces clearly during the first conversation with Dissanayake, when she says: "I think the important thing is to realize that we can't go on living the way that we are." From her ethnobiological perspective, the human species are really hunter-gatherers who have been thrust into a kind of supermechanistic, hypermediated environment that doesn't fit our nature, because we're not biologically programmed to live that way. Certainly as we continue to ignore the pressing ecological realities around us, it begins to look as if we may be a maladaptive species, living in a terminal culture, unless we can change.

Even though I believe we have already entered a time when we are likely to have to live through the devastating consequences of what capitalist exploitation and technology have done to the natural world, I was still unprepared for the next thing that happened. The second conversation in this book loomed into view on its own, uninvited, when I unexpectedly received a letter in the mail that gave me a shock. The memory of that moment remains: it was as if a rocket catapulted into my life. The letter came from an artist about whom I had written previously in *The Reenchantment of Art,* Rachel Dutton, and her husband, Rob Olds, who is also an artist. It stated that they had destroyed, or were simply giving away, all their work, and were abandoning their careers as artists, in order to study ancient survival skills with a well-known tracker called Tom Brown, Jr. "Time is running out," the letter said. "An immense spiritual crisis, brought on by hundreds of years of trying to live apart from the earth, is coming to a head. The frail separatist structures of civilization are crumbling from within. We felt we no longer had the luxury of waiting for the slow progress of images through galleries or museums."

Something about that letter set my teeth on edge. Maybe it was just raw fear, combined with my sense, deep down, that the environmental crisis *is* going to require radical changes not only in public policy but in individual behavior as well. It certainly seems as if an unquestioned trust in science and technology to come up with all the answers, and to solve all our problems, has eclipsed industrial society's ability to stand apart from itself and see the wider perspective of what is really happening to our world. But the Draconian view these artists were presenting seemed inordinately harsh, and I didn't know how to respond. "When Rob was living in South Central Los Angeles," the letter continued, "he saw visions of this beautiful world exploding. Some of his figures express fear, others are so blind that an *Angel* bursting into flames passes them like dust in the road. And since then, this world has gotten worse."

"Most artists," I wrote back, "will shrink from the idea of destroying their work, or just giving it away. Even more unthinkable is ceasing to make art at all. What will you say to them?" In one penetrating moment, as if suddenly aware of its own limitless depth, the question transformed itself into the need to create this book, which would let others unfold and say whatever they needed to say. It would be the product of many people's minds, people for whom the place of art in contemporary society is a vital concern, who would talk about how they personally assess and evaluate these issues. We would sit together in all our vulnerable humanity and consider the earth's diminished radiance—and maybe someone would help me make sense of why it is that humans are so destructive of the environment.

"This is part of what I consider dialogue—for people to realize what is on each other's minds without coming to any conclusions or judgments. In a dialogue we have to sort of weigh the question a little, ponder it a little, feel it out. You become more familiar with how thought works." Thus writes David Bohm, a theoretical physicist who first established his reputation working on the Manhattan Project with J. Robert Oppenheimer, in his seminal essay, "On Dialogue." During the final years of his life, Bohm began to develop his radical ideas around the principle of dialogue, because he believed that in dialogue, people give serious consideration to views that may differ substantially from their own, and they are willing to hold many conflicting possibilities in their minds simultaneously. "Then everybody is sensitive to all the nuances going around and not merely to what is happening in his own mind," Bohm states. We need to listen to each other and open up to all the different opinions so that the whole structure of defensiveness and attack can collapse and change to one of participation and sharing. This sharing of consciousness is absolutely necessary, Bohm felt, for society to survive. Otherwise it will fall apart.

If certain segments of the community are not heard within these pages, it is only because in creating a space for individual opinions to come together, I did not arbitrarily draw up a shopping list of people to talk with. Obviously the size of the book could have been tripled with ease, and many more diverse points of view might have been included, but I made the choice, when I began to put the book together, to include only those individuals who were, in some way or another, on my path. Because of this, something has taken place here, I think, that stands for more than just an episodic collection, or anthology, of separate and diverse conversations. Standing in reciprocal relationship with the others, each conversation gains in resonance when read in the light of its companions: they interact with, and modify, each other. And although no single story line dominates, they all hang together and should be read in their proper sequence, like the chapters of a novel.

The discourse encountered here ranges over many fields, and encompasses the thinking of individuals both inside and outside of the art world. Some of these people share my sense of urgency with regard to the perils now facing the earth, but others do not. Christopher Manes, the third person I spoke with, who is the author of a book on the radical environmental movement, believes that industrial society's principle of endless growth, and its vision of the earth as an assemblage of interchangeable resources to be sold to the highest bidder, are leading humanity to ecocide. Theodore Roszak, a proponent of the new "ecopsychology," claims that environmental problems have become the psychopathology of everyday life for the contemporary world, while Hilton Kramer, a well-known art critic, feels that we're not as doomed as we are being invited to believe, and that our civilization is not incompatible with the long-term survival of the planet. Walking the middle road is environmental historian Carolyn Merchant, who argues that science and technology, in tandem with a world view based on the image of a machine, have produced an ethics of domination, manipulation and control with respect to the natural world, which causes us to "read" nature in terms of our own economic projects for it. Nevertheless, one may hope "that a sustainable global environment, society and ethic will emerge in the twenty-first century," according to Merchant.

If the apocalyptic strain in my own thinking was in some ways the trigger, the starting point from which this book was launched, it was not necessarily the place where it ended up. When conversing with people, frequently I found myself in the role of merely feeding the meter—creating a spaciousness through listening, and relying on something new to emerge out of the moment. Inevitably, it did. Gradually the process itself led me to still another difficult edge, and I found myself peering down into the yawning chasm of the contemporary culture war: all-encompassing, wild, and threatening to intrude into the insular world of encapsulated aesthetics.

The 1993 Biennial Exhibition at the Whitney Museum of American Art—the first multicultural and political Biennial in which racial and ethnic minorities were given free reign to speak up for themselves—became, as I sifted through the tensions in the field and reached out into the unknown in an open and unstructured way, the truly compelling character of my story. The Biennial was a landmark situation, and it challenged the art world's identity and professional elitism at the core, putting its turgid, unaccommodating spirit right on the razor's edge. Suddenly it became apparent to everyone that the old cultural paradigms were under heavy siege, and that all the provocative, uncomfortable issues about inclusiveness, race, gender and merit—especially issues of the supplanting of the aesthetic by the political—were there to be dealt with, not just intellectually or theoretically, but in-your-face. The same fragmentation of culture into what Arthur Schlesinger once condescendingly described as "a quarrelsome spatter of enclaves, ghettos and tribes" that has been convulsing university campuses for many years now, abruptly repeated itself with a vengeance in the aesthetic citadel of the Whitney Museum. Previously, museums had avoided these abrasive culture clashes, along with the social conflicts and struggles that underlay them, but that pattern was disturbed irrevocably when "cultural diversity," standing for groups of people who have been oppressed by dominant categories and institutions, were invited into the museum and then transformed it into a theater of victimology. Certainly the moral uproar and social conflicts generated by the Whitney show, which formerly had been kept at bay through exclusion, proved to be miserably recalcitrant for aesthetic philosophies that belong to the prevailing power structure of the art world and that do not, in any case, see these social and political problems as part of their business.

Although I did not start out intending to write about political correctness or multiculturalism, that is where the flow of energy finally led me. The Biennial first presents itself in my conversation with the Guerrilla Girls, who assume credit for the show, having revealed in their posters how sexist and racist Whitney biennials have been in the past. My own role in relation to the show revealed itself later on, when I was invited to the "Crossing Cultures" conference in Barcelona, organized by Mary Jane Jacob, which propelled me directly into the heart of the conflict and where I found myself exposed to a range of views and positions that began to "cook" my own awareness. From a larger cultural perspective, what became clear in the aftermath of the Whitney was that the move away from autonomous art—art that is cut off from any social or communal definitions—is happening whether we like it or not, and is bringing about a very different relationship between artists and the public sphere. In giving contour and features to this state of affairs, several of the conversations here allow the culture war, in all of its dramatic, evolving complexity, to speak for itself.

One of the key points of contention in the culture war is the issue of intellectual and aesthetic merit. This is the painful edge that is still unprocessed, where all the heat is to be found. Because much of the art being made today focuses on social problems rather than on "self-expression," the broader context of political, social and environmental life is often the artist's work arena, rather than the more traditional withdrawal behind closed doors in the studio. This means that the *site* of aesthetic experience is shifting, as the conversation with Jacob indicates, away from the self-referential orbit of museums and galleries. Rejecting the isolationist tendencies of modernism, Richard Shusterman questions the whole enterprise of defining art as a specialized category of objects or activities separate from their influential connection with real life. His perspective is reinforced in different ways by other individuals in the book. Satish Kumar presents his own dimension to the discussion by describing how, from the traditional Indian point of view, art is never conceived of as pictures to be put on walls or sold in galleries, but is a living process centered around daily life and vital human concerns. Ellen Dissanayake emphasizes that this has been the case for most of human history, until the anomaly of modern aesthetics. In discussing the functional significance of art, Carol Becker argues that artists need to be understood as social agents, who are integral to the social and political life of the community, while Thomas Moore suggests we bring the artist back into everyday life so that we don't just have "this fringe art world that doesn't really touch on the values of the way we live." Moore feels that artists need to feel conviviality with society rather than alienation, and to bring art into the public life around us.

If multiculturalism is viewed by certain people as a stripping down of intellectual and aesthetic standards of excellence that is undermining the cultural hegemony of the West, for others I spoke with, the debate in terms of "the West versus the rest"—i.e., the colonial paradigm that has shaped and validated the history of Western culture—simply doesn't wash anymore. In my conversation with Barbara Kirshenblatt-Gimblett, she defines the meritocracy as a form of gate-keeping: a way to keep some people in and some people out. According to Coco Fusco, many people with power are not used to sharing it, and that commonly leads to a backlash, which is what we're living with right now.

In this very diverse and interdisciplinary group, it is the voice of Hilton Kramer that represents the conservative and traditional modernist position. Something of a lone voice in these pages, he nevertheless belongs to a vociferous band of critics of "PC," who decry the changes that are happening, and for whom catalytic situations like the Whitney Biennial of 1993 are ultimate proof that the riffraff are moving in and gaining the upper hand, contaminating the arts with a crude ideological agenda of race and gender and destroying Western civilization's aesthetic and intellectual standards. Since my conversation with Kramer took place prior to the opening of the Whitney show, I did not have the opportunity to ask him about it directly. However, his views on the "encroachment" of multiculturalism have been well publicized elsewhere. In the *New Criterion,* for instance, Kramer describes the dismantling of the meritocratic system as an "ideological plague," and in a special issue of *Partisan Review* devoted to "The Politics of Political Correctness," he proposes that attacks on literature and the arts from the "PC brigades" have to be met with the kind of political response that can effectively defend our accomplishments and traditions from being trashed by the promotion of "newly sanctified mediocrities and nonentities simply because they meet the requisite criteria of race and gender." With these few significant comments, we can demarcate the combat zones of the culture war, notice its cutthroat language and "dismissive othering" of people not firmly established in the dominant cultural body, and we can glimpse one of its combatants spoiling for a fight.

"No one in his right mind goes to an art-museum to worship anything but art, or to learn about anything else," the painter Ad Reinhardt declared in 1962. "The one thing to say about art and life is that art is art and life is life." What happened at the Whitney was drastically different in terms of tone, style and objects of attention, and interfered in a deep-seated way with the basic set of assumptions that has shaped the modern tradition of Western art. A dominant narrative that had understood itself to be at once lofty, universal, timeless and "race-free" was immoderately foreclosed in a single, massive cultural critique rendered by the Other. It was a clear signal communicating to the art world that the pressure for change is on. That change, eloquently described by Leo Castelli in the final conversation here, needs to be understood as "a sea change, not just any change." Aesthetics can no longer protect itself with a thaumaturgy of "formal" and "purist" values, or a notion of art isolated unto itself, separate from the experience of other things. With no surrender of his own integrity, Castelli offers an elegiac farewell to "the wonderful days of the era that I participated in, and in which I had played a substantial role," because he understands that they are over.

Ours is definitely not a time for the faint-hearted. Mindell makes it clear that in its attempt to balance its different parts, a field can accidentally annihilate itself if no one is there to appreciate, unfold and work with the polarizations, escalations and deescalations that are taking place. A less demonic alternative is to become a "compassionate listener." Then one automatically moves beyond the dualisms and divisiveness that tend to inhibit the natural developmental process of cultural unfolding. I am deeply grateful to all the individuals in this book who have so generously collaborated with me in therapeutic rituals of conversation, and whose thinking (to borrow a phrase from Ralph Waldo Emerson) "sheds wisdom like perfume." Their diverse perceptions and heightened sensitivity to what is happening to our world will be of help, I believe, to anyone who is trying to negotiate this extremely complex moment of passage in our culture more prudently.

As we near the end of the twentieth century, I hope the practice of dialogue may become more widely recognized for the special sort of harmonics that it offers: a latticework of thoughts and points of view that interweave and complement each other. Allowing the truth of the subject to emerge not from any one point of view but from many makes any entrenched position open to question: it will always be destabilized by another perspective. For this reason the very process of dialogue can, of itself, transform the world view of self-assured individualism and radical self-sufficiency, since when individual consciousness breaks out of the limits of its own preconceptions and expectations, it travels out more freely, in many different directions. The present book will have realized its deepest purpose if it provides even a momentary glimpse into the potency of this most exquisite discovery.

What Is Art For?

ELLEN DISSANAYAKE

*E*llen Dissanayake and I first met in the late 1970s when *she visited me in London. She had read an earlier book of mine* (Progress in Art), *about which she wanted to ask me some questions. At that time Dissanayake was living in Sri Lanka, but had come to Oxford for six months to use the library, and had started writing a book about her view of art as a biological need in the human species. When she returned to Sri Lanka, we stayed in touch through letters.*

Our friendship grew when Dissanayake came to New York in 1983 to teach in the Liberal Studies Program at the New School for Social Research. We'd get together on my visits to New York City, and we even appeared together once at the New School in a special symposium she organized about the biological, social and cultural importance of art in life. In a brainstorming session while searching for a title for the symposium, I suddenly thought of a question I had recently found in a book by Doris Lessing: "What are we here for?" We looked at each other and said: "What is art for?" Eventually, that became the title of Dissanayake's first book, which appeared in 1988. (I also used the title myself for a magazine article.) The question acknowledges our mutual interest in the fundamental role of art, though at first glance our starting points—hers pre-Paleolithic and mine late twentieth-century—seem very far apart.

In 1992, Dissanayake's second book, Homo Aestheticus, *was published; in it she argues that human societies throughout history have always displayed some form of behavior that can be called "art," and that this behavior fulfills a fundamental biological and evolutionary need. In societies other than our own, according to Dissanayake, this behavior plays an integral part in daily social life, and functions as a communal activity, whereas "the dominant idea about art in our culture, ever since the idea of 'art' itself arose in the eighteenth century, has been that it is superfluous—*

an ornament or enhancement, pleasant enough but hardly necessary." Dissanayake feels that by idealizing aesthetic experience and assigning it only to certain culturally sanctioned objects, our modern view of art controverts its biological and evolutionary significance. It is only by discovering the biological origin of this intrinsic human imperative to make art that we will truly come to understand what art means for human life and what its future might be.

There is a great deal of confusion currently about where art fits in to society, and what function (beyond that of salable commodity) it should serve. In the modern era, art's role was to challenge and disrupt by means of its "otherness" and inaccessibility. Today the question of "community" is much debated—not only "what" art is for, but "who" it is for. Eleanor Heartney summarized the turmoil in an essay called "Quality Control" in the New Art Examiner recently: "Do we want art that is harmonizing or disruptive? Should it build bridges or shake us up? Should it express a community or an individual vision? Does art suffer when it is instilled with an agenda? Does it lose something when it begins to approximate the models of social work and therapy?"

Dissanayake's biological perspective suggests that it is not "art" in some elitist sense, but "making special" that has been socially and culturally important. What artists do is

Ellen Dissanayake • 39

merely an intensification and exaggeration of what everyone does quite naturally—make important things and activities special. This is most evident in premodern societies, where artmaking is practiced by everyone. If the notion that everyone is an artist seems foreign to our highly professionalized society of specialists, it is only because art has been falsely set apart from life, in the course of which it has lost its communal nature and function.

For Dissanayake, art is as normal and natural in human evolution as is the use of language, or tools. Normally we refer to humankind as Homo sapiens, meaning "wise," but Dissanayake claims that we could just as legitimately call ourselves Homo aestheticus, since human beings universally display a unique propensity for aesthetic behavior. The fact that art forms vary so widely from one society to another would seem to suggest that they are cultural and learned, but Dissanayake draws an analogy with language—i.e., the innate proclivity is there, although the specifics are learned. Until the Enlightenment, she suggests, there was no such thing as "disinterested" aesthetic experience, and certainly no "art world," composed of critics, dealers, gallery owners, museum directors, curators and art-magazine editors, whose function it is to validate and explain the art works. Dissanayake's insistence on a more vernacular view is a recurrent theme in these conversations. "Only a few societies have thought of it even remotely as we do," she says. In traditional societies, "art for life's sake," not "art for art's sake," is the rule.

To understand what art is, or might again become, Dissanayake claims that it is useful to consider the bigger span of human history and not just the restricted field of modern Western society, in which art has become identified with salable objects rather than with kinds of behavior or ways of doing things that embellish and enlarge life. Although small-scale, less specialized, premodern societies may not possess the abstract concept "art," they do offer all their members frequent opportunities to be "artists," and to be a vehicle for group meaning. The paradox of the isolated, elitist view of "art for art's sake" is that art is simultaneously sanctified and dismissed as rubbish; it becomes the subject of complex exegesis and yet is totally ignored; it commands millions in the auctioneer's salon and yet is irrelevant to most people's lives. According to Dissanayake, we are in this paradoxical spot because Western society treats art as a dispensable luxury, when it is really an innate behavior that is essential to our human, biological nature. Art, in her sense of making special, is important to the lives of everyone, not just to an elite group of artists in an art world. A fundamental human need is being expressed, and met, by artistic activity.

The following conversation took place in my home in Blacksburg, Virginia, on Saturday, June 28, 1992.

SUZI GABLIK: I guess one thing that I was hoping to hear you speak to, Ellen, is whether your theory of art as a form of biologically based behavior, reflecting a universal human need to make things special, relates to issues in contemporary art as well. Does this same principle operate today? And if not, why not?

ELLEN DISSANAYAKE: Before trying to answer that, I should probably say I realize that the idea that art comes from a need to make things special may sound, at first hearing, very simplistic. My rejoinder for that is to say that my fundamental quest has been to find a germ in very early, pre-Paleolithic peoples from which a "behavior of art"—including what we think of as art today—could originally have arisen. Looking at the artifacts and things that we have from early times, one can see that early humans were attracted to things that are extraordinary or special, and at some point began to try to make them special. This doesn't occur in any other animal, leaving aside the bowerbird, which is actually a different kind of thing. It is something that sets humans apart from animals. There is this germ in human behavior that wants to make special things you care about, to show your regard for them. You want to do something special to show that investment and concern.

SG: You state in *Homo Aestheticus* that the human behavior of art is wider and deeper than simply the practice of art by artist-specialists and the exhibition of their works in museums and galleries. You also say that "it may be a surprise to realize how peculiar our modern Western notion of art really is—how it is dependent on and intertwined with ideas of commerce, commodity, ownership, history, progress, specialization, and individuality—and to recognize the truth that only a few societies have thought of it even remotely as we do."

ED: It's true that we're very anomalous—since the eighteenth century we've been a really anomalous society. That's what's called "modernization," and it's what we're all complaining about now—that it's turned the world topsy-turvy. If you look at the arts cross-culturally, like an anthropologist, it's clear just how aberrant the Western concept of art is. This is why I've been concerned to consider art *biologically,* that is, as a universal behavior that characterizes our species, rather as a student of animal behavior might consider nest-building in orioles or territoriality in walruses: these behaviors have contributed to the survival of the individuals and species that practice them. I'll admit this seems an unusual way to look at art. But when you view art as a "behavior" of making important things special, it seems quite evident that this is universal, even though every culture may not paint or sculpt or make installations. Particular arts and forms of art are definitely learned and culture-specific, but my thesis is that there is an underlying biological proclivity in humans that needs this extra dimension of experience. The underlying need can have many different manifestations. It may even be starved, or distorted, because there are no opportunities for its expression within the culture.

SG: Going back to my original question, is the idea of art as "making special" something that can be applied to, or connected with, our understanding of art today?

ED: Yes, I think it can, but it's important to realize that the caring part is often missing today, too. People in modern times become so concerned with getting on with the next thing that they don't have time to consider their experience, and then to mark it, to care about it and to make it special. When you have the time to think about it, then you see within a particular experience, for example, that something someone else says suddenly connects, something you read about connects, something you remember from a long time ago connects: that, in a way, is making your experience special. That's making an art work out of your experience; it's what artists do when they make art.

SG: It's something that many people would agree describes the creative process.

ED: Right, the recognizing of what pertains and then putting it all together. My notion of making special is very broad—some might say too broad—but I think it encompasses both the housewife who is making a flower arrangement and the acknowledged artist, poet, choreographer, composer.

SG: Does it encompass the photojournalistic work of Barbara Kruger, for instance?

ED: The signs that she makes? Sure, because she's singling those phrases or ideas out. She's putting them into a frame, instead of just telling somebody, "Oh, I had this really amusing one-liner thought today: 'I shop therefore I am.'" She actually takes the trouble to set it down, and then to set it apart, and then to put it somewhere, which is also a special place.

SG: So any art, then, is making special; it doesn't matter whether it's good or bad.

ED: No, there's no value judgments, and this, some would say, is a limitation on my idea. But I'm concerned with elucidating the fundamental "germ" of the activity of art.

SG: If generically all art is making special, how can that be reconciled with your notion that we moderns don't care in the same sense about making special?

ED: We do and we don't. I think it's a natural behavioral proclivity like wanting to play, or wanting to talk, or to be with other people. But whereas traditional societies provided a kind of avenue, or channel, in which people could make things special as part of their life, it seems that in our society those opportunities are fewer and fewer, and they're more commodified now. Instead of making something special, you buy it—Halloween costumes or your trousseau, et cetera. Or you vicariously let "artists" do art for you.

sg: Maybe what we need to look at, then, is the difference between your notion of making special, which encompasses things like decorating for a festival, or a ritual, or a holiday, or embellishing one's living quarters or certain objects that one has, and so on, in relation to the modern idea of the professional career artist. What about that?

ed: Again, I would look back to earlier societies, where decorating or adorning were ways of showing that one participated in a social order and was a moral member of society. The decorating of one's body or of one's possessions was a way of joining in the community expectations, whatever it meant to belong to that tribe. You weren't really a full member if you didn't do it.

sg: Art today certainly isn't a manifestation of belonging to the tribe.

ed: No, it's our individuality that we're asserting again. We're a very different kind of society, so I'm not saying it's a bad thing to do. But I remember you asked me at one of my talks if "making special" was just mere decoration. And I had to think about it, because that does make it sound like "mere" pattern-making. But since then I have read a couple of anthropological accounts about societies where decoration is not "mere"; on the contrary, it's the way to participate in the social order by showing who one is as a bona fide group member.

SG: Well, this brings us directly to the issue that concerns me the most at the moment, which is how our modern understanding of, and models for, art are *not* about participation in the social order. They seem more like a means of escape from the world, as in that Flaubert quote I like using so much: "Life is so horrible that one can only bear it by avoiding it. And that can be done by living in the world of art." Today there is this excessive sense of art— along with everything else in our culture—being an individual pursuit, an autonomous activity that is not connected in any profound sense with the world, but is used more as a kind of solace, or retreat, from it. Like psychotherapy, it's done mostly behind closed doors, without any great concern for the state of the world outside. In his book with Michael Ventura, James Hillman indicts therapy for being too personalized and individualized, and claims that it is actually contributing to the disease of our indifference to the world. Paraphrasing Hillman, you could also say "We've had a hundred years of modern art and the world's getting worse," and maybe we need to look at that. If "making special" translates itself into the individual's way of connecting with the tribe, then maybe that aspect is the component which is lacking in our own idea of art. Hillman also says that we have become so individualized and conditioned to experience ourselves as separate, we now have an actual fear of community. Certainly we have no real experience of it, as others have pointed out. What do you think might help us to reconnect with this more communal need of our nature?

ED: I'm not sure I can really help you with this, because I'm probably more perplexed about community than even you are. We self-contained academics who like to read and write are involved in solitary pursuits that, by definition, almost have to be done alone.

SG: Aha, you see, here's the point. The book by Hillman and Ventura really breaks new ground. As far as I'm concerned, it's as radical for us as the invention of collage was for the Cubists—because their entire book is created from dialogue. I know there have been joint authorships before, where the text comes out of a single voice and you never know who wrote what. And then, there's the mode of the interview, where somebody is presumably the interesting person, who is being interviewed by somebody else. But this is a whole book in which two people, each of whom has an equally masterful mind and point of view, respond to each other like two jazz musicians, improvising as they go along, letting certain ideas play themselves out, sometimes doing a solo, sometimes merging into a single voice. To me, this seems like a new thing, and I'm as excited by it as if I had discovered collage, say, for the first time, or something comparable. I go on at some length in *The Reenchantment of Art* about moving beyond the mode of monologue, the mode of self-expression that is nonreciprocal, where an artist or writer imposes images or ideas on the world, but nobody can really answer back. Shifting into a mode of dialogue creates an interactive, participatory kind of situation that is more relevant, I think, to the process and systems thinking of our time. The very principle of dialogue begins to break the spell of the notion that art or writing has to be a totally solitary, or individual process. Let me read to you what Hillman and Ventura say about writing and thinking as dialogue:

JAMES HILLMAN: Two people talking is, at least conceptually, open to the community. Open to interruption. . . . That's part of the value of writing-as-dialogue, the important interruptions each makes into the other's thought, the sudden turns. So the page is more alive in that it's more like life, it moves like life.

MICHAEL VENTURA: Books are by their nature private *and* public—a book is a public thing, but it's read privately—but writing-as-dialogue is open to the community in another way: not everyone can write but everyone talks. So this is an open form, in that if people talk about the book in a way they're *doing* the book, extending and rewriting the book.

ED: It's a way of both doing it yourself, and then, by telling it, going back and forth, correcting each other and adding to, or enhancing, what the other said. That really is something that I preach and in that sense everyone is, or can be, an artist, by doing that. And then, if they feel moved to create something more out of it, fine.

SG: You know the section of *The Reenchantment of Art* where I discuss Dominique Mazeaud's river project, *The Great Cleansing of the Rio Grande River,* and how she ritually cleans garbage out of the river once a month. She gets to a point where the relationship she has with the river takes over and becomes more important than the original ecological thrust—although even that came more out of her pain at seeing the state of the river than from a purely pragmatic desire to clean things up. It came out of her need to try and heal the river and be with its pain. And then it felt like just being in dialogue with the river was enough. But for many people, this is very problematic as art.

ED: I don't find that problematic at all as an art work. I suppose it has something to do with the intention and the state of mind of the person while they're doing it. It's not just organizing a brigade and let's go, let's sweep up this neighborhood and get it cleaned up; it's done in a ritualistic way. It's done with some kind of forethought and some kind of afterthought.

SG: And, with your idea of making special. The river becomes special to her, becomes almost a partner and a beloved.

ED: That's it, because she's noticing it. People talk sometimes about cultures where art and life are one, as in Bali, for instance, or with the Hopi, where almost everything they do has a ritualistic significance. This sort of thing *can* become very habitual and routine, but on the other hand, it has a kind of shape, or consciousness, that makes it aesthetic—when what you do has some kind of connection with other things and you are aware of that. You're not just doing it; you're doing it in a ritualized way with regard to something larger than yourself.

SG: What do you think about what is happening now, in terms of the breakdown of the canonical system and traditional modes of perceiving art as masterpieces, and so on? Where do you think this is ultimately heading?

ED: I really don't know where it's heading. I suppose as long as we still have this competitive society and people continue to invest in art for their financial aggrandizement, a lot of it will keep on going just the way it is.

SG: My sense is that there's a strong grass-roots movement to change all that.

ED: Certainly there is this recognition—Hillman speaks to this too—that community has been neglected with all the individualism that has characterized our society for two hundred years. But I think you, Suzi, have a more visionary kind of mind and goal than I do. I'm content pretty much to prowl around in libraries and take notes and connect things that have happened in the past, and connect other people's ideas to my own. I'm a scholar, and I enjoy being a scholar, and in this sense I guess I belong to what is called by some today "the patriarchal culture." I'm not sure I like being pigeonholed in what is regarded by the labelers as a negative stereotype. But I am unapologetically a Darwinist, and I find that the Darwinian view of human evolution explains a lot of things about why we're in the state we are now— for instance, we're not living in the environment for which we were adapted as a species. So I don't know whether this project of talking about the state of the arts today between you and me will really go anywhere—whether we're enough on the same wavelength, or not.

SG: Part of this approach via dialogue is not so much to construct arguments or launch attacks on different points of view, but rather to ensure that all the points of view get expressed. This is what Arnold Mindell, in *his* new book, calls "deep democracy." It's not a matter of one position wiping out another, or dominating another, but rather that all the positions need to have a voice, and should be heard. So all the better if you find yourself in conversation with somebody who doesn't share your point of view; then the different sides will begin to address each other. I see my role as catalytic; my writing is doing its work in the world if all the disagreeing sides begin talking to each other. A lot of the art I've written about takes place in a dialogic mode, and my current thinking is that I should begin to work collaboratively myself, so that my thoughts can interpenetrate more directly with others. But going back to what you alluded to earlier—the more academic or scholarly modes that you espouse in contrast to my visionary ones. You don't see your work, then, as directed toward the transformation of any of these systems?

ED: Oddly, I think it is. I've talked to any number of people who have come to this bioevolutionary way of thinking, who say that, to them, it has been like a Copernican revolution in their thought, once they understood it.

SG: This is also what people say about the new "ecophilosophy" in the understanding of our interconnectedness and our separateness. Is the philosophy you write about in *Homo Aestheticus* connected at all to ecological thinking and deep ecology?

ED: Yes, I think it's exactly the same, because it sees humans as part of nature. If it is accepted that humans evolved, like other animals, into an environmental niche, living in small bands in a hunter-gathering way of life, then we are really hunter-gatherers thrust into a kind of supermechanistic, anonymous, hypermediated environment that we're not preadapted to live in. There's a limit beyond which we cannot change and adapt, the effects of which we're seeing in all the social and personal malaise today. So it is a question of restoring, if we can, a more human environment and way of life, one that fits our nature. I think the important thing is to realize that we can't go on living the way that we are. So changing art, or thinking differently about art, is just part of thinking about everything else. My feeling is that if society changes—if we finally realize that we cannot go on living in ways that are so mechanical, materialistic and hard on the environment—then perhaps we'll change our way of living, and another kind of art will grow out of that.

SG: This hints at something I've been feeling and even sometimes saying to people, which is that we're maladaptive—we're a dysfunctional species—and we're probably not going to survive. It's such an unmanageable thought that I nearly fell off my chair when I read the last twenty pages of the Hillman book, because Michael Ventura makes a similar claim, that our civilization isn't going to survive. I'll read some of it to you.

ED: Before you do, let me just say that I think the problem is more that we've somehow created a world to which we cannot adapt, in which we cannot humanly live. It's the present kind of society that is maladaptive, or dysfunctional, it *requires us* to become inhuman. But go ahead and read.

MICHAEL VENTURA: The issue is: our culture is over—

JAMES HILLMAN: —and how do we go through the rituals of the dying of the culture?

MICHAEL VENTURA: —you can't negotiate with an avalanche. Nothing, nothing, nothing is going to stop the shipwreck of this civilization. The forces, the momentum, are too great. . . . But accepting the story, accepting that this civilization is ending, doesn't mean you don't fight for what you believe. You take part in the story. You do the portion of the story that is given to you. . . . See, we get such hubris about, "Well if the world is getting so bad then I shouldn't do anything. If that's the story then fuck the story." Which is like saying, "If I'm gonna die why should I live?"

SG: What is clearly not possible, he says, is to find your own psychologically safe and stable little place.

ED: It's almost as if people have evolved with a built-in resistance to even acknowledge the predicament. It really does seem hopeless, I agree with you.

SG: I find it liberating—because he puts the truth out on the table. It takes us more deeply into life rather than having to retreat from it. It's as if he's flicked an invisible switch that allows us to feel the pain and live it and not have to smother it. But I think that acceptance isn't the same as resignation.

Ellen Dissanayake • 55

Doin' Dirt Time

RACHEL DUTTON AND ROB OLDS

Rachel Dutton and her husband, Rob Olds, were visionary sculptors until they decided to give up making art
a few years ago from a sense of environmental emergency.
Dutton's work, constructed from hay, mud and papier-
mâché shaped around an armature, was like a hallucinatory
dream-memory of our atavistic link with the animal world,
evoking a pretechnological, more spiritual era when humans
could merge their consciousness with animals and harmo-

nize with nature. Olds's works—I recall seeing a couple of homeless men hovering around a garbage can, all made from a lavalike substance that suggested the ruins of Pompeii— were like terrifying holograms of the coming environmental and social anarchy. When I first met Dutton and Olds about eight years ago, they had just decided to leave their studios in South Central Los Angeles and "take to the woods," choosing a life of isolation from the world of people in order to become surrounded by nature. Homesteading in a remote part of New Mexico, they had slowly altered their physical reality by progressively shedding their dependence on twentieth-century technologies, and devoting themselves instead to a simple, circumscribed life, attending to the daily matters of sustaining a desert existence and enjoying their activity as artists.

Then came the letter. It stated that they were giving up everything, selling their land and studios, and using whatever money they had for a lengthy series of courses, in order to learn tracking and wilderness survival skills from a man called Tom Brown, Jr., in the Pine Barrens of New Jersey. "It has been wrenching to decide to leave the generous peace of this place," the letter stated, "the expansive silence of the plains, the clean water, the clean air, but we feel we can no longer hunker down and enjoy our little piece of paradise just for ourselves. . . . We have simply put together my sense *of ancient nature living in us all beneath the veneer of civilization, and Rob's sense of apocalyptic awakening as that civilization cracks away, to empower a life based on the compassion hidden at the core, a life of simple acts, offered as a prayer."* By the time they had written me, they had already given away or destroyed all their sculptures and drawings, to release the energy bound up in the forms, and had canceled their forthcoming shows. To accompany the works that were given away, they had composed a short contract, which stated that they could never be sold but must only be given away, and only to someone who truly loves the earth. The letter had an electrifying effect on me because it put into such sharp focus the danger I sense is coming; but I found myself wondering what had happened to unleash this radical set of decisions. Why would artists who had chosen solitude then decide to take the urgency of the environmental crisis so directly into their lives and change their behavior at such profound levels—whatever that might mean and wherever it might lead? What had so radically altered their frame of mind?

Dutton suggested that I read Tom Brown's books. His tracking school, she told me, is booked up two years in advance. By studying footprints, Brown claims to be able to read a person's moods, thoughts, actions, diseases, strengths and weaknesses. When he was a boy, Brown was taught ancient survival practices, like how to make bows, clubs and arrowheads, and how to trap, track and stalk by an old Apache warrior and scout called "Grandfather," who was born in the 1880s. Brown had started his tracking school in order to instruct people about how to survive without modern technological civilization, because of the vision of its destruction that Grandfather had received during a vision quest some time during the 1920s—much of which has already become reality. Part of Grandfather's vision was composed of this message: "The Earth is dying. The destruction of man is close, so very close, and we must all work to change that path of destruction." There would be four warnings, or signs, which if heeded would offer humanity a chance to learn the lessons and, by changing its ways, alter its probable future. The first two warnings are famine and a disease born of monkeys, drugs and sex that will destroy mankind from the inside. The third warning is in the form of holes in the sky that cannot be healed. If at this point the decision to change has not been made, all will be lost. Then will ensue the final vision of destruction: the sky turns blood red, and all is poisoned. During this time, the earth will heal itself and man will die.

The same world-shaking intuition that galvanized Brown had torn Dutton and Olds out of their isolation. Grandfather's vision and its imagery seem clear enough at *this juncture, but those who have such visions are despised, shunned and rejected in their own time. In a book of essays called* Facing Apocalypse, *David Miller writes: "Surely we all know all too well this apocalyptic fantasy, its reality, for we are chiliasts all, were we to face it. . . . And of course, this is not the whole laundry list of what we face, not the end; it's only the beginning. No wonder the face of chiliasm is repressed, in both self and in society."*

Dutton and Olds finally came to Blacksburg to tell me their story. They were on their way back to New Mexico after their first week of training with Brown. Once back in the desert, they put their house and land up for sale. Within a few months, I received an address and phone number for them from a town called Parthenon, Arkansas. Then the number was disconnected, with no referral. I have not heard from them again.

The following conversation was taped at my home in Blacksburg on July 20, 1992.

RACHEL DUTTON: To me, art's "specialness" is still a sub-category of separation. I think we need everything to become holy, or numinous. Everything has to be equally holy: the mountain, the ant, the person, the blade of grass, the dinner, the sky. One trouble I have with art right now is how it isolates certain moments or certain acts. If you're really living utterly in tune with the life-energy, every single moment and every single event becomes numinous. And that's something we've lost that art supposedly addresses and tries to bring back.

SUZI GABLIK: How has that attitude influenced you to stop making art—and to burn or give away your sculptures? Do you want to give me the scoop on all that?

ROB OLDS: Well, it starts so far back, in South Central Los Angeles. When I first was there, I started having these images of people bursting apart, bursting into flame, as they looked up into the sky.

SG: You and Nostradamus.

RD: Yes, definitely.

RO: I was working as a baker and getting up at two a.m. and driving through these streets with packs of wild dogs and people living under the freeways and trash-can fires. It was just like the end of the world. It was already happening.

SG: So at that point, you both decided to pull up stakes and go live in the desert and do your art, right?

RO: Well, I'd made the images. I made carvings of people just ripping apart, angels falling with broken wings and images of martyrs. It was a slow process, and I didn't even know what was happening. I didn't even truly understand it. And then when Rachel and I met, she was doing images of hunter-gatherers, of the hunt itself, the actual sacrifice of the hunter and the hunted. We knew we needed to get out of L.A. and move somewhere. At that point we were leaving the city in order to survive monetarily and have a simple way of life.

SG: And to live in beauty.

RD: To live closer to nature.

SG: But now it seems as if all that has changed again. It's another moment of total transformation, just as that one was, when I first met you.

RD: You actually asked the question when you were visiting us at that time—because we were saying how we didn't like the city and we never went anywhere and we never did anything. You actually said, "Then why do you live in the city?" It was a great question, along with a lot of other things that happened to us at that moment, and we started asking ourselves, "What do we want to have learned by the time we die?" It certainly wasn't how to survive in Los Angeles.

RO: And we weren't interested at all in the art world. It was the image itself, and what this image was talking to us about, what it was trying to tell us.

SG: I don't have any problem in understanding that previous moment of passage, when you left the urban environment and went off to the quiet atmosphere of the desert to make art. What is less clear, since receiving your letter, is why you're giving up that beautiful place you love, and why you feel there's no time to make art anymore. And not only the decision not to make any more art, but then destroying what you've already made and giving the rest of it away. I feel a sense of urgency behind all this, but I really don't know the story. What brought you to this point?

RD: It seemed to me when you looked at Rob's images that they were about people just sort of bursting open at the moment of death—like seed cases ripping open as civilization cracks away. The images in my work were what would grow from that seed if it had a chance to grow; it was a new way of living with nature, something that's different from what culture provided. So we went out to live closer to nature and continued to make the same images, and we're surrounded there by meadowlarks and antelopes and an immense silence for twenty miles in every direction. Where we live it's real open; you can see for hundreds of miles in a couple of different directions. You have this sense of the earth as a living being that's so immense. You're working in your garden and you just turn your head a few degrees and you have infinity stretching out in front of you. It's like a vision quest place. And you live in a relationship to immensity long enough and you begin to drop away most of what you think is your personality and your culture, because obviously culture doesn't matter *at all* in the great scope of the huge, grand earth. And I think it just lost its—

sg: Allure.

rd: It lost its allure, and it's useless. It's all about separation. We went through a whole series of changes just cleaning up the actual physical living of our life. We got rid of the television, the VCR, the tape deck, the microwave we were given as a gift. We turned off our refrigerator two and a half years ago, because refrigerators are monuments to ill-usage of energy on the planet. It's made out of chemicals that hurt the ozone. It's designed primarily for products of extractive agriculture; it's for dairy products, it's for meat, it's for the kind of vegetables that are raised and shipped on trucks. And it's all quite recent.

sg: So how do you manage in the desert without a refrigerator?

rd: We cook dried beans and dried rice. We have a small greenhouse where we grow vegetables. We have a garden outside for fresh vegetables. We don't use much dairy. We clarify the butter and make ghee and it keeps for four months in hot weather. People lived for hundreds of thousands of years *without* refrigerators. You're not going to die if you turn the damn box off.

We had these two huge barns built for studios, and we camped in one and put all our sculpture in the other. We lived in one barn for nine months while we built the little house. Then we moved into the little house, and the living of our life on the land became our art form. When we were in L.A., and even before then, I lived my life *for* my art. I destroyed relationships, my body, my health, all kinds of things, for the art. That's the ideal of the artist in this culture. Living on the prairie, in the context of the larger nature that has nothing to do with culture, we slowly started living life *as* an art. It's as if washing dishes, if done with presence, is as much of an art form as painting a picture or making a sculpture.

sG: Did your desire to make the kind of art objects you had made before simply dwindle, and die out in you?

RD: It just faded away.

RO: Actually, when we were first on the Rio Grande, we walked down to the river and when I stopped there, I immediately thought, "I'm never going to carve another piece of sculpture again."

sG: What made that thought come to you then?

RO: I have no idea. It was there. I knew it. I felt it. It wasn't just a thought.

SG: In retrospect, you can't see what it was?

RO: Not then. I do now. Now I see that the art that I made in South Central Los Angeles was *not* art: it was a message to me. It was like being shown visions that came in strange ways—they had to come through my hands.

SG: So you feel you got the message, you got the teaching, from your own art. And what was the teaching?

RO: The death of humanity, the death of our planet. The teaching was in terms of the hunter-gatherer; it was in regard to lost knowledge. Here are two homeless people, standing outside at the point at which the earth is going to die. And one person is completely introverted, doesn't see a thing, doesn't even see the fire that's below his head. And the other guy is just ripped apart in his chest, just spreads apart, seeing that moment, up in the sky. The shock of it. That's what I felt. But at that point, I thought it was just something to live with, or to keep going, in this society.

SG: You mean, how you carry the vision of apocalypse.

RO: The more we lived on that land, the more we realized it is here. It's going to be very soon.

SG: How did it come to you that it's so soon?

RD: We left L.A. because it felt like it could blow up. The place that we lived in I'm sure burned in the riots in the spring. A lot of your work, Rob, was about homelessness as a metaphor for spiritual homelessness, and you can't feel that level of disconnection that acutely without knowing something is tremendously out of balance, and that a system so divorced from what supports it is bound to collapse.

SG: So the knowledge that everything is in a state of collapse, or is already collapsing, is what caused you to stop making art?

RO: One thing about art is that, let's say if we had another forty years and we were to continue our careers, maybe some of that art would go out and be seen. But art takes years to come out, to go into the gallery system, to be written about, la de da de da.

RD: There's no time.

RO: There just wasn't time. That's what we felt. No time.

RD: Art is also a closed world. There's a small group of people who look at art and think about art. It doesn't move out very far. The general populace may stand in line for Van Gogh, but the art world is a fairly enclosed little world.

SG: Let's swing around to my generic question for these conversations, "How do we live, then, in a time of decline, or maybe even collapse, and what role does art have?"

RD: None.

RO: None. None.

RD: For me personally, making art was a powerful act, but it was a powerful act because I had no other access to anything more powerful. I had no access to making a daily life of prayer. If you can live your daily life as a prayer, it is inherently more powerful than going to your studio.

SG: What would daily life as a prayer look like?

RD: Daily life as a prayer is that everything is holy. You are holy, everything around you is holy, rinsing a vegetable in the sink is holy. This is a quality that has been utterly lost from contemporary civilized society, which lives apart from nature and sees everything as dead—except people. And the dead world is a lonely world. We live in an area where it's grassland, and with that huge molten sky in the desert, you *know* nature is alive. You hear one of those thunderstorms coming, you know that's alive. It's like when you step on the grass, you have to thank the grass because you're stepping on it—you have to say excuse me. This is a kind of living that is so alien to us; it takes a lot of work to be that reverent.

We're a long way from it, but I have an inkling of what I would like it to be.

SG: Joseph Campbell once said we don't want to understand life; we want to experience it as richly as we possibly can.

RD: That's it. But I have no interest in documenting it. I have no interest in presenting it as art. I have no interest in even calling it art. My interest is in living it.

SG: So the price of reenchantment is direct experience. You've set out to live the implications of your vision, which is breaking your cultural beliefs and is taking you beyond the traditional path of the artist.

RD: Right. We went to a lot of trouble to get rid of toxic things in our environment. We still have a car— that's a tough one. We got rid of the refrigerator. We got rid of the camera. We gave it away, because we didn't want to use photochemicals anymore to promote ourselves. That's the end of your art career right there, if you have no more camera. Another thing is what I would call a "toxic ego." You're asked to have a degree of separation and personal identity as an artist in this culture that is just as toxic as a refrigerator. I had trouble with that—I handled it badly when I had one.

SG: Hopefully you handled your refrigerator better!

RD: I didn't want to have a toxic ego any more. I wanted to be separated from the separation and go back to being part of a large family of living beings rather than having to peek in the window. And I was tired of making symbols about something that I knew had to be true—I wanted to live it instead.

SG: You've shifted worlds from chronicler to participant.

RD: That's why we finally decided to take these wilderness survival classes with Tom Brown, and learn the actual ancient skills of living with the earth, the ancient, reverent, daily-life skills of the hunter-gatherer.

SG: You wanted to do something to break the patterning of your own thinking, to experience a form of reality other than our particular cultural trance.

RD: We just recently learned things that any eight-year-old Neanderthal person would know.

RO: A five year old. We're more ignorant than a five-year-old Neanderthal child.

RD: We are so ignorant! And between the two of us we have four degrees—

SG: Hey, wait a minute! Let's be fair. We're ignorant because those things have not been relevant to the lifestyle and set of behaviors that we use in modern life.

RO: That's why we're here in this place of feeling the end of the earth—because we don't use those skills. And the skills were not just physical, they were spiritual.

SG: What is it you learn from the tracker?

RD: He guarantees that after just the standard class you can survive anywhere in North America, any season, any terrain, with nothing—no equipment, not even a knife. But survival is just the beginning. For him, it's an opening for another way of being. The skills and knowledge enable you to live so directly with the earth that you can experience completely that your life comes from the earth.

RO: One of the things he teaches is that if you go through learning these physical skills and start to become more aware of your world, you will really get an understanding that you will never hurt the earth again. You won't take the earth for granted. It's not just a physical way of surviving out there in the wilderness; it brings you further into being a part of all the things that are there. We'd been reading Brown's books ever since Los Angeles, and we had tried to do the things that were in his books all through those years when we were living in the desert.

sg: So your de-escalating from technology is something that came out of reading him?

ro: No, not that. He never said anything like that.

rd: He was teaching ways of walking, ways of opening your vision, the dynamics of meditative looking and moving into the landscape, where your perception comes out of the landscape rather than at it. At the same time that we were losing some of the accoutrements of civilization, we were adding in what little bit we could figure out of the ancient skills from the books. For instance, we made fires from a bow-drill that we constructed from special sticks we found in the woods. You create friction by working the bow-drill, and then with a little bit of dried grass and sunshine for tinder, you blow on it until it bursts into flame. You make fire with your own breath, and it's incredibly magical. It's primary magic. At one point, we got some cow tendons to make a sinew-backed bow. Tendons are incredibly useful in a survival situation; they make the strongest cordage you can come by. They're really powerful. They come from the part of the muscle that provides the tension on joints. We went to the slaughterhouse to get a few tendons to dry, in order to learn about this material—and the only way you could buy them in Albuquerque was by the twenty-five-pound box!

ro: An Achilles' tendon—only Achilles' tendons.

SG: Who the hell uses Achilles' tendons?

RD: The Japanese. They eat them. No one knows how. So we brought this twenty-five-pound box of Achilles' tendons home. They're very rubbery and tough, so they're scary to clean with a knife, because it's very easy to slip off them. They were from cows, and they weren't clean.

SG: What did you do with them?

RD: First we dried them. Then we tried to make a sinew-backed bow.

SG: As in bow and arrow? A bow you could use to shoot game animals with in the hunt?

RD: Uh huh. To learn how to do it.

SG: Did you bring the bow to the tracking class? Did you show it to Brown?

RO: No, no. He doesn't want to see it.

RD: And also, it didn't really work.

SG: It didn't work? How many tendons did you use to make this bow?

RD: Six or seven.

SG: What did you do with the other twenty?

RD: We used them in a sculpture class I gave for a couple of weeks. I handed them out—

SG: To make sculptures?

RD: I showed the students how to make cordage out of them by pounding out the fibers. You know, when we first told our friends in L.A. in the art world that we were giving up the work, that we were giving it away, we got a lot of letters back.

SG: What kinds of responses did you get?

RD: Well, from some of the art people a horrible response, and from others, really great support. One of the things I noticed with some artists is that there is this horror that life outside of art is hideous, so appalling and dismal that the only thing that gives one hope is being in the studio. And all I could say was that when we decided to cut loose and really give this other stuff weight, all kinds of things started happening to us. Opportunities, new people —we've met more new people since we decided to put our house on the market and give the art away than we've met probably in years. Just in a couple of months. And it felt like that sense of discovery and newness and unexpectedness and vitality that I always associated with studio time is now life time. When we first decided to sell the house, we decided to be real quiet about what we were up to. We were very vague, for instance, with the real estate ladies about what we were doing, and with the people we bought the land from. And then, at a certain point—

RO: We started talking.

RD: It just seemed like it was more important to say—I mean, the world, the earth, is *dying*. Human beings have to change how they live with the earth, and they have to change it soon. It felt like it was more important to say that, and if people thought we were weird, it was OK. But more people have said, "Gee, I think what you're doing is wonderful. I wouldn't have the courage personally, but I'm glad you're doing it." When we finally came out of the closet—

SG: Are you actually planning to totally leave the money culture, then, and live without money?

RO: The basic plan is to sell the house, and pay off the mortgage; and then we're going to just live someplace as simply as we can. We've already put a lot of deposits down on Tom Brown's classes. Even before we went to the first one, we had this feeling that this was it. We've also realized that you don't need all this stuff that we live with today. You don't need to have a mortgage, to have a house that keeps you warm; you don't need to have this infrastructure in order to have food. There is enough food in the wild to feed us if we are able to live *with* the earth.

So we've got a lot of classes to learn, as many as he's going to allow us to take. And then, we'll keep the rest and live simply and—

RD: Practice the skills.

RO: He calls it "dirt time."

RD: You find tracks and you follow them. We all went outside, and we did it. We even saw deer tracks in the *gravel*. This is after only one week of being exposed to the concept. Being exposed to the fact that you can see these things, that they exist out there. You don't need a clear track in the mud. That's why I say it's like art. It's like pattern recognition. I'd heard for years that in other cultures the things that are now called art in this culture were part of daily life. And this is one doorway into that. Tracking utilizes a huge amount of what art has been about, only it's not a specialized, separate activity. It's something that allows you to be closer to nature and to realize that it all comes from nature. It all comes from the earth and we just rearrange things obsessively. Now we see tracks *everywhere!*

RO: Yes, and everybody can learn how to do it. It's amazing! But you do have to do dirt time.

SG: Dirt time means putting your nose to the ground? I was just looking at his book here, the one we bought earlier, and it says:

This book deals with the many reasons that one should come out of wilderness, and why. The decision to leave a life of purity and enter a world that is impure and removed from the spiritual rapture is one of the most difficult choices a person must make in his or her life. ... The question I am most often asked by students is, "How can I take what I learned here in wilderness back home with me into society? How can I continue to live what I have found in the purity of creation?"

I guess my question is, how is being able to recognize whether the deer had a full bladder or an empty bladder when it passed by—how is that going to help you live in society today?

RO: Tracking is not one thing. It's a part of awareness, and being aware of our world.

SG: Most people's lives, as they are currently being lived, don't have any deer, or deer tracks.

RO: You'll find tracks anywhere. One thing that Brown did for a number of years was to stalk in New York City. He would hide in the crevices, the little corners of buildings in the city, and he watched homeless people. He watched people going to work. He watched *everybody*.

RD: Foxes, raccoons.

SG: He watched people going to work, and he watched foxes at the same time?

RO: At night, he saw foxes. He'd follow snakes and opossums. In the city. He said he found all kinds of things. Of course, that's one of the skills that you are taught at the school—stalking. And all of that is a part of awareness; you can't stalk without being aware of everything else around you.

SG: So what you're really trying to do is to use your brain differently.

RD: Get out of that pattern of focused, fixed vision— this exists in space in front of me, I know where it is, I know what it is. Rather, this is movement, flick of tail out of the corner of your eye. When you shift like that, you can catch all kinds of movement at the corner. The thing about the full bladder and the deer is—

SG: How is that relevant to modern life?

RD: It's the idea that other creatures are living and complex. If you can look at a single deer track and notice that the deer paused, notice that the deer turned, what it might have looked at, whether it's troubled, whether it's at ease, it allows you to extend your— what I would call your heart out to that creature.

SG: That's shamanic vision. I guess that's what is meant when they say that the shaman *becomes* the animal, becomes the tree.

RD: Exactly. Really becomes it. It's a participatory world.

RO: Brown says that as you go along in tracking, if you really get into it, you will be able to see the deer make that track.

SG: So in a sense this is developing the deepest level of empathy?

RD: Yes, very definitely. And that's the irony of it, because a lot of environmental people probably would be horror-stricken if I say I want to learn to hunt. But the thing is, if you have to viscerally take a life to support your own life, you're hardly going to go out and do it excessively. I mean, if you feel it, if you really feel the gift of another life, you're only going to take it when you absolutely need it, and you're going to make sure you utilize absolutely everything about it, to honor the spirit.

SG: Are you putting all that you have, spiritually and economically and psychologically, into these tracking courses in order to learn these feelings, then, or to actually try and live this life?

RD: To learn the skills that go with the feelings, which to some extent we've already accessed in some ways on our own. I mean, we came to this with an affinity for it—

RO: And some day, to live it.

SG: When you say live it, do you want to live the life of the hunter-gatherer?

RD: Yes, actually I would love, more than anything, to be allowed to do it. We got to the point in the book where it says you have to come back into society and try to help, and we said, "Oh God, oh shit, do we have to?" I mean, selling the house has put us back into society. Giving the art away has put us back into society. We were very comfortable out there living without anybody around.

SG: What was it, economic pressure or spiritual pressure, that drove you out?

RD: It was spiritual pressure—we wanted to learn more than we could have just from reading the books.

SG: It's interesting, because when I started these conversations, I didn't have anything more in mind than "Let's do this," let's open up the dialogue as a way of blending energy, but already certain things are beginning to come through. It's Mindell's "timespirit" idea: you can become a vehicle for certain things that need to be said just by opening yourself up and allowing the conversation to take place. You let the spirits talk through you and take you to that place where the forbidden communication stops being forbidden.

RD: As an artist, you always think you have to have a product, and so as soon as it wasn't going to be sculpture, it became very convenient to tell family and friends that we were going to write a book, because they would understand that. There was this terror that we wouldn't be doing *something* that was along that line. The kind of interactions we've had with people just since starting to sell the house, and talking to the people we gave the pieces to, it seems like human, face-to-face communication is—I wouldn't call it our art form, but it's apparently what we do now. We live in a culture where most of the information comes removed—in movies, television, books—whereas, say, almost all the wisdom in the Upanishads says you must have direct communication with the master. You can't learn this without a direct transmission from another human being. To some extent, we've lost direct transmission in our culture. Talking only to one person is not enough. You must reach ten thousand people, or forty thousand, or whatever. But suddenly now, a conversation with friends—it's like spreading pollen.

SG: There's also the living quality that James Hillman talks about; talking is a living art. You allow for the interruptions and unexpected turns, and you don't try to monitor or edit. You can be artful afterward, somewhat, in how you shape it, but what you don't want to lose is the vibrancy of the moment, the intensity conversation has that is very different from something that is thought about over time and then written down. Conversation has another quality. I never imagined that even a writer could work interactively this way.

RD: It's a lot like tracking—you don't know at first what is ahead on the trail. Brown's teacher, Stalking Wolf, whom he called Grandfather, said the ground is like a manuscript, constantly being rewritten by the movements of feet, wind, rain, leaves, instead of by letters. One of the many reasons that we're so interested in working with Brown is that what he inherited from Grandfather is not culture-specific. It's more the essence of what some of the Native American cultures were about. Grandfather was an Apache, but he wandered alone for sixty years, up and down all of North America on foot, meeting and studying with a lot of people—elders from many different tribes. He put together a kind of essential core of the spiritual attitude, without all the custom layered over it. As we got rid of our art work, one of the biggest things we were doing by stepping away was letting go of external symbols and going for the energy at the core. What Brown presents is just the core of that reverent attitude. He has a quote in one of his books that's a Chinese proverb that says: "Seek not the ways of the men of old; seek instead what they sought." It's that idea of going to the essential human skills for living on this planet, the very basic, reverent way of living truly with the earth, that we're after, rather than trying to jump into a whole other culture. We have to have the right skills in order to live simply, from the heart, without propping ourselves up, without all the things that have become so destructive. In many ways learning these skills is essentially a prayer you're offering, a prayer that this becomes the way of life again on the earth.

RO: Hunter-gatherers are the apex of human civilization. We need to go back to that point. All else is a bastardization and a plague. We can't assume what is comfortable for society, pick and choose. You've got to do it all the way, or not at all. Or we die.

Making Art About Centipedes

CHRISTOPHER MANES

When I learned that I would be speaking on a panel together with Christopher Manes at a conference on "Art and Ecology" at the University of Montana in Missoula, I bought a copy of his book Green Rage: Radical Environmentalism and the Unmaking of Civilization, and read it. Immediately I could tell that I was going to encounter someone with a beautiful intensity, a knight-errant with bulldog courage, who was bravely questioning the assumptions, values and goals of Western industrial civilization. Once again, I was confronted head-on with the specter of ecological collapse: the end of the world as we know it in the form of "biological meltdown," the destruction of diversity and species extinction.

Nominated in 1990 for a Los Angeles Times Book Award, Green Rage advocates confrontational tactics in support of environmental issues, even while it claims that the environmental crisis has made our culture obsolescent in ways we have yet to contemplate. According to Manes, we still do not understand that unlimited growth is impossible in a limited system, and, to our grief, we are just beginning to realize how costly and unsustainable our economic system is as the health and cleanup bills from years of environmental abuse come due. The realization that our culture is lethal to the ecology that it depends on, and has been so for a long time, perhaps from the beginning, requires doing something we are trained to avoid—taking a serious look at whether our culture is compatible with the natural world and its limits.

From an ecological perspective, which Manes claims is the only one that matters in the long run, "industrial societies must be considered a fleeting, unpleasant mirage on the landscape rather than a vision of the future to be emulated." Still in the embryonic stage of a project whose stated inten-

tion was to reexamine our culture's relationship to art and to the presumed superiority of our Western industrial paradigm, I wrote to Manes and asked him to dialogue with me.

Christopher Manes, it turns out, is a man of many hats. Besides being an unapologetic environmental activist (he also produced a documentary film called Earth First! The Politics of Radical Environmentalism *in 1987), he is a scholar in the field of English literature. He is also a medievalist, who studied Old Norse in Iceland as a Fulbright scholar for two years. When we finally met at the conference, he was studying for a law degree at the University of California in Berkeley. I also found myself talking to an artist and an avid basketball player.*

In reimagining the whole question of our ecological identity, Manes rejects the hierarchy of an evolutionary continuum, with higher and lower life forms as postulated by the notion of the "Great Chain of Being." Our species arrogance assumes that man is at the center of things, in a position of dominance, but as Manes says in our conversation, "Everything is just as advanced as everything else." Plants and rivers have a point of view; insects have feeling, intelligence and will, and obscure fungi in the dark, damp places of the earth are biologically more important to the overall flow of things than human beings are. We need to amplify our human consciousness so that it can mythically assimilate the world's other species, all of which are unique with their own consciousness—and learn to stop talking only about ourselves, taking ourselves as the only important subject.

As for art, Manes suggests that we move it out of the exclusively human world so that insects, mountain lions and trees can also have a voice. This would help to reinstate the sense of ourselves as members of a species within a complex ecology that includes all of the world's flora and fauna, which have their own right to exist. Beyond the "isms" of art history, artists need to recognize their own place within an ecosystem. "Concern for images of the Other is becoming more important than concern for images of Self," writes Peter Bishop in The Greening of Psychology. Learn to think like a centipede, recommends Manes. In place of the idea of man's limitless rule of creation, deep ecology substitutes the idea of the equality of all creatures, including man: we are all cocreators in a vast, intertwined network of energies and information. But somehow we have lost the feeling that this world is our home. Our survival depends, not on visions of the wondrous innovations of science and engineering, but on a return to forms of simple, ecological modesty. According to Manes, the environmental modesty of preindustrial cultures is not utopian. "On the contrary," he writes, "our way of life is utopian, in the sense that it is *unrealistic and naive and cannot realize its fantasy of unlimited affluence and power free from all ecological restraints."* For the growing ranks of radical environmentalists, it is civilization itself—with its privileging of technological progress and its claims of hegemony over the natural world—that is unstable and destructive to the very environment on which it depends. Perhaps it is time for all of us, suggests Manes, *"to make the choice between the natural and the cultural world."* The world is *"a web of interdependent living communities,"* he states mordantly, *"not a department store."*

The following conversation took place at Goldsmith's Bed and Breakfast in Missoula on September 17, 1992.

SUZI GABLIK: I think the idea of yours that's most striking for me is your notion that mankind is not at the apex of the pyramid at all, but that fungi are far more important, at least from an ecological perspective.

CHRISTOPHER MANES: That's simply a biological fact. Fungus is more important biologically, as biologists will tell you. The fact that this is so needs to be reiterated as much as possible, because, listening to the discourse of humanism, listening to the discourse of Man—this homocentric fiction that I talk about—you would think fungus is unimportant. We say that it's on the lower end of the evolutionary scale and we're on the top end of the evolutionary scale, and yet it's simple biology: fungus is more important. We need to reiterate that. If our project is read-justing and replacing humanity back into the realm of biological communities, we have to realize that we live with a certain fiction, the fiction that we are somehow special, ontologically different.

SG: At this point, unfortunately, it seems like more than just a fiction, because Man and his artifacts and his whole civilization are so overwhelming. It's hard to imagine that we're not more important than other things, because we are so powerfully all over the place.

CM: This is the fascinating thing, and it's what ties the things I'm saying into issues about the relevancy of art. And that is, all we really have are stories. This building here, or that university building we spoke in yesterday, are there because of stories someone told in the twelfth century. The particular story was, we need people to spread the word of the Bible; they have to learn Latin, so let's build a university. There's another story told about the necessity for vandalizing the world. The story creates a kind of reality. What I'm saying is we've been telling a story for the last five hundred years or so, and the story is: mankind is special, ontologically different from the rest of the world. Only *we* have language, only *we* are subjects. The rest of the world is a universe of "not-saids" called nature—nature is this immense silence, this immense, *irrational* silence. And that's a story. It's a bad story that's leading to the destruction you're talking about. We need to tell a story which shows that the fiction of Man is just another story, not an ultimate reality. We don't have to be part of that story anymore.

SG: All that connects with postmodern processes of deconstruction, of course, but my sense is that there's more than just a story going on. There's also this thing known as the cultural trance. For instance, George Bush must be aware of all the other stories going on out there, but he's in a trance with his story. So it may sound as if all we have to do is change the story, but the problem is that not everyone is willing to change the story. Even those of us —myself and yourself, for instance—we've already changed our story, but the destructive things are still going on.

CM: It's immensely difficult, of course. If I had the answer to that, I'd put it in a bottle and I'd sell it. We don't have the answer to that. But I think we should have a great deal of hope, because we can describe —and I've tried to do this in some of my writing— how this particular story came about, how this fiction of Man developed out of the Renaissance because of certain developments, certain institutions like the rise of literacy and the rise of Christian exegesis. We can actually talk about how, suddenly,

Man appeared on the stage. Michel Foucault writes about this at the end of *The Order of Things.* He says Man is like a face drawn in the sand. It appeared one day, and we take it for some ultimate reality. But, just as inexplicably, a wave could break on the sand, and the face of Man could disappear. Historians have learned, especially postmodern historians—Foucault has talked about it in particular—that history is discontinuous. People believed for centuries that individuals who saw visions were visionaries and prophets, and then, in one century, they decided such people were insane, and they put them all in the insane asylum—and we have a whole new institution. History changes discontinuously because of relationships among institutions that want to use ideas for their own power. To give you just one example: the Great Chain of Being, the notion that the world is a giant filigree of natural forms going up from zoophytes to Godhead, with mankind in the middle.

SG: Just under the Godhead, you mean.

CM: A little less than angels, and a little higher than the brute beasts. This was a notion that in medieval theology was actually a restraint on the destruction of nature. Thomas Aquinas writes—and he could have been writing as a conservation biologist today—that there are some people who believe it's better to have two angels than a stone and one angel. But Aquinas says it's better to have an angel and a stone, because the more species you have, the more you're able to see the perfection of creation. He even uses the word species, although he meant it in the philosophical, not scientific, sense. So, at least within the hushed, cloistered cells of monasteries, people used the Great Chain of Being as a restraint, saying, don't go out and destroy things. There is a perfect order, and we're just part of it. That's what medieval theologians were saying. But all this shifted with the rise of the Renaissance. Suddenly, the Great Chain of Being was an argument for human domination; and you had people like Hamlet saying, "What a piece of work is a man! . . . the beauty of the world! the paragon of animals!" And you had Francis Bacon saying that if you take Man out of the picture, out of the *scala naturae,* the world would be without aim or purpose, because it's all been made with him in mind. And ultimately, with the rise of the scientific revolution in the seventeenth century, the theological, or divine elements of the Chain are lopped off, and we're left at the top of the Chain. And this becomes an argument for the human domination of nature, so that even with the rise of evolutionary theory, where Darwin is saying there's no such thing as hierarchy, or advance, or progress, in nature, evolution gets absorbed by the Great Chain of Being. My point is this: ideas can be used and can have their meaning changed by institutions—profoundly, in very short amounts of time, inexplicably. And if we know that, we have the hope that the ideas we've created over the last five hundred years can be used toward preserving the earth, and preserving biological diversity, and getting back into communication with the other biological communities around us.

SG: So the new, more sanguine story, if I understand you correctly, is the story of deep ecology, and within that story, Man becomes superfluous.

CM: Superfluous in the sense of being part of what Aldo Leopold calls just a plain member of the biological community. We're here like anything else. Which is greatly liberating, if you ask me. We can enjoy ourselves. We don't have to be the vanguard of evolution anymore.

SG: It should liberate us from our overweening hubris because, as you say, from an ecological perspective, if we disappeared, not too much would change, whereas if the fungi disappear, everything might collapse.

CM: That's not a deep ecology view, that's a fact of biology. Ask some biologists; ask those people who actually look at nature and, at their best, don't bring ideologies to their observations, but who just listen —to what the fungus has to say. How does the fungus work? We won't bring our stories to *it;* we'll let the fungus tell its story. At its best, science is really humans trying to communicate with nature and letting nature have its say. I think that's what Darwin was doing.

sg: Do you think we have any part in the Chain at all?

cm: Yes, we're here. It's not a chain. It's—

sg: A circle? A web?

cm: It's a home. We live here, with other things. And we're more or less related to them. We have a system of genealogies, of family trees, in which we're ultimately all related; and everything that's here is just as advanced as everything else. The challenge is how do we talk about it, since obviously humans are important to us. How can we tell stories about ourselves, how can we talk about human freedom and human dignity, without depreciating and occluding the rest of the natural world? For that reason, we need a new language that leaps away from the Enlightenment language in which our verbal, and even our artistic, language exists. The art we produce today is the art of the Enlightenment.

sg: That's something I was going to ask you. If we're talking about a new language and a new story, how does that affect art, and our understanding of art? What role could art play in creating the new story?

cm: You can see two roles. One is the deconstructive role: giving the lie to the old story about human dominance. That's the easy part, it seems to me. You pointed out that, to a great extent, postmodern art has already done that; it's decentered all the centricities we have, of logic, rationality—

SG: The heroic ego-self.

CM: Exactly. It's been a decentering process. But I don't think it's gotten to decentering what I call the fiction of Man, because that aspect becomes much more problematical. What I would say is this. The political aspect—some of the things you're talking about, like the necessity for artists to be responsible, and to respond to the death of nature in a way that acknowledges it—I think that's important, and absolutely necessary. But there's a deeper question, and that is, who is doing this representing? In other words, we can talk about environmental problems, but if we're still "Man," if we're still this fiction, we're defining the problem in a certain way. For instance, Man is the product of the Enlightenment and Renaissance humanism, which exists through psychological, economic and sociopolitical terms. That's how we see the world—that's what this fiction is about. And we're the center of things, because of this grid of knowledge that our institutions have produced—the church, the state, corporations. That's the Man who's speaking in most of our discourse, even environmental discourse. The problem, we always say, is economics—we're not using our resources right. Well, who's saying that? That's not me as an animal in the world; that's Economic Man, *Homo economicus.* That's a creation of the Enlightenment. No one else could have said that —a classic Greek couldn't have said that.

SG: What would it take to not be that person?

CM: I don't know, but I do know this. It seems to me something that artists have to ask: who is doing the representation? Because if it's "Man" doing it, it will always define the problem in a way in which nature will always be silent. And that's what we have to get away from. Now, how we do it—that's the issue, and it's very difficult. Let me just suggest a couple of things. I think first of all that we need to look at what aboriginal people are doing, because they have a different taxonomy. We have a taxonomy that talks about higher and lower life forms. It has no analogue in the real world. It's the fiction of Man talking, and there's a directionality there that doesn't exist in nature. There is no higher and lower. Everything that's evolved is just as evolved as everything else.

SG: What about the idea of certain creatures having more complex nervous systems, and by the time you get to man, a whole thinking apparatus and ability to cogitate and reflect, and to create artifacts and civilizations, which other animals don't have? Doesn't that appear to be a superior set of skills, or endowments?

CM: It is if you say it is. Now, if you say lovemaking is more important, then banana slugs are more skillful, because they can make love for three days and are hermaphroditic. We can't do that. If longevity is what you really care about, then bristlecone pines are the most superior beings. They live for several thousand years. If you pick the quality and privilege it—

SG: Complexity, I guess, has usually been the privileged notion.

CM: Yes, but why privilege complexity? And, by the way, how do you gauge complexity? Do you gauge it by the number of cells? Did dinosaurs have more cells than we do? And blue whales? A dolphin's brain is pretty complex.

SG: Well, it all has to do with forefinger skill and stuff, doesn't it?

CM: Well, that's forefinger skill. But termites can identify each other digging holes fifty feet away, and they can wind up having the holes come perfectly together. We don't know how they do it. Now, to me, that's a wonderful skill. So does that give them the right—and the duty—to dominate evolution? Obviously not. It's random. We privilege things. It's not a coincidence we privilege ourselves.

SG: In her book *Homo Aestheticus,* Ellen Dissanayake claims that Man is the only creature who makes art, who makes things special, who has created civilization.

CM: She mentions bowerbirds, and of course, bowerbirds do create art. But, if you ask me—and this is really fundamental—in the observation of nature, as opposed to old books about things, if you watch almost anything in nature, it does basically what we do. Edward Abbey said, if you watch a centipede for fifteen minutes, you realize it has a life, and a way of being, that's just as important to it as mine is to me. Centipedes go out, they hunt, they mate, they sleep, they calculate, and they sit around and look at things. And when I think about my life, that's exactly what I do! There are very few things in nature that don't do basically what we do.

SG: A centipede doesn't play basketball!

CM: No, but I don't have poisonous fangs. And I don't hunt worms. The centipede has all kinds of qualities I don't have. There are animals that have extraordinary, complex behaviors that we can't even fathom. Basically, this is something we have difficulty coming to terms with. We're animals—that's what we are. The only thing really odd about humanity that makes us different is that our hair grows in front of our eyes, and that doesn't happen to a lot of animals. But there's no quality—this has been a thousand-year search—that makes us different. You can't find anything. First, it was language. Then we found out that chimpanzees have language, dolphins have language. For a long time, it was toolmaking; we're *Homo faber*. Then we found out that Darwin's finches make tools.

sg: But surely they don't make tools on the scale that Man makes them?

cm: Oh sure, there's a scale question there.

sg: What about that? Do you just ignore it? I mean, finches can't make atom bombs, right?

cm: That's true. But we don't make formic acid, as ants do. There's no quality we have that can't be counterpoised by another quality in nature that we don't have. We have qualities, and the rest of nature has qualities, but basically they overlap.

sg: What about the question of power? We now have the power to destroy the world. Ants, as far as we can tell, do not have the power to destroy the world.

cm: On the contrary, we don't have the power to destroy the world. We have the power to destroy this beautiful period of the world in which we evolved, the Cenozoic period, where there are ocelots and flamingos and ferns. A nice place to live. But we can do everything we want to do to destroy this, and nature is going to continue. It's pretty difficult to destroy spores. And there'll be spores here no matter what we do. And in a million years, there'll be a planet here, without us. The issue really isn't saving the world; the issue is saving this particular period in geological time in which we evolved. And why waste it? It's a world where we evolved, and it's beautiful. I like being here. Ultimately, this is not about a dreary subject. What I'm talking about—rediscovering our place in nature—is not about some kind of devolving into a lower life form, where we have only some basic existence and we don't have beautiful things around us. What I'm saying, and what I think environmentalists and artists should say more about, is recapturing the rich, poetic, wild ways in which we can relate to nature and ourselves. Our potential for relating to each other is really complex and beautiful, whereas our civilization has reduced it, and made it one-dimensional.

SG: Mechanical.

CM: Yes, that's what Man is. Man is this mechanical creature, who sees himself at the apex of evolution, and who defines everything in terms of psychology and economics and a few other privileged categories of the Enlightenment, of humanism. But we're not limited to that. We merely have to point to aboriginal people, who engage the world in profoundly different, and rich, ways. We have this potential to relate to each other so richly, and wildly, and poetically. And really, that's what environmentalists and artists should be talking about—enriching ourselves. Our lives aren't enriched by nuclear power plants.

SG: How do you teach that to George Bush?

CM: I don't know. That's not my role in things. Maybe you want to teach him. Maybe he can't be taught.

SG: But what does that say about human consciousness, if we take him as a paradigm figure for those who can't be taught? I mean, what's wrong with us that what you're saying, which is so clear to you and to me, can't be seen by so many people and isn't understood by them?

CM: This is the effect of power. Power privileges and reifies its stories, so it's not even a story to George Bush, not even a story to most people. The domination of humanity over nature is a *fact* to them. There's no other story to be told. But that's the role of intellectuals, that's the role of writers and artists —to break down this pyramid, this Egyptian pyramid of domination that looms over our culture, and then to start telling other stories. As I say, it's easier said than done. And it might be impossible—we might crash and burn. But we have a responsibility to try, and everyone has to try what they feel they need to do. I personally like interpreting the shift from the medieval period to the Renaissance in the construction of nature as silence. I find this notion of nature having no voice to be much more productive than the usual discussion of the rights of nature, for instance. I use that locution sometimes myself, but generally, rights are an outcome of the Enlightenment. No one talked about rights until the Enlightenment. It seems to me we have an obligation to get away from the language of the Enlightenment.

SG: Is there any art, beyond the writings of deep ecologists and poets like Gary Snyder, any visual art that you feel fulfills the kind of vision you're talking about?

CM: I really think that it's time for our culture, and artists, to change the subject. For the last five hundred years, all we've talked about is Man—his political existence, his economic existence, his psychological existence. And that's all part of the fabric of this story. I think we have to take that subject and just put it aside, not talk about it anymore. We need to start talking about this other kingdom.

SG: Now we've gotten to the heart of the matter—making art about centipedes!

CM: We need to make art about centipedes! We need to have art in which a centipede is speaking. I think it's very similar to Pleistocene art. It's very similar, perhaps, to Mycenaean art, in which the natural world is there and speaking as itself. It's not there as a moment of contemplation for the fiction of Man. One of the reasons I think aboriginal people have been able to stay on the Red Path, as Black Elk would say, is that they used ritual to make sure the rational part of the brain never took over. Maybe the reason for that was to keep in balance the rational and the irrational. I mean, they wouldn't see it as that kind of dichotomy, but this one calculating part of our existence, as opposed to the intuitive and creative and holistic part—we don't have any of that balance in our society. We need logic to get by in the world, but it becomes hypertrophic at some point, in that it keeps on growing. It's like elephant tusks, the mastodon tusks. At some point they cross, and they become burdensome. Maybe our minds are like that. We need to develop techniques to keep the rational mind in balance. I think art does play a role in it.

SG: How much time do you spend making art yourself?

CM: Not very much. I've been painting since I was nine, but I don't paint much anymore. I just do it when I get the inspiration.

SG: Can you describe one or two of your works?

CM: Yeah. I started as a Surrealist. In fact, I was very interested in Hieronymus Bosch—I'm a medievalist, so that makes sense. And then, I got very interested in Dalí. In fact, Dalí taught me how to paint.

SG: What interested you about Salvador Dalí?

CM: First of all, his draftsmanship. Whatever you want to say about Dalí—maybe in the end he's just a charlatan, that's a possibility—but he was a great painter as far as his draftsmanship. He really studied the Dutch painters. And so, he's very useful for learning the techniques of painting. Then I got interested in Pleistocene art, the purity of it. It was this gaze—the perspective of the viewer that was just this gaze on the animal world, without the intervention of psychology and economics. So now, I like using cave art images in the background and using a pastiche of modern images over them. I'm interested in Ice Age art because it is clearly a way of looking at the world distinct from the Enlightenment, Renaissance, humanistic point of view, where the world is a repository of symbols that are interpreted, in which meaning resides in us, or some putative divine being who speaks through nature, so that these other animals out there don't have a life of their own. What's amazing about Ice Age art is that it's absolutely anatomically correct. These people studied those animals. They obviously studied them very, very closely, as all hunter-gatherers do. Hunter-gatherers understand the other animals—they have to. They have to listen to them. Cave paintings are not some generalized, vague, formalistic portraits—they are detailed listenings. Hunter-gatherers obviously sat down and watched these animals for a long time.

SG: In our life of office buildings and factories and shopping malls, how do you think we can acquire those skills again? How can we learn to hear the animals?

CM: That's a good question. Maybe what I'm feeling when I'm doing my art is how the Pleistocene megafauna is right under the surface. It really is. I mean, our cities are phantasms that are just fleeting images on the landscape. They're probably unsustainable. And nature is always ready to boil up and return. I think you simply have to realize that this is not the real world—Los Angeles is not the real world. It's a strange digression. The real world is old-growth forests and deserts, and places where evolution is happening. It's just an amazing idea, the thought that evolution may be coming to an end because of our disruption of the ecological community. We've so undermined, and we're so managing, the natural world that evolution—something that's persisted for three and a half billion years—is being disrupted. It's enough to make your blood run cold. However, it can only be disrupted for a while.

No Art in the Lifeboats

HILTON KRAMER

After the conference in Missoula, I had occasion to share the lecture podium in Madison, Wisconsin, with Hilton Kramer, for many years the lead art critic of the New York Times, *until he left to become the founding editor of the* New Criterion *magazine. Currently he is also the art critic for the* New York Observer. *Kramer is well known for his hard-hitting, conservative views and for his blunt opinions about the political correctness movement.*

Not only does he take a dim view of political correctness, but he is categorically opposed to the "politicization" of art; to describe any art as "political" is sufficient to discredit it in Kramer's eyes, without further discussion.

Knowing that his views on art, and indeed on most things, are diametrically opposed to my own, it was with some trepidation that I wrote to Kramer, asking him to do a conversation with me while we were in Madison. I explained that my purpose, which at this point had clearly emerged, was to activate the oppositional force fields in our culture, and to make use of empathic dialogue as a means for healing these conflicted relationships. Beyond that, I told him, I had no fixed purpose, only a desire to create a space for others to talk.

"How can you share," Bohm asks, "if you are sure you have truth and the other fellow is sure he has truth, and the truths don't agree? How can you share?" My conversation with Kramer, I knew, was the one that was going to put Bohm's whole philosophy to the test, not to mention my own. I was acutely aware of Kramer's resistance to the kinds of collaborative, community-oriented art projects, aimed toward social, cultural and environmental change, that I talk about when I am on the lecture circuit.

As an unyielding, capital M Modernist, Kramer believes in aesthetic autonomy as crucial to art's value; a well-

honed, universal canon defined by quality; the prototypical model of the artist as a lone genius struggling against society; and a vision-generated, vision-centered paradigm for art. When an interviewer for The, *Sante Fe's monthly magazine of the arts, recently asked David Ross, director of the Whitney Museum, what he thought of Kramer, Ross replied: "Hilton Kramer is a tremendously gifted, neoconservative critic who hasn't liked any new art in, probably, thirty years, and whose taste in things old I tend to appreciate. I wish he would open his mind up to look at the things that are being made today and recognize the qualities in them, but I fear that he never will." Since I had already encountered his aggressive antics and sharply pointed tongue elsewhere, I knew Kramer was not afraid of a rumble. Evidently the organizers of our duo performance at the University of Wisconsin were anxious about this, too, since they organized separate dinner parties for each of us.*

"The defense of opinions," writes David Bohm, "separates people. Each of us defends his own opinion, and then we don't meet. We don't really listen to one another; we try to win." On the podium, this is exactly what happened. Kramer (who spoke after I did) proclaimed, with the force of a typhoon, that art is at its best when it serves only itself and not some other purpose—that is, when it is created and appreciated as art and not as something else. Then he

proceeded to lowball the kind of art I had put forward,
stating that things having no relation to art were now being
legitimized and accepted as art (Mierle Ukeles shaking the
hands of New York City sanitation workers in a perfor-
mance piece became his designated bête noire), and claiming
that art is incapable of solving any problems but aesthetic
ones. Kramer feels it is disastrous to imagine that social or
environmental issues can be addressed in the artist's studio
(no mention was made of the fact that many artists have
chosen to leave the studio for new zones of practice), or to
think that political or social change could ever take place in a
museum or an art gallery. With an edge that was sometimes
arrogant and often brutal, Kramer declared that the de-
mands being made, as he put it, to "chain art to some
anonymous collective purpose" is a move toward totalitari-
anism, since the great achievement of modernism has been
to free art and give it autonomy. The purist ideal, which
regards social isolation as essential for art, was summed up
pretty accurately for me by Grace Hartigan, who was quoted
not too long ago in the New York Times *as saying: "Art is*
still the only place in the world where you can do exactly
what you want, if you pay the price, which is having no one
else want it."

In our private conversation, the tone of things was
quite different. Gone was the hostility and cynicism that

practically drips from Kramer's public persona. In place of the lacerating style, he was unhesitatingly open about himself and his life. "In the dialogue," states David Bohm, "we just talk with each other, and we are not committed to accomplishing anything. Nobody has to agree to anything. We simply listen to all the opinions." Listening to all the opinions, Bohm claims, will bring us together at a much deeper level. We don't have to make any decisions. That is how it felt when we spoke.

The following conversation was taped at the Elvehjem Museum in Madison on October 2, 1992.

SUZI GABLIK: What I'd like to do here, Hilton, is open up the possibility for you to speak about whatever's really important to you at the moment, in relation to your sense of the direction that art is going.

HILTON KRAMER: One of my principle concerns these days is for the embattled feelings that I observe in many younger artists who are working in what I suppose now would be called "traditional" media—drawing, painting and sculpture. Because of the politicization of the art scene, meaning the museums, the universities, the art journals, and so on, including even the mainstream media, they feel very endangered, facing a prospect of marginalization in the art world. They're being told that it's not the route to success in the art world to be doing these traditional things. Obviously, among the best of them, that is not a deterrent, because they seem to have made the distinction between what it means to be an artist, and what it means to have success, and they aren't inclined to confuse the one thing with the other. But they feel that all the signals of the cultural world are suggesting to them that what they're doing is no longer of significance, whether it's because they're white males, or because they're Americans in a culture that's going to be dominated by other parts of the world. They feel there's a failure in the cultural world they inhabit to reinforce the values that mean the most to them as aspiring artists.

SG: I find these comments interesting, because in describing traditional art forms and the artists who are using them, you seem to suggest that they are in the position of underdogs at this point. I myself have been focusing more on artists who often do not pursue traditional genres at all, and I can only say that I have found the same thing to be true of them. They also feel misunderstood and not included. I'm frequently told that nobody speaks for them but me. So, if neither the traditionalists—your group, if you will—nor the nontraditionalists are getting the recognition, then who is getting it?

HK: There is that great miasma out there which we can generally characterize as the art world of fashion, just to use a convenient shorthand. And that art world of fashion doesn't allow many points of entry for either of the things we're talking about. That world is defined by the Gagosian Gallery, Mary Boone, Pace, Castelli, and so on, and the museums, critics, collectors and people in the media who look to them to signify what is of most importance, and what should be supported and promoted as the most significant art of the moment. They always have to allow for the induction of new members, but these tend not to come, certainly, from the artists I'm talking about.

SG: Are there any artists working today whom you feel *are* getting the reputations they deserve, or are all those with the big reputations overconsidered, while the others are underconsidered?

HK: I think there are certain artists of the older generation who have earned big reputations deservedly— Richard Diebenkorn, for example. I think his work is marvelous. He's earned his reputation without engaging in any dishonorable shortcuts. He's been in total personal control of all of his aesthetic decisions in a way that, it seems to me, somebody like Julian Schnabel or David Salle is not. Among artists younger than that, there are some that I admire a lot —Helen Miranda Wilson, for instance, who is a wonderful landscape painter. She's the younger daughter of the writer Edmund Wilson. She has a show every few years, and people buy her paintings. They're very small pictures, and they have relatively modest prices. She has a real following, but as far as I can recall, I've never seen her work in a museum collection; I've never seen an article in an art magazine about her. I've never heard her complain about it, by the way. She's followed, really, her own course. She's pursued what seemed, fifteen years ago, an eccentric, almost reactionary position, and she's made something solid of it, I think.

SG: So would you describe this situation we're talking about as a kind of real dysfunctionality in the art world?

HK: Oh, I think a large part of the art world is dysfunctional now. But I think a lot of it—and I'm not reluctant to make moral judgments, as you know—has to do with the *size* of the art world, and the quantity of works that are put before the public, the sheer quantity of galleries, the quantity of objects, the quantity of people making claim to the status of professional artist. The map of the art world has so greatly expanded in the last twenty-five years.

SG: Would you be willing to use the word "value-structure" instead of, or in addition to, the word "map"?

HK: I don't think the value-structure has significantly expanded. We may mean different things by value-structure, but to me, there's been a decline in the confidence that people have the right to say of a work of art that it's failed—or indeed, that it has succeeded. I mean in aesthetic terms, not monetary terms.

SG: Do you see that as a flaw in our critical apparatus?

HK: It is a flaw in our critical apparatus, and I find in it an analogue to the declining confidence that people have in describing any form of personal behavior as moral failure. I don't think there's necessarily a causal relationship between moral failure and the inability to make aesthetic judgments, but I think there is a parallel development.

SG: Do you feel there is a moral imperative to art, then, or some kind of connection of the moral life with art? What would it be?

HK: Yes, I think there is a moral imperative in art, but I think it consists of living up to one's highest abilities.

SG: To make art?

HK: To make art.

SG: What about issues like Picasso's much discussed reprehensible personal life, and that sort of thing? Do you think any connections ought to be drawn here, or are we meant to focus only on art when we talk about higher principles?

HK: Nobody has a lower opinion of Picasso's moral life, his personal life, than I have. I think not only in his treatment of the women in his life, but also in his treatment of the men in his life, he behaved like a scoundrel, from start to finish. I cannot say, however, that in the most important works of art he created—which for me are his Cubist works between about 1907 through the 1920s—that I feel these works of art are in any way diminished by the flaws in Picasso's character.

SG: I would certainly agree with that. I guess the question that is really most on my mind is whether you consider that the state of the world at the moment —being, as we probably are, at the edge of potential social and environmental collapse—should in any way affect how we view art, and the role that it might play in our culture at this time?

HK: Well, I hope that it doesn't. Because I think to sacrifice our interest in art to any higher collective good would be so damaging to the spiritual life of our culture that even if we succeeded in dealing with the social, political and ecological problems that we face in this society, we would be so diminished that it might not be worth our success. That is, I don't think you can expect to achieve victories in a society at the expense of art.

SG: How do you feel about the "fiddling while Rome burns" scenario, then, or rearranging the deck chairs on the *Titanic?* How do you get around that?

HK: I don't really see our society in that condition today. What I'm much more bothered by in our society today is, for example—this will sound familiar—the disintegration of the family. I don't think that art, high art, has any role to play in that. I do think that popular culture—movies, television, rock and rap music, et cetera—plays a tremendously *destructive* role. I'm not even interested in censoring them, because in our kind of society every attempt at diminishing freedom of expression boomerangs. But I don't feel that the condition of our planet is that of the *Titanic*.

SG: You don't! Well, I guess that would be our biggest disagreement—even more than anything else we've talked about today.

HK: Probably. I think we have very grave problems, but I also think that in piecemeal fashion, they're being addressed. I don't want to live in a world in which they're being addressed in anything but a piecemeal fashion, because large collective mandates for dealing with the environment are going to be so diminishing to individual freedom and initiative that they will result in a society not worth living in.

SG: So will the escalating destruction of all the life-support systems of the earth lead to a livable society?

HK: If I believed total destruction was that imminent, I suppose I would have to rethink the question.

sg: If you were more inclined to the *"Titanic* view," would that alter the ideas you've been putting forward about art and its relevance?

hk: Well, if I really believed that the ship was sinking, I would certainly want to get into the lifeboat, and in the lifeboats, there's no life of art. But there, you're sacrificing art to survival. You're not sacrificing it to any higher good than that.

sg: When you say you would jump into a lifeboat without art, what would the lifeboat consist of?

hk: The lifeboat would consist of social action. But I think we know from history that we're not facing that kind of catastrophe.

sg: You don't see our particular civilization as totally incompatible, then, with the long-term survival of the environment?

hk: No, I don't.

sg: I'd love to hear you speak more about that.

hk: Well, I can't put myself forward as an authority on the environment. I've done my share of reading and listening as other people have, but from Malthus on, there have been prophesies of imminent catastrophe. I guess I'm both temperamentally and intellectually not susceptible to believing in them.

sg: You mean, to apocalyptic visions?

hk: The apocalypse to me is a form of simplification.

sg: There's no possibility that there's any kind of denial or blindness in this? You don't think, as one environmentalist has put it, that there's an elephant in the room, which we're not seeing?

hk: There's always a possibility of denial or blindness, but I feel I'm acting like a rational human being, weighing one thing against another.

sg: And your instincts tell you that everything's going to be OK?

hk: My intelligence tells me that we're not as doomed— I'm not going to say we're going to be OK—that we're not doomed in the way we are being invited to believe.

sg: So what does your picture of the future encompass?

hk: Unfortunately, my picture of the future encompasses a society in which the pressures are all going to be, on the one hand, for a good deal more of what I would call "atomized" freedom.

sg: What do you mean by that?

hk: That is, people are being encouraged to live more and more aspects of their life without any moral restraints. And on the other hand, we have large social pressures to conform to mandated modes of behavior in nonpersonal ways. There is now no value in the name of which you can say to any child, or youngster, that any form of sexual behavior, or any form of sexual perversion, is a bad thing. On the other hand, the pressure from society to prevent that child from smoking a cigarette will be enormous. So you could say the vision of the future is the child who is given a condom and has his cigarettes taken away from him.

sg: Is this a vision you feel comfortable contemplating?

hk: No, I very much disapprove of it.

sg: If you could effect some change yourself, what would it be?

hk: I'm not hopeful about effecting changes, but I think that without some restoration of real conviction in the traditional family structure, there's no hope of avoiding the drift into a greater and greater atomization of the individual. Because I think it's only in the context of family that people learn to live in society in an amicable way. I say this without any illusions about family life—I've had plenty of difficulty with my own.

sg: Do you have children?

HK: No, I don't have children.

SG: But you have a wife?

HK: Yes, I have a wife. I've been married for twenty-seven years.

SG: With some difficulties?

HK: I am talking about the family into which I was born. I was the youngest of four children. Nobody in the family really approved of the way I wanted to spend my life. My parents were Russian immigrants—my father was a tailor. Fortunately, they had the good sense to get on the train in Boston and go north; and they got off at the last stop and it was Gloucester, on Cape Ann. That's where I was born and raised, which is a beautiful place to grow up in. But it was my teachers in public school who gave me my real start in life.

SG: And your love of art?

HK: That I picked up outside of school, because Gloucester was still a summer art colony in those days. All summer there were people painting everywhere.

SG: That was your first contact with art?

HK: That was my first contact with art. The kids I knew all painted from the time they were very young, as I did.

SG: You painted, too? When did you stop?

HK: I stopped when I was around fourteen, when I went to the Museum of Fine Arts in Boston for the first time.

SG: When you saw the real thing?

HK: When I saw the real thing.

SG: So art intimidated you, Hilton?

HK: No, no. It taught me a great lesson in reality.

SG: Was it a kind of shock and disappointment at the time?

HK: No, I was already drifting away. My interests were shifting to writing and reading.

SG: Since we're on to something a little more personal, maybe you would share how you got into art criticism.

HK: Like most things in life, I got into art criticism by a kind of accident. All of my formal academic education was in literature and philosophy. I went to Syracuse University as an undergraduate, and by that time I had a fair experience of looking at works of art, old art. I wasn't really interested in modern art at that time. Particularly because of the Boston Museum collection, I was very interested in Indian and Indonesian art: Coomeraswamy had put together that great collection.

SG: Becoming a modernist was a big jump then.

HK: I hadn't really seen any—there were no modern paintings in the Boston Museum in those days, and I probably didn't even know about the Fogg. I had wonderful teachers in literary subjects, but none of them ever told me that the Boston Museum was there; I just fell into it one day. In any case, when I went to college, it turned out that most of my friends were artists, either art students or art teachers. Even though I was majoring in English and philosophy, I signed up for one art history course. The first day we were given the list of slides we would have to memorize for the examination at the end of the term, and I thought it was ridiculous to memorize slides of pictures you had never seen, and so I just got out of the course. And I never took a course in art history ever again; though in later years, I taught art history—first at Bennington, and then in other places.

SG: How did you get from philosophy and literature into art criticism and the *New York Times?*

HK: I came to New York in January 1950 to go to graduate school at Columbia, also in comparative literature and philosophy. From time to time, I went to hear Meyer Schapiro lecture, but I never had a course with him. I was spending more and more of my time in museums and galleries—1950 was a good year for that. It still never occurred to me to have a career in the art world. I thought I was going to have a career as an English professor, and I started writing literary criticism and publishing it in the literary quarterlies. It was in 1953 that an artist friend of mine, who had been studying at the Art Students League—we used to go to galleries together—suggested, apropos of an argument we were having about some shows, that I try my hand at writing about art. I'd already published a couple of articles on T. S. Eliot, and so on. That was how I got started: I wrote an article. I sent it to Philip Rahv, the editor of *Partisan Review,* whom I had met at the School of Letters in Indiana, and he published it in the summer of 1953. To my absolute amazement, I woke up the next morning, so to speak, to discover that the art world regarded me as an art critic. I was showered with invitations to write about art.

SG: When did the *New York Times* come into the picture?

HK: That was much later, in 1965. I first went to work for the old *Arts Digest,* which we transformed into

Arts Magazine, and I became the editor of that, at the end of the 1950s. I left that job in '61, went to Europe for awhile; 1962–63 I taught at Bennington, and at the same time worked for a year as art critic for the *Nation.* It wasn't until the fall of '65 that I got a call one day, asking me if I'd be interested in coming to work for the *New York Times.* It was amusing in a way. I was free-lancing at the time, and when my wife, Esta—who had formerly been married to the painter Al Leslie and had a lot of experience in the art world—came home from her job at *Arts,* I told her the *New York Times* had offered me a job. She sort of recoiled in horror, and said, "Well, you're not thinking about taking it, are you?"

SG: That's wild!

HK: [Laughing] You must remember what a bad reputation the *Times* art page had when John Canaday was carrying on about everything. She felt that she'd never be able to face anybody in the art world again! As for myself, I had just given a talk, which was going to be published, at an American Federation of Arts conference in Boston, about what was wrong with art criticism, citing the *New York Times* as the prime example. So when I had my interview with Clifton Daniel, the managing editor, and he asked me what I thought was wrong with the art criticism at the *New York Times,* I was able to say, "Well, I'm just about to publish a paper on the subject!"

sg: The things you felt were wrong then with art criticism—do you feel the same things are wrong now, or that different things are wrong now?

hk: I feel different things are wrong now.

sg: What was wrong then?

hk: What was wrong then was a kind of basic philistinism.

sg: You mean there was no depth, no controversy?

hk: It was all bland. The controversies that Canaday caused by attacking, you know, Robert Motherwell, or someone like that, as being an incompetent artist —they weren't interesting controversies. It was just the same old philistinism. And it came as a big surprise to me that the editorial management of the *Times* was getting very restive because they were receiving a lot of complaints about it. Turner Catledge, who was then the executive editor, said to me the day that he hired me, "They tell me you're a very bright fellow and you know a lot. We need that now. The papers, even the *Times,* used to hire art critics for the worst possible reasons—old sportswriters, people who couldn't do the difficult beats any more. It was a form of semiretirement for them," he said. "But our readers are too smart for all that now, and we really have to give them a more informed account of what's going on."

SG: So did you come in shooting from the hip, on high moral ground?

HK: I came in, in the beginning, very determined not to be amusing, because that was sort of the *patois* of writing about art—that it was all a bunch of yaks. I presented myself as dealing with very serious matters right from the start. It really upset an awful lot of people.

SG: Do you remember what some of the issues were that you took up, initially?

HK: My first review was of a Jules Olitski exhibition at the Poindexter Gallery, and I talked about what had happened to abstract painting in the sixties, and the shift from Abstract Expressionism to Color Field painting.

SG: Was it more than just a description of events? Was there some imperative, or thesis?

HK: It wasn't an enthusiastic review, but I wanted to make clear that the judgments I was making of the art were aesthetic judgments. They weren't the old philistine ideas—ideas that anybody can do this sort of thing—which had been the subtext of the Motherwell-bashing kind of stuff. I came to work in the fall of '65, when things were still quiet politically. The Vietnam protests were already in place, but a year or so later, everything was hitting the fan, politically and culturally. I got involved in those issues, not unlike today, trying to defend the integrity of art against the attempt to enlist it in political causes. Compared to what's going on today, it was almost an age of innocence.

SG: How do you feel about the point of view, which many people hold, that formalist art is itself a very politicized kind of art that derives directly from the capitalist ethos, which wants value-free products and commodities?

HK: I don't believe in it. The whole point of the main essay in my book *The Age of the Avant-Garde,* published in 1973, was that it had been a mistake in perception to think that there was anything permanent about the conflict between the avant-garde and the bourgeoisie. The avant-garde was unimaginable as a cultural development in isolation from the middle class. It functioned historically as the aesthetic conscience of the middle class, and was allowed to develop as vital an art as it did because of the liberalism of the middle class.

SG: Would you refute the idea that modernist art is a contextual art, in the sense that it is not pure, or universal, or value-free, but that it reflects a particular social moment and has been used to support certain political and economic ideologies?

HK: I agree to this extent—that modernist art has proved to be, though not by the intention of most of its creators, the most appropriate art for a democratic, capitalist society.

SG: In what ways?

HK: I think modernist art represents the dynamism of bourgeois, capitalist societies.

SG: You mean the need for new products?

HK: No, I mean a propensity for changing technologies. Because I don't see the need for new products as the driving force of capitalist enterprise. I see the drive for new scientific and technological discoveries —it's only within the capitalist context that these technological developments are harnessed to provide the comforts and improvement in standards of living of the society.

SG: And you see art as somehow linked to that pattern of behavior?

HK: I see modernist art as linked to that pattern of innovation, yes—what I call the "ethos of innovation."

SG: Does your present vision of art encompass the priority of this "ethos of innovation"? Do you still consider that innovation is a primary force in the artmaking process?

HK: I think its ability to produce art of what I would call real quality is much diminished from what it was.

SG: In other words, it's a process that has more or less spent itself.

HK: It is certainly in a fallow period at the moment.

SG: But could easily undergo a rebirth?

HK: I think it could undergo a rebirth, but that would probably depend on the revival of a certain kind of moral confidence, which was a very important driving force in bourgeois society until very recently. I think it has a lot to do with the kind of confidence that the art of high modernism enjoyed.

SG: Now you feel that confidence has been sorely undermined.

HK: I think that confidence is very much undermined.

SG: Do you want to discuss the factors that have played a part in this?

HK: I think the reason for the undermining of what I call the "ethos of confidence" has to do with the nature of liberalism itself, which has an almost fatal tendency to blame itself for the woes of the world. There seems to be, built into the liberal ethos, a guilt factor.

SG: Could you give an example of what you're talking about?

HK: Yes. That we are somehow responsible for the catastrophes that have overtaken, say, the nations of Africa.

SG: It's strange that you say that, because my sense is just the opposite. The way we live in our country is always to experience such calamities as happening to exotic others over there, but it has nothing to do with us over here.

HK: I don't think that's supported by the evidence—the whole idea of the Peace Corps, of foreign aid, of the immense quantities of money and technology that agencies of the American government and Western European governments have poured into the new nations of Africa. I think there is now an almost runaway tendency in a liberal society like our own to feel that we have somehow failed in our mission to bring to the rest of the world what we enjoy ourselves.

SG: What about the notion many people have today that a lot of what we enjoy ourselves is at the expense of the rest of the world?

HK: I don't think it's true. I don't believe that for one minute. I myself think that the people of Africa, specifically, would have been much better off— would have prospered socially, financially, medically, and in every other way, even culturally—if the decolonization process in the aftermath of the Second World War had been a much slower and more drawn-out process than it was. I think even India, for instance, would have experienced much less bloodshed if the British had not made such an abrupt departure. We all know the reasons for it, and we were all on the side of that abrupt departure at the time, but in my opinion, the consequences were devastating to those societies. It's taken India decades to regain the ground that was already in its possession under the empire. But I think Britain was also affected by that liberal guilt, and to go back to our own culture world, I think that no society so radically defined by guilt can produce an art based on high confidence.

SG: Let me put one more question out there before we wind down. Do you think that in today's world—the world we're living in right now—an art of high confidence is possible?

HK: I think it's difficult, but I do believe it will be possible again.

SG: Do you want to add any final words as to how you think that might come about, either ideally, or hopefully?

HK: No, I'm not a big believer in critics attempting to prophesize the future. The reason I feel—and I don't regard this as a prophesy so much as a conviction—that it will come again is that I think human nature is very resilient. I think there *is* a human nature. I don't think that the accomplishment of high achievements in art is an accident of history; I think such accomplishment answers a fundamental aspiration of human life. And as long as there are human communities in a state of advanced development, that aspiration will ignite the ambitions of gifted people.

Ten Thousand Artists, Not One Master

SATISH KUMAR

In January of 1991, I left London, where I had been living for more than twenty years in an on-and-off fashion, for good. I moved to a house on a mountain, on the outskirts of a small university town in Virginia. Three days before my over-and-done-with departure from London, George Bush embarked on Operation Desert Storm, in what seemed to many to be his private war with Saddam Hussein. On the day before I was to surrender and conclude one life in order to make way for another, headlines reverberated ominously in the London newspapers: "Heathrow Surrounded by Tanks!" I was lucky. I got out of there without incident, and threw off the urban, Anglican yoke forever.

Two years went by before I roused myself from my Appalachian dreams to return to England for a visit. It was time to check out the old story, see how friends were faring. Just as I was leaving, George Bush—who had recently been voted out of office by an American electorate absolutely desperate for change—began dropping bombs on Iraq again. So the trip had an eerie, déjà vu feeling about it.

When I was living in London, I occasionally published articles in an ecophilosophical magazine called Resurgence, which has been edited since 1973 by an inspired and engaging Indian man, Satish Kumar, who rode camel-carts with his mother during childhood, drank buffalo milk, and became a disciple of Gandhi's philosophy of nonviolence. Today he is the founder and director of an eminent think-tank for reframing our relationship with nature and for studying the global ecocrisis, known as Schumacher College, in Devon. Kumar had invited me to lecture there, and I was eager to visit the place where people like Fritjof Capra, Theodore Roszak and Joanna Macy come regularly to offer courses in systems theory and ecology that are the conceptual foundation of new paradigm thinking. People go to study *at Schumacher College (which takes its name from E. F. Schumacher, author of* Small Is Beautiful*) from all over the world, because of their desire to understand the roots of our environmental predicament more clearly. My visit turned out to coincide with that of Arne Naess, a founder of the deep ecology movement, which redefines humanity's interactions with, and place in, nature.*

It's difficult to describe Satish Kumar without resorting to colorful words like "magnetic" and "sparkling." His flamboyant personality positively radiates the cosmic connection—perhaps because he comes from a society that has not lost its roots with the divine. As a boy in India, he trained to be a Jain monk (a mendicant order) from the age of nine until the age of eighteen, when he defected by running away. A short time later, Kumar was sitting in a café in Bangalore, when a friend made an astounding proposal: to undertake a peace walk together around the world, traveling exclusively on foot and carrying absolutely no money with them. (The story of their amazing journey, No Destination, *written by Kumar, was published by the Black Pig Press in Wales in 1978.) Staying with whoever would give them food and shelter, the two men walked their way through remote villages and towns in Armenia, Georgia, through the Caucasus Mountains, the Khyber Pass, along the Black Sea, through all of Europe and much more, for two years.*

Kumar directly challenges Hilton Kramer's conviction that Western modernism and Western thinking are standards by which other cultures can be measured and judged. In our conversation, Kumar argues the case for a resacralization of art and nature, deploring the linear, product-oriented thinking that characterizes Western industrial society's relationship with both. From an Indian point of view, art's primary function is to define the communal, not the individual self, and to express the unity between humans and nature. We in the West have paid a great price, he claims, by viewing creativity not as the birthright of everyone, but only of the artist as a special genius. The dichotomous thinking that has separated art from life, and segregated aesthetic experience to the exclusive realms of the museum, art gallery, or concert hall, means that we are left to live in an otherwise ugly world. The arts belong to all of us, not just to a select few. Kumar claims a role for art that not only would return society's attention to our interdependent condition with nature, but also (in the words of poet Gary Snyder) to "the natural dignity of life at its normal, natural, ancient, slower pace."

The conversation that follows was taped at Schumacher College on January 18, 1993.

SUZI GABLIK: Let's talk a bit, Satish, about your time in India at the Indira Gandhi conference, which you were describing last night at dinner as a kind of multicultural forum for the arts. Perhaps you'd like to explain more precisely what this conference was about.

SATISH KUMAR: It was a seminar organized by the Indira Gandhi National Center for the Arts. This is a very big organization, designed to bring the arts into Indian contexts, because Indian art, at the moment, is very much being influenced by Western modernist thinking and modern art. So this center was established in the memory of Indira Gandhi, and the government gave it an endowment of twenty-five million rupees, which is quite a lot of money, in Indian terms. And this seminar was organized on the environment—on nature—to see how art plays a part in our environmental understanding and our ecological consciousness. The center, very interestingly and very encouragingly, believes in the traditional Indian point of view, that art is *not* an end product you either put on the wall, or sell in the galleries to make money. It's not a product; it's a living process. If you take the traditional Indian point of view, there are two examples I would like to give—one very famous and one, my own mother. The famous one is Coomeraswamy, who said the artist is not a special kind of person, but every person is a special kind of artist. So that represents truly the traditional Indian way of thinking. The other example is my mother. She was a very great craftswoman. She used to make beautiful embroidery work, beautiful mirror work on shawls, skirts, blouses—anything she made. And when she'd give it to my sister, sometimes my sister would say, "Mother, this shawl is too beautiful. I can't wear it. I must put it on the wall." And my mother's answer would be, "Don't put it on the wall—it's for you. I made it for you to wear. The day you start to put beautiful things on the wall, you start to put ugly things on your body. And that is not right." So those are the two ends, you might say, of Indian culture. And that is what this Indira Gandhi National Center for the Arts was trying to encourage in this seminar.

SG: Your point about not putting art on the walls is especially interesting to me, because much of my own thinking in relation to Western culture at this point involves the way that many artists are creating a more participatory and interactive kind of art—trying to get it off the walls, so to speak, and to make it happen in places other than the studio or the gallery. So I'm quite keen to understand what people in India think is the role that art might play in terms of ecology and the environment.

SK: Integration, I'd say, is the concern of everybody—because art and life have somehow become separated. How to bring art and everyday life together is the concern. When you have a sense of art—which means a sense of aesthetics—it means a sense of the sacred, from an Indian point of view, because aesthetics and the sacred are two sides of the same coin with us, or even are interchangeable. When you say the earth is sacred, that is an imaginative, creative, artistic point of view. Because when you set out to do a painting of the landscape, you will not paint just any old landscape, but you have some kind of heart connection with that landscape—that's why you paint it. You have a feeling of reverence for nature, a reverence for the environment and for the landscape, and that is the spiritual, sacred point of view. In Indian thinking, we would say the earth is sacred, the trees are sacred—a tree is not just useful because it will make a nice beam for our house, or nice planks for our furniture, but it is a divine manifestation. It is the home of God, and therefore the tree is sacred; it becomes an object of worship. You have a tree temple, a shrine. The Buddha gets his enlightenment under the bodhi tree.

SG: What is the artist's role, then? Is it to mediate images of the sacred—is that how you would put it?

SK: I would say that the artist's role is to create, among people, and to somehow be the bridge, or the instigator, for developing a sense of reverence and beauty. Beauty and sacredness go together. Because if something is natural, then it is beautiful. In India, even a thorn, or a worm, even an earthquake is sacred, because something is happening where the earth is maintaining itself, correcting itself, balancing itself. In this natural happening, there might be some pain, some suffering, some difficulties for human beings, but if you look at the earth as a whole, all natural phenomena have their place, from the Indian point of view. So that is why the work of artists is meant to be an inspiration to people—to help them see that beauty in nature. You develop a sense of the sacred, and then you see everything as divine. And therefore your relationship with the tree, with the rivers, with the land, is not utilitarian; it's an I-thou relationship with nature, rather than an I-it relationship. And that reverence for nature has been the work of artists throughout the ages. The artist in India is not somebody who paints paintings to put on the wall.

SG: But surely some of that art about the beauty of nature would be in the form of images, and pictures; what happens to those images? Wouldn't they go on the wall?

SK: Most images are connected with some divine manifestation, like religious icons, which have been the most prevalent. And those will serve as symbols of the sacred, to evoke spiritual and sacred feeling. They function as objects of meditation that help you to focus. Just as a particular tree may be turned into a wayside shrine, a picture or a sculpture becomes Shiva. Whatever is made artistically is connected with that sense of the spirit; it is not just an object created by human beings for the glory of human beings.

SG: Or for the glory of one's career.

SK: Not for the career, but to further the development of spiritual consciousness, compassion and devotion, all of which are necessary in our day-to-day relationships with each other.

SG: In my own thinking, I've really looked hard and long at ways that compassion can become part of our model for art. It has led me not so much to images and icons and the concept of worship, but more toward a kind of activism—not political activism in the sense of demonstrations in the street, but an activism where the artist is engaging actively with, or intervening in, particular situations, and using his or her creativity to create a space for some kind of healing to occur.

SK: I think it's very good that you're engaged in that kind of approach to art, because from the traditional Indian point of view, art is a way of replenishing the soul. And also the society. Because we are constantly using ourselves, there is a wear and tear of our souls. We become angry; we become fearful; we become emotional. We use our intellect; we use our body; we use our thinking—so we are using ourselves all the time. When you sit down by the river and have a little drawing pad in your hand, and make a sketch of the flowing water or a tree standing by the river, that way you are sitting quietly, meditating and replenishing your soul. That is the reward in itself. The picture is not being painted as a product I can sell, so that I can become famous and my name will be known. That's not the idea: it's the replenishment of the soul, and that is the important thing.

SG: How would you respond to James Hillman's idea, then, that our emphasis in psychotherapy has been overly directed toward the notion of the soul as being only "inside" of us? And while we strive so hard to heal the individual soul, the soul in the body of the world, the *anima mundi,* is undergoing great suffering, and is very damaged. Hillman's plea is that we reconnect with the soul of the world—that we turn our attention away from ourselves and try to heal the world in the form of our dysfunctional cities, our dysfunctional institutions. It's an idea that is very compelling to me in relation to art, which has also been viewed as a vehicle for introspection and for self-healing, when perhaps it could actually help to heal the world.

SK: From the Indian point of view, soul is inside you, and you are inside the soul of the world. It is not one or the other; it is not either-or. The nondualism of the Indian tradition leads you to think in a nondualistic way. When you are healing yourself, you are also healing the *anima mundi,* because the *anima mundi* and the soul inside you are not two separate entities. You are part of the *anima mundi* and *anima mundi* is part of you.

SG: So what do you make of Hillman's thesis, in *We've Had a Hundred Years of Psychotherapy—And the World's Getting Worse,* that we've had a century of people doing therapy and healing themselves, but ignoring the fact that outside, the world is unhealed, and is dying?

SK: Absolutely! I totally agree with Hillman's proposition that psychotherapy has been too much engaged, almost obsessed, with the inner psyche, rather than seeing that you cannot heal the individual psyche unless you have a healing world outside you. So you can go on not only for a hundred years of psychotherapy, but you can have the next five hundred years of psychotherapy, and people will still be sick and ill, because the individual psyche cannot be separated from the communal, social and universal psyche. That's why art in India is also a healing of society, because they say, for example, that we have received so much from our ancestors, and our teachers: from the Buddha, from Shakespeare, from Beethoven, from Bach, from Van Gogh, from Rabindranath Tagore, from Tolstoy, from all the great architects. So when we contribute something, it is not for our own ego-satisfaction, not for our ego-boost, but it is so that this great flow of art and architecture and poetry and music and paintings continues. Our contribution is in the flow of art started by many, many great artists—so the *anima mundi,* and being part of that one continuum, is very much part of Indian thinking.

SG: As an Indian, how do you feel about the history of the Western tradition of great art, which has been very much a tradition of heroic, individual masters —and mostly, we now know, white, Eurocentric males? It did give us a wonderful body of art that everyone loves, didn't it?

SK: Yes, but at a great cost. Having a great body of works of art in museums and galleries and art collections has also resulted in an ugly world all around us, since the Renaissance, since the Enlightenment and the Industrial Revolution. That vast ugliness, the desert of ugliness all around us, with then a little bit of oasis consisting of these few, special works of art—it's not right.

SG: How has that happened, in your thinking?

SK: Because art became very much ego-centered, in the sense that *I* am doing art, it's coming from *me,* whereas in India, art comes from the community. Traditional Indian art never came from the ego-centered individual. This cult of the individual since the Renaissance has destroyed the true art in society. It has reduced art to a few great masters, who become trendy and fashionable and can make lots of money for a few art dealers. And society is suffering, we have paid a big price for these great works of art. We are living in an ugly world as a result, because we have put all this art in one little corner, in a compartment, or in art schools, where you go to become an artist. And then out of ten thousand students going into art college, ten might become the masters. What a waste of energy and money and time! In India, we want all ten thousand—every single one of them—to become artists, and therefore, no single master. That is the price we have paid.

SG: You mentioned last night that at this conference, no modernists were allowed—they were not invited. Why is that?

SK: This center is trying to rediscover, or reconnect with Indian roots, rather than with modern roots, or modern developments. Modern art in India is very much influenced by Western movements, and two hundred years of British education. All our universities and colleges and art schools and fashion and business and commerce and industry and technology—everything is dominated by Western thinking and Western trends. So this center is trying to, just a little bit, reverse that process, by reaching back to Indian roots. That's why, in this conference, they invited people from the villages, tribal people, rural people, who sang beautiful folk songs and songs of Kabir, and that was presented side by side with classic Indian dances and music, and also a certain amount of European classics: we read something from Dante and some Russian poetry. In all cultures —European, Indian, Chinese—there is a holistic tradition of the arts, and the Indira Gandhi Center is trying to find the holistic, integrated view of art and ecology and nature, which gel together, rather than having nature separate, art separate, industry separate, politics separate, religion separate, and they never meet. This seminar was trying to bring religion and art and tradition and environment, all these trends, together.

SG: When I was traveling in India about ten years ago, I wrote an article about art in India. Most of the artists I met were definitely trying to work in the modernist tradition, doing offshoots of Cubism or Surrealism, for example. Many of them had gone outside of India to study somewhere for a period of time, like England or America. Would you say that this is still a primary aim for artists there? Or is that changing now?

SK: It's changing only slightly. There is some small movement in reverse, because a few people—but only a small minority, such as the director of this Indira Gandhi Center and some of her colleagues —have seen how the Indian view of art has been corrupted by this onslaught of Western, ego-centered, artistic movements. But still, I'm afraid and sorry to say, the dominant art movements in India are based in the cities—Bombay, Calcutta, Delhi— and are commercially oriented, modeled on the West. But if you go out ten or twenty miles from these cities, if you go to the villages, they have not heard of modernism yet, and they are still painting their traditional walls and doing their beautifully decorated pots—and they don't think they are artists! They don't know the word "artist." Rural India is still the majority, and there, the corruption of modernism has not reached. But if you go to the artistic centers, you will see the intellectual elite of India is dominated, still, by Western thinking.

sg: There's usually a five- to ten-year time-lag in the way these philosophies travel, but you must be aware that even in Western culture, there's a cultural war going on, part of which involves a deconstruction of the whole tradition of modernism, whose assumptions are unraveling. Modernism is considered to be over by many people, although it is strongly defended as the one true gospel, and the only true art, by certain others. When I was traveling in India, modernism was still the uncontested spirit of the times, whereas in the West this is no longer the case.

sk: I think modernism, even in India, is in retreat. It's not the powerful and unchallenged force that it used to be. Nevertheless, it's an unfortunate situation that with our modern, educated city people, modern art is still seen to be the dominant factor.

sg: In terms of Western culture where we both live, what do you think is the true function of the artist in our declining civilization?

sk: The function of the artist is very, very important, and I think if the world is going to be saved, it is not going to be saved by the politicians, or by the industrialists, or by the business people, because in my view—and it's a harsh thing to say—they are the culprits of this ecological, environmental and spiritual crisis that we are facing. Why the world is facing this crisis is because we have become dualists, we have separated ourselves from nature. We see nature out there, for us to dominate and use and exploit, for us to manipulate for our benefit, for our comfort, for our convenience, for our luxury. Whereas the artist can still see the relationship of unity between human beings and nature.

SG: Which artists are you talking about? Modernists tend to be more drawn to culture than to nature.

SK: Alas, it is only a small movement, and there are only a few people that I can name, but I'm thinking about someone like Andy Goldsworthy, for example. To me he is a sign of hope, because he doesn't see nature as just out there—as something we need to make a painting of—he sees the earth and nature and humans as one continuum. That is the kind of artist I have in mind, and from time to time, I try to find such artists and present them in *Resurgence*.

SG: For how many years have you been the editor of *Resurgence?*

SK: For eighteen years. It's a long time! And I very much enjoy editing *Resurgence,* because it gives me an opportunity to establish a close, friendly relationship with a number of writers, poets, photographers and artists, who contribute from their holistic point of view to this world. Although it's a very small magazine, with a circulation of only seven thousand, nevertheless, it gives me great pleasure that there is a forum for a minority of people who will not find a voice anywhere in the mainstream media, because they don't fit into the commercial market. So it is a small voice, but I think it is an important voice.

SG: Have your aspirations for the magazine changed in any way from when you started, or have they just evolved more or less in the same direction?

SK: Same direction. I'm always finding new people who are articulating the same concerns in a different medium or vocabulary. And that is very good, because we don't want to be static; we want to keep moving. But the basic spirit of the magazine has always remained the same. We want to find an integral view of life that is holistic, ecological, spiritual and artistic, in the true sense of the words.

SG: Are you feeling more hopeful at this time that these ideas are gaining ascendancy, actually becoming transformative, within the culture?

SK: It is very difficult to feel hopeful in the kind of world we are living in. The forces are still very strongly against everything *Resurgence* stands for. In the last twenty years, since the Stockholm conference on the environment, say, to the more recent Rio conference, we have fewer forests left; we have a serious ozone problem and global warming; we have more traffic, more psychological problems. We have so many crises all around us, and they are not abating. They are not declining. So that doesn't give you much room for hope, or optimism. However, I feel that in spite of all these negative forces, the consciousness of people is changing. And now there is much more interest in the things that *Resurgence* stands for than there was twenty years ago. So I'm still hopeful that in the next ten years, before the turn of the century, we will see some real change in mindset, and that is the basic and foremost change that we need. Nothing else will change unless we have a different mindset. From our dualistic, industrial, commercial, ego-centered, individualistic mindset, if we can come to a more social, holistic, ecological mindset where we see each other as part of one another, and not indiscriminately damage everything to get short-term personal benefit at the cost of somebody else, if *that* can change, then other things like politics, economics and commerce will follow.

SG: It was in the 1970s that the Club of Rome first published its report and said there was a ten-year "window of opportunity" to turn things around. We've passed through several decades since then, and that window of opportunity—well, it may already have passed. And yet, there are many people who consider that things are not as bad as we are being made to believe. I was wondering if you'd thought about inviting Al Gore to write a column for *Resurgence?*

SK: I don't know if he would have time now that he has become vice-president! But we have a sort of Al Gore type of person in England, in a different way, and that is Prince Charles. I have been publishing Prince Charles's contributions in *Resurgence* quite regularly, and I would be very much interested, if Al Gore makes any public speeches on the new world order, in publishing them. I would be happy to publish things by him; I think his book is quite good.

SG: He does seem to think deeply and sensitively about the environment, and to understand that it has to be the bottom line for all our activities now.

SK: What I would like to suggest to Al Gore is that he create fifty new settlements, one in each of the United States, consisting of, say, ten or twenty thousand people, as pilot projects to find out whether ecological, conservation-oriented communities are viable and possible. I mean communities where transportation, education, energy-use, and lifestyle are different, so we can see whether what we are talking about is only ideas, or, can it work? If it doesn't work, then only fifty settlements will have failed; and if it does work, then they can become examples for other people to start a new way of life.

SG: It's a little bit like what you've already tried to do yourself, in establishing the Small School in Bideford, isn't it? Isn't that a kind of pilot experiment for a new kind of school?

SK: That's right. Our model for the Small School is the family rather than the factory. Most schools in Britain look like, feel like, and function like factories, whereas our Small School is an extension of home. So you have an open fireplace; you have carpets and curtains. You have friendly people—only thirty of them, so you know everybody. You are on first-name terms with them. Your head-teacher is not an ogre sitting behind a desk in a big office, where you are called for punishment. Fear doesn't reign in the Small School. In large British schools, children are afraid. They are afraid of missing class, they are afraid of being told off, afraid of punishment, afraid of their teachers. They're afraid of failing exams, afraid of being cast as failures and of not succeeding in a competitive atmosphere. They are undermined and underestimated. They're never given a chance to flourish and be themselves. So the Small School gives that kind of example, that kind of opportunity. A trusting atmosphere rather than a fearful atmosphere: that is the philosophical difference. But we have practical differences also. We incorporate art and gardening and farming and building in our education, whereas in normal schools, you don't teach children how to cook, how to grow food, how to build a house, how to sew clothes. The basic things we need in our lives, nobody teaches them. Nobody teaches them at home; nobody teaches them in school. How are they going to learn the skills for a new kind of environmental, ecological society? So we teach these basic skills, in addition to French and English and literature and science and math— all the academic subjects. Learning the art of living, how to relate to people, how to relate to nature and the environment around us, and how to live a more satisfactory life: this is what we try to teach.

SG: Have other schools begun to model themselves on the Small School?

SK: A few schools have started along similar lines, one in Liverpool, one in Derbyshire; and another one is starting in Bristol. So there are some schools, now, beginning to follow our model.

SG: I think this is an important development, because if you start with a very young person and give them a different modality of education, you'll probably end up with a very different consciousness at the end, and maybe even another kind of person—and that, possibly, is really the heart of the matter.

SK: It is very important, and I can see that if ecological thinking and lifestyle are going to develop, it has to come into our schools, because adults like you and me have already got a conditioned mindset, and our patterns of behavior are set. It's very difficult to change those habits, whereas children are still growing. So if they can learn to recycle, if they can learn to use things properly and take care of them and relate to them in a more spiritual way, and not be wasteful, if those habits can be learned early on, then it will be so much easier for them to continue these patterns when they are older.

Creating the Space for a Miracle

DAVID PLANTE

*A*fter talking with Satish, I spent a few days in London with my dear friends Nikos Stangos and David Plante in their apartment on Montagu Square, just a few streets from my old place. Looking out the windows at the overcast January sky, it was almost as if I'd never left. I'd spent the morning roaming around the neighborhood, revisiting my favorite haunts. Everything seemed more or less as it had been before I left: Barclays Bank on the corner of the High

Street, the South Indian restaurant, and even my former travel agent, Brian, who was sitting at his desk and greeted me warmly. Something was different, though; I think it was that my soul had moved on and I no longer felt a part of this story.

It is my last afternoon in London. David Plante and I settle down in his study. He tells me that I made the right decision to leave, because England has pretty much seized up as a place where any meaningful dialogue can take place, as if the English had become so soulless they think any such dialogue would be pretentious and embarrassing. Plante is a writer (one of his novels, The Family, was nominated for a National Book Award in 1978), and he feels that the world of novel writing in England is particularly dry. He finds himself more attracted to the charged political atmosphere in Russia, where he has recently been the first Westerner to have taught at the Gorky Institute of Literature in Moscow.

If dialogue exists at all, in England, it exists in the world of art, which makes Plante more enthusiastic to talk with artists than with novelists. Despite its messiness and contradictions, the world of contemporary art is more of an inspiration and an influence for him than the world of novel writing. When I spoke with him, Plante had recently completed a profile for The New Yorker about an old friend, the painter Francis Bacon. His most recent novel, Annunciation, *is about an art historian who, in her longing for art to mean something that will make a difference in her life, finds herself, to her own amazement, kneeling before a painting of the Annunciation and praying. Art historian friends have told him he is sticking his neck out, but Plante feels that is what artists are called to do. Rodin, Van Gogh and Rouault were not embarrassed by the moral and spiritual lives of their work, which makes him wonder what has happened to cause such embarrassment today that an artist like Robert Ryman, for instance, prefers to ignore the moral and spiritual depth in his work, and will even deny that it is there. Can art get over this embarrassment? Should art today risk embarrassing itself? "I think it should," says Plante, unequivocally answering his own question.*

Plante's measured, elliptical manner of speaking resembles his writing, which sometimes can be as stylized as a Chinese tree. It wasn't long before we became entangled in his unclassifiable mystical atheism, which seems to hint at a trust in some hidden current, or force in life—although the force may not always be benevolent or necessarily help things to work out positively. Plante believes in the saving ability of images, rather than ideologies, and in his writing seeks to create a space in which miraculous images might occur. I am reminded of the poet Samuel Taylor Coleridge, who once dreamt that he passed through paradise and had a flower presented to him to show that he had really been there. But if he were to find, upon awakening, that the dream-flower was in his hand, what then? Creativity may not be demonstrably paranormal, but for Plante it does involve an assault upon one's basic perception of the world, and it certainly has a magical, visionary quality that is not easily explained. There is an outburst in one of his novels, The Accident, *in which the narrator (who is really Plante) defends his atheism with this astounding declaration:*

> For a religion to be a religion it has to descend on you, descend and descend and descend on you, and knock you to the ground and make you believe whether you want to or not . . . something that you hate because it's going to kill you but that you can't stop. That's the only religion that is convincing. The only one.

As for humanity's future, Plante's vision is only a stone's throw away from bleakness. "I don't know, Suzi love," he wrote me recently in a letter. "You used to question my pessimism, as I recall, and I would be reassured by your questioning it, as I'd think that there was someone who was aware and yet who thought there was a possibility of salvation, but I wonder if you, too, have come to the conclusion that humans are simply basically destructive and have no salvation. I do despair."

The following conversation was taped on the afternoon of January 19, 1993.

DAVID PLANTE: Suzi, you invited me to start off, so I'll begin in reaction to part of the tape we listened to a few minutes ago, with Satish Kumar saying, very movingly, that in India a tree is sacred, a river is sacred, nature is sacred. There's nothing I could agree with more, insofar as I think that's the way things *should be.* I have to agree with the ecological movement, which a lot of people belong to, but only in terms of the way things *should be.* Now it's true that the Ganges *should* be a sacred river. Though I've never been to India, I have seen lots of pictures of the river and it looks sacred only insofar as a sewer can be sacred. I know trees in India *should* be sacred, but I see many, many photographs of totally devastated trees, which look absolutely uncared for. I myself have lived among Italian peasants. Before going to Italy, I had a belief that they would find the earth sacred. They hated the earth! They used whatever chemicals they could find to make things grow as quickly as possible. They felt they were slaves to the earth, really. Now the way things *should be* is the way I would want the Italians to think the earth is. The way things *are* is the way the Italian peasants treat the earth—and the way the people in India pollute their rivers and devastate their countryside. One should, of course, say to oneself, "The way things are is so terrible that they have to be changed, and they have to be changed into what they could be." And I would agree with that. Of course things have to be changed; otherwise it's total devastation. But the problem is—and this is where I become a total pessimist—whenever an intention, or an idea, is imposed upon reality, it never, never results in what the intention hoped to realize. Most often, it ends in chaos and greater destruction. We've learned the lessons over and over again of the attempt to realize ideologies. These are ideas, and the imposition of the ideas is beyond anyone's control. I become a total pessimist when I see it's impossible to realize a vision of the way things should be.

SUZI GABLIK: As a writer, would you say that your own writing is involved with any kind of a vision at all?

DP: Oh, absolutely! I think my writing is filled with the grief of the impossibility of intentionally realizing a vision. But I do believe in something which is not intentional, and is greater than our intentions. I'm an atheist. I don't believe in God, but I believe in grace. I believe also, from my own highly particular Franco-American Jansenist background, that grace comes unintentionally. You might try to be very, very good, but you're not going to get grace. On the other hand, you may do all the wrong things, but grace will come to you. Grace is beyond one's intention.

SG: Somehow it is either given, or not given?

DP: I think the most that one can do, the most that I can do as a writer, is to create a space in which the grace can, I hope, occur. The word "occur" is very important to me in my own vision as a writer. Whatever worth there is in my work has nothing to do with me, I believe, but occurs of itself, and all I can do is allow it the space in which it can occur. Now that word "space" might seem ambiguous in terms of writing. What I mean by that is I describe without commenting, a room, let's say, in which the sense of that room occurs of itself. I don't know how this actually happens; one of the great mysteries of description is that if you get a very vivid description of a room or a landscape or a person, something occurs within it which gives it life. The moment you impose yourself and qualify it by saying, "The person looked sad," or "The room felt melancholic," or "The landscape looked drab," you kill it because you're imposing your own interpretation on what should occur *of itself* within the space of the description.

SG: Are you saying that the important thing is to see the world at that moment as if through the room's eyes, or from the landscape's point of view, or what?

DP: Well, you try to keep yourself out of it as much as possible. You try to see it in its details.

SG: You mean, in its suchness, in the Zen sense.

DP: That I don't know enough about, but it might very well be Zen. I see it in terms of details, telling details. Of course, the master of that is Chekhov. For example, in a description of a room where a murder has taken place, he creates the space completely by having a bowl of boiled potatoes fall off the table into a puddle of blood on the floor. So you've got these white potatoes absorbing the blood. It's an amazing image. Even more than details, what I have in mind is images. Chekhov might create a room by describing it all rather banally, or simply, and then find one image—for example, an old pair of shoes tied in a handkerchief—which fills that space with something that is impossible to qualify. In the end, I believe that writing, as all art, is something you can't talk about. You can't define it. I think writing has to defy definition.

SG: What is your relationship, then, to the idea of subject matter? Do you simply find your subject as you go, or is there a particular subject that is close to your heart and that continues as a thread throughout all your work?

DP: I think I have to use as subject matter what is most familiar to me, because that is what I've experienced. And that is also what gives me the most immediate images. So if I've had the experience of living with farmers in Italy, that has given me extraordinary images, and I might one day write about that. My family life brings an image of cinders thrown on a snowy sidewalk to keep one from slid-ing. The whole suggestive image of throwing cinders on the snow is in itself absolutely wonderful: cinders and snow. It comes from my childhood. So my sub-ject matter is what I've experienced.

SG: Would you agree that, in a sense, it's also a search for the perfect image—for that which is waiting to be said, or something like that?

DP: It's the search for an image which will most evoke what can't be said, what can't be defined. To me, that is the joy of reading; it's the joy of looking as well. I most love reading when it's very visual, though I must say, an image in literature is essen-tially different from an image in painting, or in sculpture, or photography and film. And the differ-ence is so great that it would require me a long time to go into that. But essentially, an image in literature, though we say it's visual, is not visual at all. And that's also a great mystery. An image that occurs in writing is closer to the mystery of awareness to me than an image that you actually see with your eyes. Images that occur when you close your eyes are very mysterious things and don't relate, except perhaps in common parlance, to what we see when our eyes are open.

SG: As a writer working now, does the present dysfunc-tional state of the world affect your sense of the work you do? Does it affect your sense of your role as a writer?

DP: Absolutely. Absolutely.

SG: Do you want to elaborate on that?

DP: Well, as I said earlier, I'm terribly pessimistic about intentions, to the degree that any visionary who comes along and says, "This is the way the world should be," I distrust, on the grounds that I know the realization of the vision will be entirely other than what he or she imagines it to be.

SG: Do you think there is any role art *can* play, that might have some effect on the general state of affairs?

DP: It can play a role in giving one a sense of possibility, because things are so out of control, and so uncertain. And by giving one a sense of the possibility of what there is outside of one's control, outside of one's intentions and in the darkness, it offers the possibility of grace. I believe grace is possible, and I believe that writing and art can inspire grace.

SG: Are you talking about grace being bestowed on the individual? I read somewhere recently that to be in a state of grace is to feel the play of cosmic forces in oneself, to be penetrated and suffused by them. Is that what you mean? Or are you talking about some form of grace for the whole planet, that somehow we might actually be saved?

DP: Yes, I would like to think that. Again, I wouldn't want to promote any kind of ideology, any religion, which would then say, "This is how you're going to get grace. If you do this, that and the other, grace is going to occur to you." Because I know that by doing this, that and the other, grace is not going to occur, but something else.

SG: Your sense of grace sounds as if it were something that is totally haphazard and unpredictable. Or is it something that is actually bestowed by some greater force we don't understand?

DP: Well, you see, I believe in inspiration. I know inspiration exists. I've had it.

SG: In other words, something extraordinary arrives in your consciousness from you know not where, because it wasn't a thought that you would have had just on your own.

DP: And usually, the inspiration comes with an image, and the very occurrence of the image is, to me, extraordinary and mysterious.

SG: Do you think life itself follows this pattern, or is this something you only experience when engaged in the process of writing?

DP: There are moments in my life which have had transcendent meaning, which have united me with the world. It happens reading poetry; it happens reading novels; it happens listening to music; and it certainly happens looking at pictures. If I go to the National Gallery in London to the new Sainsbury wing, I know that I'm in the presence of some of the greatest works ever produced by humankind, and they do give me a sense of something that unites the whole world. When people say art doesn't civilize, or poetry or music don't civilize, I think they're wrong. They do. But they'll say, "Yes, but Hitler used to listen to Beethoven's *Ninth Symphony,* and he wasn't changed much by it." Well, there's no argument for that. Perhaps he was as deeply moved by the *Ninth Symphony* as I, but I do know when I listen to it, and when other people I know listen to it, we are raised to a level of awareness which transcends ourselves and unites us in what the symphony, in its own extraordinary way, does realize.

SG: I'm not sure who's ever said that art doesn't civilize. We just both read that wonderful article by Robert Coles, who is teaching his students about a whole segment of humanity through the novels of Raymond Carver, using them as models for understanding the sociological phenomenon of the working class rather than reading about it in a sociology book. The novels offer a picture that is much more vivid, more direct and more human. Coles considers that the compassion Carver shows when writing about this lower economic group of people is a better teaching tool than what the students would get from reading a dry textbook on the subject.

DP: But there are people—W. H. Auden, for instance, who said that poetry does nothing, that poetry exists in the valley of its own saying. The fact is Auden wrote some of the best poetry of the twentieth century and has had a great influence on other poets, which belies what he said. But thinking again about salvation, you see, whereas I don't believe in ideologies—because I can't commit myself to them, in that I've seen too often in history how an attempt to realize an ideology ends in disaster—I do believe in the saving ability of images, which are somehow above ideology.

SG: Could you give an example?

DP: Well, the great religious imagery of the world: nothing is greater.

SG: Christ on the Cross?

DP: Christ on the Cross; the pregnant Madonna; the contemplative Buddha. I don't know much about Eastern religions, but I know that when I go to a museum like the Oriental wing of the British Museum, the buddhas I see are very, very effective. They are saying something to me in purely visual terms, in terms of an image which rises above the dogma, or statable defined beliefs, the ideology even, of their religion. And I think images in prayers, images in words, do something even more to me, because images in words are, as I've said, more mysterious. Think of the images in the Litany to the Virgin Mother, for example—Tower of Ivory.

SG: You began by saying you were very pessimistic, and I know this to be so from other conversations I've had with you over the years. How do you deal with your own despair?

DP: I try to see it as darkness. And I try to see images in the darkness. And I tell myself the only way these images occur is because of the darkness. If you close your eyes, those images I mentioned before—those mental images which occur from one's reading rather than when one is looking at something—they occur in darkness. And I tell myself, to help myself perhaps, that the only way they can occur is because they occur in darkness. And it's the darkness that somehow gives them the meaning and the greatness and the deep mystery that they have. That is, the darkness, as stark as it is, can still give one a great sense of wonder and possibility about the miraculous occurrence of images in one's life, and in the world.

SG: Do you see your pessimism as somehow rooted in your own nature and your own perceptual modalities, or is it something that's a consequence of what you would consider a reality-check of some kind? In other words, is it produced by what you see happening in the world?

DP: I think it has something to do with my religion, this very, very dark religion I was brought up with, which evolved over hundreds of years in the North American woods. I'm an eleventh-generation North American, and I'm one-eighth Blackfoot Indian— my great-grandmother was a Blackfoot Indian. I come from a long line of *habitants,* French farmers, who had to survive in the woods, and did. And they evolved their own religion, which I believe is a very particular form of Catholicism, which exists uniquely among my people, my tribe.

SG: What's its special characteristic?

DP: Very great darkness.

SG: About human nature? About what?

DP: The overriding belief, if I think about it carefully, of my religion, is the belief in impossibility. The doctor won't come in time to save the dying mother; the rain won't fall in time to save the crops.

SG: I wonder a bit about some of this being one's own negative scripts. I've tuned in recently to some of these in myself. You know, I was utterly—and I mean unshakably—convinced that George Bush would be reelected president, for instance. Nothing could dissuade me of this conviction until the night when he lost the election. Of course, I was thrilled to be wrong, but nevertheless, my pessimism was so overwhelming, and so convincing, that I believed absolutely that he would win.

DP: I think one has to accept the fact that a lot of what one feels is scripted, either psychologically, or because of one's social upbringing, or the religion one was brought up with. On the other hand, having said that the belief in impossibility is native to me now, I read enough every single day in the newspaper to make me feel that perhaps it really is impossible to save the world. With anguish, one reads about yet another oil spill. One reads that yet another river in some country one was hardly aware of is dead. It used to be, when growing up one had a romantic vision of far-off countries being pure somehow, being protected. And then you find out that the Aral Sea is completely dead. And you think, well, there's no point in traveling. What's the point of going to China? You might see these lovely tourist spots, but you know that all around is pollution and devastation. And Russia, wonderful Russia—

SG: Does all this darkness affect your will as a writer? For instance, you know that in one of these earlier conversations with two artists, they claimed to have become unable to continue making art at all, because their sense of impending catastrophe is so intense, and they feel that art isn't efficacious, isn't fast enough. It's not a vehicle that can be used in dire circumstances, which is a very extreme position, of course. But I guess my question is, since I know you're not someone who is likely to give up writing, do you see that your art could serve this dilemma in any direct way? Maybe the important thing is that you choose to keep on writing at all, which perhaps is a bit like trying to hold on to *something* as the ship is sinking.

DP: I do go on writing with the sense of holding on to something—that's absolutely true. But more than that, again, I believe in the power of images. For example, I would give all of my writing to be able to come up with the image of the Annunciation.

SG: You mean a contemporary Annunciation?

DP: A contemporary Annunciation, or some equivalent of what is one of the greatest images ever conceived of. And what is so marvelous about that image and makes it particularly meaningful to me is that virgins don't become pregnant. It's inconceivable that a virgin should conceive. So it's an image that is conceiving the inconceivable. Now that's a very great image.

SG: It's the image of a miracle.

DP: Exactly.

sg: So are we moving toward saying that what will have to save us is a miracle, and if we could but conceive of that image, then we could be saved?

dp: Yes, I think so. You say it's the image of a miracle —the image itself is a miracle. And images are miracles, because we don't know how they're produced. No doubt there may be an explanation, but so far there isn't one. Images are miracles. I believe that paintings are miracles. Sculpture, photographs and films are miracles. But the miracle that most inspires me is the miracle of an image in a poem or play or novel. We are inspired by miracles, not in terms of what they intend, not in terms of any dogmas or definitions or commentary they support, but in terms of an awareness of something greater than what we ourselves can do.

sg: Is there any particular book on the contemporary scene that fulfills this kind of prophetic imagery for you?

dp: Very little that I know of in contemporary literature. Raymond Carver could come up with some extraordinary images. I'm not talking about metaphors or similes. In Chekhov, they're not metaphors or similes. The boiled potatoes in the blood is not a metaphor, it's a straightforward image.

sg: It's an event.

DP: It's an event, exactly. Raymond Carver has that ability. A lot of writers are not visual in that way. I'm not crazy about metaphors and similes. I think they are also miraculous, but they have to be treated *so* carefully, because they're so strange and overwhelming that I would only allow myself a metaphor every hundred pages. In the writing of John Updike, for example, he overuses metaphor and similes, so the effect gets clogged. Occasionally, he'll get an image.

SG: It becomes a kind of technical device, or a technical flair, like playing a flashy arpeggio.

DP: But then, for example, in a short story called "Life after Death," which I think is very clogged with imagery, suddenly he'll describe a heron rising out of the woods, and the heron has the wings of an angel. And it's a startling, wonderful image. Now if that image had been more isolated in space—the kind of space I want in writing—rather than jammed into a clogged narrative, it would have really taken the story up. As it was, in the end it became just another simile within the context of the story.

SG: It's certainly an image with a kind of cosmic essence for our age.

DP: Oh, it's a wonderful image. But he didn't allow it enough space.

SG: Perhaps he didn't know what he had.

DP: Maybe, I don't know. But what one would like to do is cut out some of his images and paste them in an album, and then, just read the images.

SG: Do you have a favorite image like that of your own? Something that has come through you and that seems to be the kind of miraculous image you were talking about, like the potatoes soaked in blood?

DP: What I most pray for is that the image would occur of itself within a space I try to prepare for it, an image most resonant with a sense of something "other." And I believe that to be most resonant, this sense of something other must go *out* from one, must be a sense of something that is entirely objective, and not *inward*, not subjective. I am not drawn to the subjective at all, which has no resonance for me. I don't like Surrealism, and though one might say the whole point of Surrealism is images that create a sense of something other, this sense has to do with something unconscious, and the unconscious doesn't interest me at all. Anything that is meant to evoke the unconscious, or the subconscious, is of no interest to me whatsoever. I'm interested in awareness, and I'm interested in images that give one an awareness of something as objectively other as all of stellar space.

SG: Aren't you drawn to archetypal imagery then? The heron with angel's wings has a strong archetypal feel to me.

DP: Rather than archetypal I would call it universal. An image that I'm really drawn to, and which I've been collecting over the years from various writers, so that I now have a big collection, is sunsets. You get marvelous sunsets by Conrad, or Proust, or Chekhov.

SG: So you collect your sunsets in a notebook? David, while we've been talking, I've been looking over my shoulder at this book by Andrei Platonov on your shelf, *The Fierce and Beautiful World,* and I've been wondering if we'll ever see that world again.

DP: I think what is important is to have images of it, transcendent images of it. Because if we're going to have it again, it won't be in terms of dogma, but of inspiration—and that's what images can give us.

When You're Healed, Send Me a Postcard

JAMES HILLMAN

James Hillman, so much the inspiration for this book, is a Jungian analyst who for ten years was director of studies at the C. G. Jung Institute in Zurich; since that time, he has been the most provocative theorist of the archetypal psychology movement, and since 1985, together with Robert Bly and Michael Meade, a spirited leader of the controversial men's movement. He is also the author of fifteen books. His colleague and friend, the author Thomas Moore, once said of Hillman that he provides a way to think about psychology within the context of the humanities rather than the sciences —placing it among the traditions that care for the soul and thus escaping from the medical model and its "medicine complex." Today, however, Hillman says, "I like to practice therapy. I do it well. But I don't believe in it."

His maverick approach to the profession has procured him an estimable reputation as a firebrand and a troublemaker. Many hackles have been raised in the therapeutic community by Hillman's claims that the practice of psychotherapy is too self-enclosed, pretentious and commercial— and that its theoretical base has not gone far enough and needs to begin the enormous task of redefining its premises. It is wrong, according to Hillman, to trace dysfunction in the world back to individual subjectivity—we cannot inoculate the individual soul nor isolate it against the illness in the soul of the world. Psychotherapy is working only on the "inside" soul, but meanwhile, outside, the buildings are sick, the schools, the streets—the sickness is out there. Psychology—working on ourselves—could be part of the problem, and not part of the cure, because it is no longer possible to separate the condition of the individual soul from that of the world. The patient suffering breakdown is the world itself. "Let us carry Freud's notion of neurosis and the therapeutic analysis of it beyond the community of individuals to the communal environment," he writes in The Thought of the Heart and the Soul of the World.

Hillman's assault on the professional framework of psychotherapy—his efforts to extend its theoretical base and to reveal its blind spots—is as liberating for some as it is uncomfortable for others. "I'm going on protesting . . . against therapy. Something's rotten in its kingdom, and I'll go on saying so, even if I have not been able to imagine what to do about it." For my own part, not only do I look upon Hillman irresistibly as a "soul-brother," but I also identify most of all with his outspoken, free-thinking, troublemaking, extremist side. When he argues, for instance, for a world view of attachment, only to hear it said that it is not therapy's job to be concerned with the social, economic or political ills of the world, I find myself comparing and contrasting his struggle with my own, which often draws forth a similar sentiment about art from the artistic profession. Because, like therapy, art too has fashioned its practice on the paradigm of separation, detachment and autonomy. It may be no accident that both disciplines traditionally are carried on in rooms whose doors are closed. At this point, for Hillman, psychotherapy is really a digression from the more crucial issue, which is that the ship is going down. As such, it becomes an active collaborator in the culture of denial, unless it can shift its focus from saving the soul in the individual patient to saving the soul of the world.

One of the happiest occasions I've spent with James Hillman was a celebration in honor of his sixty-fifth birthday at the "Festival of Archetypal Psychology," held at the University of Notre Dame in June of 1992. The festive atmosphere was at times extremely volatile, with explosive sessions that went on for days in truly Olympian style, until it seemed as if everything under the sun had been microscopically examined, from "Phallos and the Gulf War" to "Lifestyles of the Gods and Goddesses," a topic archetypal psychologists like to ruminate on ceaselessly. Lectures were interspersed with wild performances, storytelling, poetry readings and African drumming—with sudden ruffian appearances by Hillman and Bly, who were roaming around as "wolfmen," creating as much havoc as they possibly could. On the first evening there was a big get-together on the patio of the Morris Inn. Hillman arrived with his companion, Margot McLean, an artist who lives in New York, and was wearing a spectacular necktie, decorated with luminous red beets the color of dragon's blood. I asked Margot if she had bought the tie for him. "No," she replied, "I bought it for myself."

Beauty, its sensate presence, is, for Hillman, absolutely fundamental to life; it is not a cultural accessory, or something that belongs to the exclusive province of the arts. Beauty is in the inherent radiance of the world, and its repression, he feels, is the most significant factor in our *culture, because its loss is what keeps us from caring for nature. "Nature today is on dialysis," he says, "slowly expiring, kept alive only by advanced technology." When all is said and done, it is only love for the world, and a desire for rich, sensory contact with the beauty of its sounds and smells and textures that will save us. A truly aesthetic response, in Hillman's view, could affect issues of civilization that most concern us today which have remained largely intractable to psychological resolution. Like Satish Kumar, Hillman feels that beauty has been sequestered into the ghetto of beautiful objects by museums, by the ministry of culture, and by a professional cadre of artists. Indeed, he claims we must cleave beauty altogether away from art, art history, art objects, art appreciation, because they posit beauty into an instance of it, when in fact, beauty is the manifest* anima mundi, *the very sensibility of the cosmos. In our dialogue, Hillman claims that ideas of beauty and metaphor are also necessary to art, if it is successfully to transcend the level of social commentary or politics. Elsewhere he claims that beauty is the way in which the gods touch our senses, reach the heart, and attract us into life. If beauty is not given its full place, we will probably not survive.*

The conversation that follows was taped on February 27, 1993, in a loft in Manhattan belonging to Hillman's daughter, where Margot McLean was exhibiting her work.

SUZI GABLIK: I've been quoting you and Michael Ventura so often in these conversations, James, that it's wonderful to dialogue with you directly. One of the reasons I've been quoting you so much is that I believe your assault on the practice of psychotherapy raises many issues that are equally relevant to the practice of art right now. For instance, you condemn psychotherapy for its narcissistic, inward focus and its exclusive preoccupation with the personal soul of the self. More than that, you've made a direct connection between this self-preoccupation that therapy helps to perpetrate, and the dying of the world outside, as if our loss of attention to the *anima mundi* has somehow allowed the world to fall into such a dangerous and catastrophic state. I feel a great deal of resonance with these ideas, myself, because in art, today, I think there is a similar problem. Like psychotherapy, the practice of art has become a self-contained, individualistic pursuit that has largely surrendered its connection with the world. Most artists—although this is beginning to change now—consider art an activity that is healing for the individual soul and important for the individual's own well-being, rather like therapy. What I was hoping we might discuss is whether you feel that the kinds of complaints you've advanced against psychotherapy are also relevant to art. Do you see any significance, for instance, in the proposition that, like psychotherapy, the practice of art needs to evolve beyond the world view of isolated individualism and toward a more expansive, inclusively communal model of the self?

JAMES HILLMAN: To begin with, yes. Psychotherapy has been trapped in the world view of individualism, and we could also say that the soul has been driven out of the world by three hundred years of Cartesianism, science and rationalism. But also by personalism—that is, the inflation of the individual human being, especially the individual white, Western, human being.

SG: Do you see art, then, as being implicated in that whole process as much as everything else?

JH: Certainly. On the one hand, it produced modernist art—extraordinary works of enormous beauty and value—with, since the Renaissance, the focus on this individualized, creative genius, or central figure.

SG: Basically, the heroic male.

JH: That's partly right. But let's please not reduce these extraordinary works to clichés about gender and patriarchy—that's far too simplistic. I think that therapy, coming very much later, at the end of this long period, proceeded along the same line, based on the philosophy of individualism, in which the psyche is located inside the skin of a person, and you work upon that psyche inside the skin, and possibly you work on the intrapsychic, between two people. And there could be a psychic field, but it certainly doesn't include the chairs the people are sitting on, the table that they're sitting around, or the animals or the trees, or the car that brought them to therapy.

SG: If we draw a parallel here again with art, we could say that art is in the same boat, in a sense, because like therapy, it too happens in a room, usually behind closed doors, where the artist is isolated from the normal flow of society and removed from life actively practiced in the real world.

JH: That may be the intention, but if we take the other point of view, some people might say, "Look, what you're doing in that room, alone, whether in therapy or in art, is inevitably done in the context of a world, and it is affirming a certain world." From a Marxist point of view, it's affirming the bourgeois capitalist world. But from another point of view, you could say that whatever you do—and this is what the critics of what I write say—whatever you do alone in that room in therapy *does* affect the world. It's like a ripple, and it comes out. And so, in art, it must also affect the world.

SG: I've followed some of those criticisms, and the disagreement seems to revolve around this idea of healing the self first, and that only the healed individual has what it takes to make a real contribution to the world.

JH: Yes, and I reject that. I reject that for at least three reasons. One is, when you're healed, send me a postcard. How do you know when you're healed? That's the first one.

SG: I suppose there's an answer to that, which is that the person begins to feel more together, or more ready to take on things he or she couldn't seem to cope with before.

JH: But we have to see that therapy already reinforces the fact that they can't. It reinforces the fact of inability—that's part of its job, to explore the wound. More and more of that. So that's a second reason. And a third reason is, people have been going out into the world for thousands of years, unhealed, and doing what has to be done. I don't believe human life is in worse shape *psychologically,* today, than we were in 1812, or 1736, or whatever. Some aspects are far better; others far worse.

SG: Part of the problem seems to be that because the *world* is in such a catastrophic state, on a scale that has never been seen before, the issue of responsibility for actually going out there and doing something looms like a specter in front of us all. That responsibility was more optional, wouldn't you say, in the past?

JH: Are you saying it's more necessary now to go out there than it used to be?

SG: Well, let's consider the question of art's responsibility as one instance. During the modernist era, the assumption was that art was autonomous and free of any responsibility to deal with problematic social or environmental issues. In late modernism, especially, this was not considered art's domain, and art was very determined just to do its own thing. Autonomy seemed fine during an era that could afford such an approach; but my own sense, I suppose, is that now our time of grace is over.

JH: I see. So you say the conditions are so radically different today, and you use the image of the *Titanic* —it's also the image of the shipwreck that Karl Jaspers uses, and it's an image Michael and I used in our book.

SG: Right.

JH: So if the conditions are that way, we have to start with that as the playing field, with that as the metaphor.

SG: And as the key question really, because so much seems to hang upon whether one accepts shipwreck as the bottom line, or not. Hilton Kramer is one example of someone who doesn't believe things are really that bad. He even admits he'd have to rethink his whole approach to things if he did believe this, but since he doesn't accept the idea that the Western industrial paradigm is failing, he's quite happy to continue on as he is.

JH: Doing small repair jobs, as he says. When Michael Ventura and I talked about this, I said the same thing. I said what do you do when the ship is sinking? Do you repair the plumbing on the *Titanic?* Which is, in a sense, what therapy does. That's the therapeutic view. You don't take the catastrophic view, you take the therapeutic view. You try to make the patient as comfortable as possible, because the patient is dying.

SG: But Michael Ventura says something quite different. He says that you can't negotiate with an avalanche, so the important thing is to understand the story that you're in, and to play your own part in that story. I've just recently read Theodore Roszak's new book, *The Voice of the Earth,* and he claims that even though there is a great deal of information out there about what's happening to the planet, the upshot is that we don't really know anything for sure. So we're forced, in reading all this stuff, to make our own decision as to whether or not we think things are really that bad—and this is our dilemma. Because if the information made a clear and conclusive picture, there wouldn't be a choice, and then it might be easier for people to rouse themselves and make some drastic changes. However, since there is the option that someone like Kramer takes, of concluding that things are not so bad, that's what stymies us.

JH: My recent meetings with Roszak tell me he believes it is indeed bad. But is it the direness of the conditions as such, or the need to change the world view of individualism because it is outdated and damaging? There's another problem, though. Even if you conclude it is that bad, there are still two alternatives. One is the point of view of nursing: taking care of the small things, as the ship goes down. Or, something else: the lifeboats, the apocalyptic transformations, what else?

SG: Can you translate any of these notions more directly into the possible role you think that art might have at such a time?

JH: The trouble with that question for me is it sets up a program for art. And if I stay within my old-fashioned ideas, art shouldn't have a program, right? So I can't set up a program for art, if I stay in the old-fashioned ideas. If I connect art with the going down of the ship—

SG: Yes?

JH: Then one of the ways for making it comfortable for the dying patient is art: the contemplation of beauty. That is something which goes beyond the sinking of the ship. Platonists would say it's the contemplation of the eternal.

SG: But if you're talking about art being a vehicle for the expression of beauty, or for allowing us that contact with the beautiful, this would circumscribe its role to the domain of the purely aesthetic.

JH: Well, I don't know about that—I don't think you can make that kind of separation. That's not my view of the aesthetic. *Aesthesis* means noticing the world.

SG: This is something I'd like to explore with you a bit more—whether you think aesthetics enters into the realm of responsibility, or moral obligation.

JH: Moral obligation to what?

SG: Yes, that's the blockbuster question, isn't it? I'd say, moral obligation to the catastrophic state of the planet, to what you call the *anima mundi*. Put it like this: I've read enough of what you've written currently to know how strongly you feel that therapy has failed to take the *anima mundi* into account. It's trapped by an exclusive focus on the self. Do you feel anything like this holds true for our artistic practice as well?

JH: In some ways I think the art-making process has noticed the *anima mundi* almost more than anything else. Pop Art, for instance, by taking an ordinary Brillo box, deliteralizes the box and makes it into something else: it's got soul potential.

SG: Wow! This must be the first time anyone ever attributed soul-making to Andy Warhol!

JH: Pop Art did something for my eye. It made me see all kinds of things in the world very differently. Ordinary things come alive, become metaphors, have humor. No longer just Kmart and throwaway.

SG: Minimalism does a similar thing for piles of bricks, and so on.

JH: Rusty girders, or the ruins of an old car, that's right. It makes me see that things are animated. So I don't think art is guilty for the neglect of the *anima mundi.* With the *objet trouvé,* it rescued and made use of discarded materials.

SG: You're more generous, James, in such matters, than I've been of late. I see such a dramatic difference between artists like Kurt Schwitters or Robert Rauschenberg collecting trash and then using it for their own aesthetic purposes, and someone like Dominique Mazeaud, who collects the trash as part of her monthly river-cleaning ritual, because of a concern for the litter that's left out there. I talk about this at some length in my book.

JH: Other artists, you think, are not concerned with the litter that's out there? Perhaps they're not concerned with the *meaning* of the litter that's out there —I mean, its ecological meaning.

SG: That's right. In the case of Schwitters, obviously it wasn't even an issue of the times, but now, it seems harder and harder to consider the medium of trash without being conscious of the fact that there's a lot more of it out there than is comfortable. I guess what I'm really trying to find out is, do you feel this shift into ecological awareness ought to become an intrinsic part of the art-making process? And how does it affect your view of the therapeutic process?

JH: I suppose I should start with the therapeutic—certainly it does. I've written about it already so many times: what's the use of that one hour in the analyst's office, if there are three hours on the highway, or in the subway, to get there and back? There's some terrible disjunction between these two worlds. The analytical hour doesn't seem to have enough effect on what happens afterwards, and what happens in the subway doesn't really get attention in the analytical hour.

SG: For some people, subway journeys may be so unpleasant that they need to see a therapist just to unload the stress accumulated by traveling to the therapist's office!

JH: Ideally, the therapist's position is that the work you do in therapy helps you live that time on the subway, as it would be if you were doing Buddhist meditation. You'd be able to remove yourself, or harmonize yourself, or detach yourself—it would have some effect on your relation to the subway trip.

SG: But no effect on the dreadfulness of the subway itself, which is what I think you're really getting at.

JH: Right! In fact, the meditative approach abstracts you from the subway, teaches you *not* to be caught by its discomfort. So does the recovery movement in general. It teaches serenity, not outrage; that the faults are yours, not the subway's. Therapy's interiorizing of the emotions keeps you from doing anything about the subway. By interiorizing the emotion, you're much more prone to talk about how, when I get off the subway, I'm trembling and I've got a lot of anxiety. And then we talk about my anxiety, and when it began, and what my diagnosis is about anxiety attacks, or panic attacks—all of that puts it back in the sub-ject and not in the sub-way.

SG: In terms of how we might learn to refocus our attention away from ourselves and onto the world, is there anything specific in your thinking that might help this come to pass in therapy? Beyond that, do you have any ideas of how it might transpire for art?

JH: The subway part, or the highway part, requires a sensitization to what's going on—not only to what's going on in me that I'm feeling afraid, but also to the whole thing, which is really to deanesthetize yourself.

SG: Often when artists work in their studios, it functions as a kind of sanctuary situation. It answers a need to escape from the struggles of the world outside. So, in a sense, it serves as a means of desensitizing oneself to input from the environment and its stresses.

What feels great is to enter the studio and shut the door on the outside world—to get into a meditative space and commune with oneself.

JH: Or commune with the work. I don't know about commune with oneself.

SG: But the point is, within that traditionally accepted model of the artist, based on isolated individualism, it's very difficult to perceive any strong connection or direct influence that art could have on the world. That's why, in my writing, I have been drawn to artists who use their creativity in ways that can have a direct effect. Of course, it may only be a small effect, like helping a few homeless people, or healing some environmentally sick place.

JH: We've talked about this before, and I think there's a problem about, first of all, why that's art, and second of all, what's the difference between that art —an artist like Dominique Mazeaud cleaning the river, the Rio Grande—and *l'art pour l'art?* Because in the end, her art has no worldly effect. You say yourself that it's not really even meant to clean the river: it becomes a devotional ritual. It isn't truly an ecological project; it's a communion between the artist and the river. So what's the difference between doing that at the river or doing it in a studio? At least, as far as the artist's isolation is concerned?

SG: In the river, there's often an interaction with passersby, who want to know what she's doing, and why she's doing it. And now that her project has become somewhat known, she's invited to conferences to talk about it, or to teach. So that aspect has quite a lot of outreach, as the work becomes a focus for debate. Of course, studio artists also talk about their work in this way, but in Dominique's case, her focus is really on an issue, the degradation of the river, which is what she wants us to pay attention to, and not on what a wonderful artist she is. It's an issue that ought to have our attention, wouldn't you say?

JH: But she did not begin with that outreach. It was a consequence of the work, which could be the equivalent of a successful painter, who has worked for three years in a studio and then somebody finds the paintings and recognizes them, and invites them to have a show or to talk in a college class, or whatever. But the intention of the artist at the river seems to me the same intention—the same kind of meditative, solitary discipline—as the artist in the studio.

SG: And yet, there's something different about it, right?

JH: I agree. There is something different about it.

SG: Part of what attracted me to her work in the first place was the way it transcends the museum concept of art, which tends to dominate our thinking about art in this culture. It challenges the reigning philosophical and aesthetic paradigm that separates what we consider to be fine art and its objects from ordinary life and action. Of course, I also like the fact that she wasn't cleaning the river to draw attention to herself as an artist. What's really different about it, I think, is the reason why she does it, which is her care and concern for the river, and not so much for art.

JH: Or herself, as you said. She was not doing it as a spiritual discipline in the manner of a desert monk, who is trying to climb the ladder to heaven.

SG: Exactly. Nor was she doing it in an effort to reframe our conception of what art is, the way Duchamp did when he put a men's urinal into an exhibition. In fact, she herself would say that whether or not others accept what she's doing as art is not the important thing to her. The important thing is her relationship with the river.

JH: What's the difference, then, between that and another artist's relationship with the canvas, or with the piece of wood that she's carving?

SG: These points are well taken, James, and in a curious way, they can be enlisted as arguments both for or against what we are trying to discuss. My own position, of course, is that this is art, and so I could say, there's absolutely no difference. Indeed, the river is her canvas; it is the locus of her creative effort. And it's not problematic for me to think of this as art at all, since her choice is to define herself as an artist

who is doing this, rather than as an environmentalist, who would undoubtedly be doing something
else.

JH: But then, what gets metaphorized in her work?
Doesn't she remain in the literal world? And, as
such, it's not art? *She's literally cleaning the river!*

SG: But that's a problem only if you want to define art
as a separate aesthetic realm, divorced from life and
quarantined to the museum or art gallery. And only
if you want to insist on the Cartesian split between
art and life, self and world.

JH: I certainly *don't* define art that way, but I do believe
it transforms the literal to the metaphorical and
mythical. Otherwise, the social comment, politics,
advocacy, protest exist on *one level only.* And that's
part of my problem with her cleaning of the river,
and with making pushcarts for the homeless as a
form of sculpture. For me, art is dedicated to
beauty; it's a way to let beauty into our world by
means of the artist's gifts and sensibilities. The river
does get more beautiful because of her cleaning; but
unless the pushcart has beauty, is it not merely a
better or more useful shopping cart, and as such,
not art? I think beauty needs to come into it somehow. Ideas of beauty and metaphor are necessary to
what I call art.

SG: In a conversation that precedes ours, Satish Kumar
says that in India, art was never meant to hang on

walls—it's part of life. He thinks that the desert of ugliness all around us is connected with concentrating our notion of beauty in a great body of works of art to be found only in the oases of museums. In India, art is not separated from the normal flow of life. It seems as if it's only in our culture, and since modernism, that we regard the idea of art and the aesthetic as a separate realm, to be enjoyed and contemplated as an escape from ordinary life. Among the great debates going on right now, a lot of discussion is being instigated by people who feel that until —or unless—art can reconnect with life, it's going to be meaningless and stay marginal, without any part to play in the larger picture.

JH: That's a very good point, because it shows something crucial to this civilization: that the work in the river can be put in a different context altogether, which is art in the service of . . . life. Like the way dance was originally in the service of the tribal community; it wasn't dance for an audience on a stage. It was a dance that helped the crops to grow. On the other hand, state art in Nazi Germany and Stalinist Russia was in service of the community. So you see there are *always* problems when one defines the correct intention or nature of art.

SG: In our culture, the notion of art being in service to *anything* is anathema. Service has been totally deleted from our view of art. Aesthetics doesn't serve anything but itself and its own ends. I suppose if I were to try to pinpoint the singlemost notion that my own struggle has been about—you probably have one of those, too—it would be the idea that art and service can't be linked. I would like that to change. When Hilton Kramer says that the minute you try to make art serve anything, you're in a fascistic mode—well, I don't believe that. You know it's being said even of spiritual practice these days that hanging out in an ashram, or meditating on a mountain top—spirituality without service—is middle-class self-indulgence. Isn't that what it's boiling down to for both of us? Therapy without service, working on just healing yourself, becomes another form of middle-class self-indulgence. It's like going to your studio because it makes you feel better. It's not that I'm against feeling good, but at this point in time, is that enough?

MARGOT MCLEAN [who had been listening]: What happens if you go to your studio and do what you do merely "self-indulgently"—and then you also go out and collect garbage off the street, or organize your community for recycling, or you go to a shelter and cook for the homeless, and you do this as a very devoted service to your environment?

SG: This question comes up frequently when I lecture, and my answer has usually been something like this: on a sliding scale of zero to ten, perhaps somebody doing what you just described might register five, in comparison, say, with artists who spend all their time in the studio. This may sound judgmental, and probably is from a certain perspective, but I think there are many levels of possibilities and commitment here. For me, an artist who manages to integrate their care and concern directly into the work reaches yet another level of responsibility.

MM: I guess I have a problem with this, because I myself often go out and do environmental things, similar to cleaning the river, and this direct concern for the world has a lot to do with my work in the studio. I see it as being interconnected. So I have trouble in making the distinction as to which is better: whether cleaning the river as art is better than cleaning the river and then going to the studio and making a painting after having been to the river. Because the river is getting cleaned both ways. I agree that the interaction with the public may be very different, because there's no guarantee that someone who looks at the painting will know that it was somehow inspired by the river.

SG: If we agree that there is a paradigm shift happening in our society at this time, then the question is, how much of a break is necessary from the older forms and ways of doing things? When you're in your studio painting, it is likely that you will be perceived as a "traditional" artist, whereas doing one's work in the river captures people's attention differently, makes them stop and consider what's going on. I think this is the intrinsic value of Mazeaud's project:

it pushes people's buttons, rather like Duchamp's urinal in its day, and makes them consider, why is this art? The river work challenges you about a lot of things, which is the reason I used it so centrally in my book—because it raises all the issues, and because it is such a struggle to come to terms with it as art. That is what gives it a power, in my opinion, that perhaps a picture on the wall wouldn't have at this juncture.

JH: I'd like to defend the cleaning of the river, for a moment. I'm going back to what you said a little earlier: it's the attempt to put art in the service of something.

SG: Yes, that's where the issue is.

JH: Art in the service of something. If we say that it's life, and if we think, for instance, of the Balinese village, where everything is made to be functional and useful, for celebrations or ceremonies, and so on, where you're not just making things for no serviceable reason, you're still in service to the gods, somehow. Now we don't have that—we've wiped the gods out.

SG: And we've wiped out art that has a function, or a use, too.

JH: Right. So the god that it now serves is the god that dominates the culture, which is the god of commodity, of money. So it *is* in service, it's in service to gods we don't approve of. They are the powers that art now serves. Now suppose the question doesn't become what art should do, but rather how do we find that which art should serve? It is already in service—in fact, it's in yoke—to the commodity-museum-gallery ethos, behind which is our consumerism god—the bottom-line god. The other god it serves is the self. Art *is* in service, so could we perhaps change that to which it is in service?

SG: I would say so, absolutely. But then, we have people like Hilton Kramer saying—and it's *his* absolute bottom line—that art must not be in service to anything. He believes, along with many others, that the whole power of the great art we have had in our culture comes from the fact that it is autonomous.

JH: Well, he's absolutely wrong in that regard, and he even said himself what it served: bourgeois capitalism. So it is in service. As the Marxists say—it perpetuates the system.

SG: The system of individualism and commodity aesthetics.

JH: Yes, if you're one of those who's on that privileged side. I really think everything's in service, our whole lives are in service. We just don't know what we're serving.

SG: So the question is what could art better serve than the things it has been serving throughout our lifetimes?

JH: Right. And I think the artist in the river is serving a different god.

You Don't Have to Have a Penis to Be a Genius

GUERRILLA GIRLS

*T*here are definite advantages to being a woman artist, according to the Guerrilla Girls—like working without the pressure of success, not having to be in shows with men, knowing your career might pick up after you're eighty and, of course, not having to undergo the embarrassment of being called a genius. "You don't have to have a penis to be a genius," admonishes one of their more anarchic posters, which by now have become an art form unto themselves.

Guerrilla Girls is a group of anonymous women (their actual number and identities are as undercover as an FBI file) who consider themselves "the conscience of the art world" and periodically streak through the night, disguised in gorilla masks and fishnet stockings, putting up waggish posters that zap the white male establishment for its sexism and racism. They first appeared on the scene in the spring of 1985 with an invigorating poster that listed forty-two prominent male artists, who were bracketed with the question, "What do these artists have in common?" The answer was, "They all allow their work to be shown in galleries that show no more than 10 percent women or none at all." Another subsequent poster listed twenty-two art critics who wrote about women less than 10 percent of the time.

Guerrilla Girls love to name names and point fingers with their other great tactic of "Report Cards," which evaluate specific members of the art world on their performance in relation to the underrepresentation of women. For instance, for the period 1985–86, Blum Helman Gallery received the rating "no improvement," while Mary Boone was rated as "boy crazy" and Sperone Westwater "unforgivable." Another rectifying action involved mailing a letter on pink paper to certain collectors. "Dearest Art Collector," it read, "it has come to our attention that your collection, like most, does not contain enough art by women. We know that you feel terrible about this and will rectify the situation immediately. All our love, Guerrilla Girls." Guerrilla Girls consider their pronouncements (such as "When Racism & Sexism Are No Longer Fashionable, What Will Your Art Collection Be Worth?") as "public service messages." Always well disguised by gorilla masks, they have brought their messages to panel discussions, CBS television news, and lecture auditoriums at universities. When right-wing politician Jesse Helms laid siege to the NEA, Guerrilla Girls responded with a poster directed personally to him: "Relax Senator Helms," it said. "The art world is your kind of place. The number of blacks at an art opening is about the same as at one of your garden parties."

In 1987, Guerrilla Girls targeted the Whitney Museum Biennials for their practice of racial and sexual exclusion. When the controversial Biennial of 1993 opened, it seemed as if all those years of irrepressible trouncing were finally vindicated, since the majority of the participants in the show were women, African-Americans, Asian-Americans, Latinos and gays. Even the catalogue texts were largely written by individuals from those communities. It was the first time the Whitney had ever mounted such a highly focused, politicized Biennial, and the ostensible "political correctness" of it all drew a red herring right across Madison Avenue that very quickly had an enraged art world reared up on its hind legs, sneering. Kay Larson, a critic who writes for New York magazine, sized up the situation very well when she wrote, "Those who have a lot to lose (or think they do) in an uprising of the alienated will probably risk cardiac arrest just by walking through the doors."

On all four floors of the museum, almost no paintings were to be seen. Instead, there was an abundance of video (including recurrent showings of the Rodney King video), installations (such as the reconstruction of a murder scene in a Puerto Rican apartment by Pepón Osorio), photographs and texts, pulsating boomboxes blasting funky music and hip-hop, banks of telephones with numbers like 1-900-Desire, and many other things not usually thought of as art. About thirty of the artists were there for the first time, including Daniel J. Martinez from Los Angeles, whose specially designed admission buttons—the metal tags you clip to your lapel—consisted of words that, when put together, formed the sentence "I can't imagine ever wanting to be white." Maybe a joke, but maybe not, prompting one to ask, however, "This Whitney Museum, is it a racist organization?" The mood was echoed again in Pat Ward Williams's billboard-sized photograph that had been placed in the front window, where five black youths stared insolently at the incoming crowd, spray-painted with the inscription, "What you lookn at?" In serious white man's country, it set the tone for the hardcore scene that was to be found inside. "They let us in uncensored," Martinez told the Boston Globe. "I've never seen that happen in a major museum before. This is a breakthrough, and a beginning of a new type of thinking and a redefinition of our cultural position. [David] Ross [director of the Whitney] has exhibited courage and vision at a time when it's necessary. He knows he'll be attacked for it, and he still did this show. I admire this. This is not lip service."

While writing this, it happened that I was also reading M. Scott Peck's book on building community and creating civility, A World Waiting to Be Born. Peck suggests that it is the personality of those at the top that primarily determines the culture. If those few people change, then the culture will change. In this case, David Ross (and his chief curator Elisabeth Sussman) opened up the sanctuary doors, invited in the polyglot and the free-style, and indicated to the world that the Whitney wasn't afraid of funk or of the warring ground. As top managers of an institution that needed exorcising, they gave their power away, and in Peck's sense, practiced the art of "followship."

The Whitney show had just opened when I learned that the Guerrilla Girls would be coming to speak at Virginia Tech as part of Women's Week. I managed to track one of them down, and they agreed to do a conversation *with me while they were here. Since Guerrilla Girls remain anonymous at all times, I never did discover who I was talking to, although the gorilla masks were dispensed with for reasons of comfort. Guerrilla Girls have a policy of assuming the names of dead women artists from history; I talked with Romaine Brooks, and a tall woman wearing a faux-zebra jacket who referred to herself as Guerrilla Girl I. Since we spoke, the first installment of their 1993 newsletter* Hot Flashes *has come out. It probes the* New York Times *and its current writers on art. The Guerrilla Girls' recipe for a new, improved* Times *includes:*

1. Bring back Michael Brenson; find a critic of color; put a hiring freeze on young white men from the Ivy League.
2. To achieve gender and racial parity in reviews, devote the next 100 years to covering only women and artists of color.

The following conversation took place in my home in Blacksburg on March 20, 1993.

SUZI GABLIK: What's the best, and what's the worst thing about being a Guerrilla Girl?

ROMAINE BROOKS: The best thing is, we love traveling. Doing gigs is quite a lot of fun—we've seen a lot of the world.

BOTH: Join the Guerrilla Girls and see the world!

RB: In the last couple of years, the Guerrilla Girls have been invited to Australia, Finland, England, Germany and Austria, so we've had a lot of fun, but it also shows that there's an incredible appetite for hearing what we have to say. For instance, we just went to Austria, and I think we met every feminist in Austria when we were there. A lot of them didn't even know who the Guerrilla Girls were—they weren't artists. But it's such a powerful image to women that I felt like we energized and juiced up these women, because there's so little support for feminists, and feminism, in some of these places.

GUERRILLA GIRL I: The reason that we're invited to all these places—a lot of universities in the U.S. as well as places in Europe, and we went to Brazil, Ireland, Scandinavia and Finland—is because of the great need, and interest, obviously, in our issues.

SG: Let's talk about those issues a bit.

GGI: And about all the changes that we have initiated, by the way—and that we take full credit for, I might add. [Laughter]

SG: OK! Let's have a little rundown on what that is.

RB: One thing is that we did a critique of the Whitney Biennial a number of years ago, at the Clocktower in New York, where we gave all these statistics, revealing how sexist and racist all the Whitney Biennials have been. Well, the most recent Whitney Biennial [Spring 1993] is 40 percent women, and it's probably 35 percent artists of color, and I'd say we really take full credit for this. Things that we've been pounding on and talking about for years are finally bearing some fruit.

GGI: Peter Plagens actually wrote in *Newsweek* to the effect that the images in the Whitney show looked like the *New York Post* edited by the Guerrilla Girls. I think it's a measure of our influence that he characterized the show by using us as a generic reference.

SG: I know that humor is a primary component of your work, but how, in a serious mode, would you sum up your mission?

GGI: In 1984, the Museum of Modern Art staged an international painting and sculpture show. There were 166 people in that show, and only about 16 were women, so that was 10 percent or less, and we knew we were in deep shit. So we started the Guerrilla Girls, because we felt that critics, artists, curators and dealers are all responsible for this problem, the underrepresentation of women in terms of the art

world. We wanted to target those who were responsible for a lot of the problem and make them ac-
countable for the solution. Our goal is for more
women artists to be represented in terms of their
sensibility within the art world.

SG: Give me a little bird's-eye view here. Even though I
know everything has to stay anonymous, tell me
what you can about the day all this got started. I
mean, who was there, what happened? Who
dreamed it up?

GGI: Oh God! This is like talking about the beginning of
the earth.

RB: It was actually a combination of older feminists and
younger feminists.

SG: Were you two in on the very beginning?

RB: I was not.

SG: Was there a single person, who could be identified
if that were allowed, who thought this up?

GGI: No, it's a group. What happened was we worked
out how we wanted to package it all, and the Guerrilla Girls just seemed like a great idea, in terms
of the double meaning of the word—"gorilla," the
animal, and "guerrilla," the action. We spell it like
the freedom fighters, but then we wear gorilla

masks, so that it works imagistically. It's very effective. You have this angry gorilla image combined with a female body, and the women have reason to be angry. So when you see the image, you think of what the Guerrilla Girls stand for, which is the self-proclaimed conscience of the art world.

RB: It was also to take feminism, which at that point was becoming a dirty word, and to make it sexy, to make it funny.

GGI: And to make it very positive.

SG: So has any of this anger that you started off with abated somewhat, given the current changes in the art world?

RB: I'd say we've achieved some successes but I think the anger continues, because of the backlash against feminism, and because of the recession of the nineties; I mean, the opportunities for artists across the board are much worse than they were in the eighties. In some ways we can point to situations like the Whitney Biennial and say that things have gotten better, but in fact, the times are really difficult for artists, particularly for women artists and artists of color. We thought we could go back to the jungle by now, but it seems we can't.

SG: The times are certainly difficult, but as you yourself said earlier, in certain respects they are getting much better. It certainly seems as if there are vast changes going on in the art world these days.

RB: It's true, but one wants more.

GGI: The changes aren't enough!

SG: Still, in some of the old patriarchal camps there's quite a lot of distress at what's happening. One of the conversations I did earlier was with Hilton Kramer, and—

RB: Oh yes, I'm sure he's furious. I'm sure he hates this Whitney Biennial.

SG: Well, he likes, and he's defended very strongly, traditional modes of art and traditional artists—meaning, of course, high modernism—which he feels is getting short shrift in the world of multiculturalism and feminism. So from the vantage point of someone like him, people like you are really calling the shots now.

GGI: But it still seems as if the people he's referring to are making a great deal of money and they're still getting exhibited—there is a market and an interest for their work. But it's true that other issues are more to the front now, and those issues are being addressed, for example, by the Whitney Biennial.

RB: The problem is the Whitney Biennial of 1993 might be *the* political Biennial, and then it could all just go back to what it was. We're making these advances, but this could end up being a sort of token situation.

SG: Besides taking up the cause of the short end of the stick, so to speak, that women have received as artists in the art world, is there anything about the art world itself that you would like to see changed, beyond having women achieve better participation?

GGI: That's still a big issue.

RB: Yeah, if we could do that, we'd actually have done a tremendous amount.

GGI: We're not out of the woods yet.

RB: By full participation we're really talking about the rewriting of art history, too, so it's a huge job. It's not just that maybe a few more women are in galleries, or something like that. It's that more women are being written about and being acknowledged, and that there's a real fundamental change in the way women artists are recognized. One thing we'd like to see changed is this whole network that supports male artists from the beginning, and the creation of a network for women artists that's been in and out of place since the seventies, where women support and advance each other.

GGI: You also need a network that's actually supported by all artists, museum people, dealers and writers, as well as collectors.

SG: All those patriarchs you detest so much!

GGI: Well, we want to be more matriarchal. We want women and artists of color to have more access to the system.

SG: Putting it in those terms, do you want to change the system in any other way besides giving women greater access to it?

GGI: Or are we satisfied with the system as it is?

SG: Yes. Do you think the system is OK, as long as women and artists of color get their due in it?

RB: I think the system is fundamentally pretty fucked up, but are we talking about political change, or what?

SG: I guess a related question is whether you think artists have a responsibility to work for social change?

RB: Yes, I think so. I think art should be relevant, it should matter, both to artists and to the audience. But I'm talking for myself here, and not the Guerrilla Girls, when I say this. Art should connect—it's got to connect.

SG: So you are both artists in your own right and exhibit your work in galleries?

BOTH: Yes.

SG: But you don't want to talk about, or identify that?

RB: The whole point of our anonymity is that we don't use the Guerrilla Girls to further our own careers.

GGI: We definitely want to focus on the issues and not on our specific careers, so that's why we wear masks and prefer to remain anonymous. That way we speak for more people.

SG: I'm interested in the relationship of your personal work—if you can talk about this at all without identifying anything—to your Guerrilla Girl work.

RB: I'm sure we'll have different answers to this, but I feel that they're two very different things. The thread they have in common is that being a Guerrilla Girl and going out and talking about these things strengthens my own resolve as a woman and as a feminist—I take that energy back into my own work. It's a way of channeling the anger so you don't have to turn it on yourself as a woman artist.

SG: Is there a quality of anger, then, in your work? Is your work conceptual?

RB: No, it's painting, with images. I also do public art, and the idea of addressing a large audience, which I do as a Guerrilla Girl, is something that also informs my own work.

SG: Is your work involved with feminist subject matter?

RB: Not overtly. I don't make political art, but I do find being a Guerrilla Girl is helpful in my own work.

SG: It offers a direct path to a life in the world, doesn't it? In my own case, for instance, it's the reason I ended up choosing writing over painting, because writing has given me a very active life that I think being a painter might not have done, even if I'd been more successful at it than I was. I might have gotten my picture on the cover of *Art News* or something, but I doubt I'd have had access to the educational life that's unfolded for me through my writing.

RB: That's what happens when I do my public art commissions, which involves working with other people.

GGI: I think each Girl has a different relationship to being a Guerrilla Girl as well as doing her own work. I know for me it's fairly separate. But I think that there's something very empowering, and also very positive, about targeting people with a lot of humor, and addressing issues that we have a vested interest in—not apologizing for it, but being very overt about it. Some of the women do work that is political, and some don't. Some are painters, or sculptors, or performance artists. It's a whole range.

RB: Some aren't artists at all.

GGI: Some are art professionals, working in institutions.

SG: How many of you are there?

BOTH: We never say.

RB: Before I became a Guerrilla Girl, I remember walking around the East Village on a cold snowy day a long time ago, and looking up and seeing my first Guerrilla Girl poster and just being knocked out. I felt like somebody was talking to me. Suddenly the frustration I'd been feeling, the isolation and all that —it was like suddenly there was a voice.

SG: How does one get to be part of that voice? Can you sign up to become a Guerrilla Girl? Can anyone be one?

GGI: That's funny, because one of our posters says, "We signed up to be Guerrilla Girls."

RB: It's kind of an underground thing; it's a feminist network.

SG: You have to know someone. [Laughter] It's just like getting a show in New York—you have to know the right people!

RB: We don't want to say it's a cabal, but I guess if you make it known to the right people—

SG: Is your membership spread right across the U.S.?

GGI: We're a New York-based group.

RB: But we've done enough lecturing across the U.S. and around the world that Guerrilla Girl chapters just sort of spring up, but they're more like franchises. They're independent from us.

SG: So the primary organization is pretty well New York "owned and operated"?

GGI: Yes. Also the issues and people being targeted are definitely focused on New York. I mean, the issues are broader than that, but the specifics relate to New York.

SG: Do you have monthly meetings?

GGI: We do not say. But we actually meet a fair amount; we have poster meetings to decide what issues we want to address through posters. Initially our posters started out being statistical report cards, in terms of, say, these galleries show women artists less than 10 percent, these museums have not represented women or artists of color, that sort of thing. Usually, we try to do them with humor. We discuss how we're going to handle issues; we target auction houses and other kinds of things. There was one instance where a Jasper Johns painting sold for 17.7 million dollars, and we showed how, for that amount of money, you could buy an anthology of all the women artists in history.

RB: You could buy a piece by about fifty women artists.

GGI: More. Georgia O'Keeffe, Frida Kahlo, et cetera. It's a sad comment, but nevertheless, we get these ideas and try to make a poster on them. And then we post them.

SG: Do you ever get hostile responses?

RB: Absolutely. Especially when we've made posters that attacked certain galleries. There's been a series of posters, like report cards, that we made where we grade the New York galleries. One of our most recent ones said, "These are the most bigoted galleries in New York." That's a pretty heavy word to use.

SG: Who was at the top of the list?

RB: It was all the regular blue-chip galleries, like Pace. One of them was in Soho—Jay Gorney—and every time we put that poster up, it was torn down immediately. It's almost as if the galleries sent out their minions to get that poster off the street.

SG: I guess you don't get angry letters because you have no address.

RB: We have a P.O. Box number on the posters.

SG: Do you get hate mail—and love mail?

RB: We get a lot of love mail. People send us money, and kisses. I don't think we've gotten much hate mail.

GGI: We have occasionally, but very little. You really find that people just love gorillas. It's also a photo opportunity. Everyone wants to have their picture in an art magazine with the Guerrilla Girls, which accounts for a lot of our success!

SG: This is a slight shift in gears here, but one of the running themes of these dialogues so far is the sense some people have that Western industrial civilization is unraveling, and that we may be at the end of it. Things are coming apart. I was wondering if that's anything you Girls ever think about? Does it make a difference to what art should be doing? Or are you just unidirected, exclusively toward women's issues?

GGI: I think we are unidirected, though I think some artists in the group might want to address that issue. But we don't actually tell people how they should address any issue. Frankly, our job is to poster, although the kind of thing you're talking about has actually come up at meetings.

SG: Can you describe any of those discussions?

RB: Well, in the last years of the Bush administration, we made a series of political posters. It was the first time we made posters that didn't deal directly with the art world, because we were so alarmed at the Gulf war, as well as the issues of homelessness, the environment, and AIDS. At the same time, a group called WAC (Women's Action Coalition) started in New York, which is a direct action group that duplicated some of our efforts. So we decided that maybe it was time for us to go back to our original idea, which is to deal with the art world. Our new posters are dealing more directly with the art world. That's not to say, though, that some of us aren't personally very obsessed with things like AIDS, or wondering what the point of it all is in the face of such impending disaster.

SG: Do you feel, then, that these are indeed apocalyptic times?

RB: I personally have been touched very much by losing a lot of friends to AIDS, so it does change things. It makes me wonder sometimes about the art world and all that, but it doesn't mean that I'd want to stop being a Guerrilla Girl. Many things are in question right now, for me, and for a lot of us.

GGI: We talked earlier about our agenda, which is fairly narrow, but it's actually an important agenda, because it's a civil rights issue. Many, many women go to art schools; more than 50 percent of art students are females. And they somehow get lost, because when they leave, there's not a support structure for them. They don't have access to the system, and their sensibility is lost. It's almost as if, simplistically stated, you have a black man who goes through medical school, but can't practice, as used to be the case.

RB: Today, when we visited the Roanoke Museum, there was a painting by Thomas Eakins's wife. I guess the only reason her painting was in the museum is that her family comes from around here. That's what we were told. It reminded me of a show I saw in New York just recently, a show of artist wives of famous artists, and they were all extremely gifted and talented. In one case, the woman had destroyed most of her work at the end of her life because she felt it would be a burden to her children; nobody paid any attention to her the whole time she was making the work, so only a few pieces were left. Milton Avery's wife, Sally Avery, was in the show. It turned out she'd supported him for twenty-five years, and when the woman curator went over there to get a few pieces for the show, all of Milton Avery's work was on the walls, and her work was in a pile on the floor. So the curator said, "Why is your work on the floor?" And she answered, "Well, Milton gets the walls, and I get the floor." And that is a crippling attitude. Even though it's now 1993 and things should be different, I think it's still an attitude that one encounters. You know, what happens to women after graduation?

sg: One of the things I find most compelling about your Guerrilla Girl work is its communal, collaborative approach, and that, on a certain level, you've managed to deindividualize yourselves, because you work anonymously. You share a collective vision, and there are many of you, so you represent a force because of this that you'd never really achieve just on your own, any one of you.

both: Absolutely!

sg: And yet, there's a contradiction about it all, because this very same part of you that's hooked in collectively with the Guerrilla Girls goes out and fights for the world view of individualism, for the right to have these individual careers, and in that sense, to go the way of the culture totally by following the narrow limits imposed by the established ideology of autonomous art. So it seems as if the whole communal dimension gets a bit lost, though I'm not trying to be critical here. But I have a problem, in that I see the system as a set of entrenched patriarchal institutions and forces. Of course, I agree with you that women have not fared well under that system, but I've gone beyond that issue myself to questioning just how interesting or important it is to be part of that system. Because there's something intrinsically wrong with it, something more than just the fact that it hasn't been very welcoming to women.

RB: I guess at the moment we don't have an alternative.

GGI: To actually change the system is so unbelievably complex that at this point, our interest, as we've already said, is in getting women more access to it. So that's our attitude about change, as opposed to breaking down the system.

SG: I don't think any of us as individuals has the possibility of changing the system, but writing, I've found, has some effect in the world; it does the one thing I think it is possible to do, which is to influence people toward a change of heart, or a change in consciousness. And once that happens, then the system—and the values it embodies—begin to look different to you. You haven't necessarily changed anything about it, but it does become harder to muster up the same enthusiasm for being part of it that I still sense, for instance, coming from you.

RB: [Laughter] You think we're enthusiastic about the system?

SG: Well, you're enthusiastic when women are doing well in it, yes!

RB: I think we might be delving for alternatives in one part of our brain, but at the same time, as long as we're continuing to live in New York and be part of it all—

SG: You want to participate.

GGI: Absolutely! We speak for the people who want to participate and be part of the system, no question about it.

RB: But you've got to understand that we are a collective, so that everybody thinks differently.

GGI: The kind of interview that you get depends on whom you speak to.

RB: In the end, since we are Guerrilla Girls, we'll come to some kind of consensus, but basically, we're a bunch of real individuals.

Viewing the World as Process

CAROLYN MERCHANT

A *re capitalism and ecology incompatible? There is an-*
other, more optimistic scenario than the one of col-
lapse, which, according to Carolyn Merchant, is based on
the ability of systems to reorganize themselves and to create
order out of chaos. As global warming, pollution and re-
source depletion escalate, increasing the need for environ-
mentally sustainable solutions, the contradictions within the
various levels of our civilization may force us to reverse

the priorities currently given to production and economic growth, and to seek out other philosophies that harmonize better with the constraints of the ecosystem. In this way, the direction and cumulation of social changes begin to differentiate among the spectrum of possibilities so that some ideas assume a more central role in the array, while others move to the periphery. From this organic process, cultural transformations develop that Merchant refers to as "ecological revolutions"—a reorganization of our consciousness in relation to nature that could take about fifty to seventy-five years to complete. The current global ecological revolution, if it succeeds, means that a value-system oriented to nature as process, as a teacher whose ways must be followed, will eventually replace the dominant, mechanistic image of nature as an "it" that is our legacy from the scientific revolution. The objectification and commodification of nature have sanctioned human actions toward the environment that are emotionally neutral and encourage domination and control rather than intimacy, reciprocity or nurturing.

Carolyn Merchant is an environmental historian at the University of California, Berkeley, and the author of several books, including The Death of Nature, *which traces the alterations that took place in our relationship to nature as a result of the scientific revolution's mechanization of the world picture. At that time, the shift was from an animate, organic universe to mechanism as the dominant metaphor for binding together the cosmos, society and the self into a single cultural reality. The disembodied eye, based in a spectatorial epistemology that posits a subjective self reflecting on an objective world exterior to it, is paradigmatic of the domination of the earth through the controlling scrutiny of the overseer, for whom seeing from a distance (rather than a face-to-face relationship) is the primary source of knowledge.*

When my friend John Browder, a professor of urban studies, informed me he was going to bring Merchant to speak at Virginia Tech, I wondered how it would be to dialogue with her about the new process paradigm in relation to art. John was already setting up appointments on a very tight schedule, and there was no time to write to Merchant in advance, explaining who I was or describing the project. John said he would hold open a slot for me and gave me her phone number. In the event that Merchant agreed to see me, I could have exactly fifty minutes at two o'clock on Tuesday. It took many calls before I finally reached Merchant. I found myself trying to plow as much information as I could into the potent silence at the other end of the line. It was definitely a lightning strike. I was unsure if, in just a couple of minutes, I could ignite the curiosity of someone I'd never met, who clearly had no idea who I was. When I

hung my request on the air, there was a pregnant pause.
Finally she said, "Is your 'reenchantment' related to Morris
Berman's Reenchantment of the World? *"Yes," I replied,*
"it is." "All right," she said, "I'll do it."

We met in John's office on campus on April 6, 1993,
and sat on opposite sides of his desk with the tape recorder
on. There were no preliminaries; we simply began the dia-
logue. Of all the conversations in the book, this one was
perhaps the most difficult, the most taxing. As I sat across
from Merchant, who was austerely dressed in a navy blue
suit, I was very conscious of her imposing intelligence, and
I could see that the whole situation was a wild card for her.
She interrupted to make herself a cup of coffee. Then she sat
down again, and the two of us began a slow dance, allowing
our thoughts to weave a complicated web around the sub-
jects of science, art and ecological revolutions. As it says in
the Nike advertisement, you do the tango. Just do it.

SUZI GABLIK: One of the things you say in *The Death of*
Nature, Carolyn, is that civilization has advanced
itself at the expense of nature. The problem is that
civilization has set itself above nature; this is part of
the hierarchy of the masculine "power over," which
has meant patriarchal dominance and a repression
of the feminine. We might start by talking about
whether you think there are significant changes

going on in our culture about those issues right now; for instance, do you think the culture-nature dichotomy is just as profoundly lethal as ever it was?

CAROLYN MERCHANT: I guess I would start by rephrasing what you say I say—which is not to talk about civilization in some large abstract sense, but Western industrial capitalism since the seventeenth century, as it developed in North America and Europe. Capitalism inherently contains a principle of growth that depends on turning nature, which is subject, into something that is object, commodity and resource. Capitalism is committed to growth, as is state socialism, but with different principles—the former for commodity production, the latter to fulfill basic needs and raise living standards. As global capitalism spread the market economy throughout the Americas and the colonial empires in the early modern period, and now throughout the rest of the Third World, it has brought nature into a very compromising kind of position. Nature gets transformed from independent subject into object and is used to advance the interests of entrepreneurs and elites at the expense of fulfilling basic needs for everyone, especially the poor.

SG: You've also talked about the shift in our relationship, since the mechanization of the world picture, from what used to be a face-to-face reciprocal interaction of humans with nature, to this notion of the disembodied eye that surveys and measures nature from a distance. That was particularly resonant for me, because of its parallels with the development of art.

CM: Right, the dominance of vision is part of, first, the Greco-Roman world that replaces a kind of oral, face-to-face culture of the Homeric era, and it gets amplified in the Renaissance with the empirical eye and the eye of the mind. This is the essence of science's reduction of the world to experiment and mathematics as the only forms of valid knowledge.

SG: There really is a strong parallel here with what happened to art when it became purely visual, and stopped being a participatory, face-to-face experience. It began to address what Gary Snyder has called "a faceless audience," where you don't direct your expression to anyone in particular. Rather, you're making autonomous objects that have no context until they're siphoned off into an institutionalized setting, where they become pure commodity, or spectacle, or fetish.

CM: So isn't that a kind of reification, or abstraction, of the word "art"? I mean, some art is still participatory if it includes dance, or if it involves the audience. Tribal art might be an example of what you were saying we've moved away from.

SG: Exactly, but we have very few instances of that kind of participatory involvement in our culture, at least when it comes to the so-called fine arts. The fine arts tend to exist either on stage or in an art gallery for a faceless audience for whom they become spectacle. The audience rarely has a participatory role. It has an observer role.

CM: So even with music, or with dance, which maybe involves some other aspects of the body than just the eye, it's still reduced to a sort of spectator sport?

SG: Absolutely. And ultimately, in the case of visual art, to the production of autonomous objects that can only be viewed, or commodified and sold, rather than used in some manner to serve society's needs.

CM: So do you see a way of getting back to the more participatory forms?

SG: That's actually what my book *The Reenchantment of Art* is about. It tries to show that everything in our culture is now moving in the direction of process-oriented and interactive models. My work is mostly about artists whose focus is less on making objects and more on participatory or collaborative relationships. But getting back to what we were talking about originally, would you say that we have to confront the fact that capitalism, and the capitalist way of life, is lethal to the ecology then?

CM: Yes, absolutely.

SG: Do you see signs that the necessary changes are beginning to happen? Do you feel hopeful that we will make it across this threshold of change before we completely destroy the life-support systems of the earth?

CM: I have this idea that we're in the midst of a global ecological crisis, which is a way in which society is reorganizing itself and its consciousness in relation to nature, to ecology—and that's what I call "ecological revolution." It's a process of both visionary thinking that's challenging older paradigms and putting out new ideas, and of social movements that put pressure on the vulnerable economic and social structures.

SG: Did getting rid of George Bush and Dan Quayle make you feel more hopeful?

CM: Well, that certainly was a small step in the right direction, but I'm distressed at this point to see that some of the green program is being rapidly undermined—the mining and grazing and forest issues.

SG: You say in *The Death of Nature,* and I'm quoting here, "The death of the world soul and the removal of nature's spirits helped to support increasing environmental destruction by removing any scruples that might be associated with the view that nature was a living organism." The people I know, who do have a sense of the living quality of nature, certainly have those scruples, but somehow they seem to be in a serious minority, in terms of megaindustries, corporations, government and the like. How do you think we're ever going to turn all that around? At a more personal level, it worries me that even if one is a deep ecologist at heart, it's still very hard to imagine life without the many technologies that are so destructive in this culture. Even if you manage to tone down your lifestyle, you're still hooked up to, and dependent upon, electricity, cars, planes—we all continue to use them. But in order to really save the planet, it would seem as if all that eventually has to go. What do you think?

CM: I don't think it all has to go, but I do think it has to be reorganized in a way that's sustainable. How that will happen is critical to whether we can achieve this global ecological revolution, or not. But I don't see any way that Western market capitalism is going to go back and get rid of all that—

SG: You don't think it might simply be forced to?

CM: I think it might be forced to become sustainable. It will be forced to become ecologically viable, because the contradiction between the economy and ecology is deepening all the time. And global capitalism is continually undermining its own resource base and its own conditions for perpetuation. Now, ideally one would go toward a totally different kind of system, one that we haven't seen yet on this planet, some new form of a socialist way of being with nature, not oriented toward growth, nor toward total industrialization. But probably there'll be something along the lines of green capitalism, which I don't think is enough. Certainly capitalism, at least, will have to confront its own situation.

SG: What is your sense of the viable time frame for making this turnaround?

CM: Well, my thought with *Ecological Revolutions* is that these are processes which take several decades—five, seven decades, or something on the order of fifty to seventy-five years. And so, when you look back on it you can say, yes, that between the beginning and the end—let's say the 1970s to the mid-twenty-first century—looking back from that watershed you would say there's been a real transformation in thinking, and in economic relations to nature, and also in reproduction.

SG: You sound fairly hopeful that this is already in process, and that it will take place successfully.

CM: I don't know if it will take place successfully, but I think it's possible. I don't know if it's probable even, but I think it's possible. One of the things that's changed in the last two decades is a tremendous global awareness to the issues and problems; even as those problems have deepened, more thinking has gone into looking for alternatives on all kinds of levels, and more groups have organized themselves who are trying to rethink and restructure our relationships with nature and with each other.

SG: Is it your sense that the scientific community is making some necessary alterations in world view here?

CM: My hope lies in some of these new ideas which you mentioned earlier, of process philosophy, process physics, David Bohm's work, Ilya Prigogine's work, the work on chaos theory and complexity theory. All these have inherent within them a different set of assumptions about nature. They view the world as process rather than as manipulable parts that are rearranged through external forces, which was the Newtonian conception.

SG: Has your work or your thinking ever brought you toward considering what art should be doing in terms of these changes—or is that completely outside of your sphere?

CM: I don't know if I've thought much about how art would reflect these changes, but I think it would, just as science can reflect and support them. Deep ecology, for example, is putting forth a whole new set of assumptions about the nature of reality, of ontology, epistemology, ethics, psychology: all the foundations of the modern world are being challenged by postmodernist thinking. But I don't think deep ecology will necessarily lead the transformation, just as the new art will not lead the transformation, but it will reflect it, support it, encourage and nurture it.

SG: You don't think that deep ecology is at the forefront of the change in consciousness that has to occur in all spheres?

CM: A change in consciousness is part of it, but I don't think it is the instigation, or the cause, of it.

SG: What will be the instigator, or the cause, then; the catastrophic depletion of the earth?

CM: Yes, but I don't think it will be catastrophic. I mean, I don't agree with a kind of "limits to growth" theory of exponential growth and collapse. I like better the order-out-of-chaos approach, which is that we're in a state of crisis and chaos now, and out of that will come a regrouping and a reorganization.

SG: You mean something unforeseen, something new will emerge?

CM: Right. And I think the visionary thinkers and artists see that—they see what needs to emerge, and they can imagine it. If it's participatory art, they can even involve us in a participatory way in new modes of being, with respect to nonhuman nature.

sg: Would you describe this as a kind of moral responsibility of our time to do this?

cm: Yes! What I think chaos theory suggests is the need for a new ethic about nature, not an ethic of domination and control, which is what Francis Bacon and the seventeenth-century scientific revolution led to. But rather, I call it a partnership ethic, in which nonhuman nature is active, free, alive, organic, in process, and unpredictable. We need to recognize as humans that this is part of reality. Nature can't be totally predictable, and it can't therefore be totally controlled or dominated. And that makes us more humble with respect to the nonhuman world.

sg: The dominant philosophy of Cartesian-Kantian aesthetics has really taken its cue from science, in the sense of creating a value-free, autonomous discipline that has been purged of any ethical or moral imperatives—this is what we call "art for art's sake." My work has been involved with trying to change that framework, to shift our ordinary understanding of art away from value-free, autonomous thinking. It certainly parallels certain issues in the scientific world, such as the assumption many scientists make that they don't have moral responsibility for the consequences of their work, their responsibility is simply to do research and get the information. Artists often take the same view about art: their responsibility is to make art. It's not to save the planet, or anything grandiose like that.

CM: I think there are ethics embedded in world views, so just as there was an ethic of propitiation embedded in the organic world view of the premodern world, there is an ethic of control embedded in the mechanistic world view. I think a new scientific world view will be recognized as not value-free, but rather will have values associated with it. It will be a process-oriented, ecological world view in which humans and their values are part of nature.

SG: Then it's likely to be cyclical, rather than linear?

CM: I don't know if it's cyclical, necessarily, but it's certainly nonlinear. Certainly cyclical ideas are critical to how we think about ecology, but I don't think cyclical is the only way, even if it was the way of the past—tied to sun and moon and tides, and so on—because I don't think we can go back to what a premodern consciousness was like.

SG: If you had to take a mindset like that of George Bush, and it was your task to make this person understand deep ecology, what would you try to do first? Do you think such a person could undergo a change in understanding—this is something that has come up in other conversations—or is somebody like him a lost cause? Would it be better just to focus on a different sort of person altogether?

CM: I think that most change takes place through young people, and the old ways of thinking, or the old strongly held opinions, die out, just as linear thinking dies out, and nonlinear, or nondeterminative thinking, or a partnership ethic, or process-oriented thinking, comes in with young people, who become concerned and interested. It also comes in with new ways of teaching. Society reproduces itself and perpetuates itself through the laws and governance of the social order, which Bush represents, and which our government represents, but it also allows points of change and transformation—it's not cast in stone. However, it is very difficult to change something that has gotten so large and bureaucratic and consumed with its own perpetuation, as, say, the federal government has now.

SG: I see other problems, not only in the overwhelming aspects of our institutional structures, but also in the addictive nature of the whole culture, which is something that Anne Wilson Schaef writes about in *When Society Becomes an Addict.* So many of us have grown up with a way of life—I had this experience in a major snowstorm recently, when it seemed like the power might go out—in which, well, we just don't have any hunter-gatherer skills! [Laughter]

CM: That's why I say we can't go back.

SG: I have artist friends who have given up everything and are learning survival skills with a wilderness tracker, because they believe industrial civilization will soon collapse. But when I confront my own fear that they could be right, I find it very difficult to contemplate learning how to forage for food, or learning how to hunt and trap and make shelters and all that. Can you do those things?

CM: No, and I don't think that's the answer either.

SG: I'm glad to hear it!

CM: I mean, I don't see that kind of collapse happening, because I think we're a lot smarter than to just let it happen. What I see happening over a period of time, that in retrospect we might call a revolution, is a series of changes and adjustments—you might even call them painful changes—towards sustainability. These will be in the things that are the necessities of life: food, clothing, shelter, energy, health care, old-age care. In food, for example, through sustainable agriculture. What does that mean? It means a way to treat the soil as the living thing that it is, not the dead matter you assume it is when you put pesticides and chemicals on it. It means developing ways that will use biological controls rather than chemical controls, which are based on a different paradigm and a different ethic. In sustainable forestry, it means using methods that are not self-defeating, and forestry is moving in that direction. It isn't there yet, but there are very strong pressures to become sustainable, such that we're not undercutting our own resource base.

sg: Do you feel deep ecology is moving us away from the mechanized world picture, and back toward a more organic, animistic vision of reality?

cm: I'm not sure that deep ecology's project is to move us "back." Away from the mechanistic, yes, but I'm not sure calling it animistic is correct.

sg: How *would* you define the new world picture, as it moves away from mechanism, if it isn't definable as the old animism or organicism?

cm: For one thing, it's a problem to call it a picture, because that's exactly what we're talking about with spectators and vision, and the idea, as Heidegger said, that it's not that the picture of the world changed, but that it became a picture at all, with the emergence of modernism. So it would be, as you said, something more participatory. It would be new and different ways of knowing and being-in-the-world. It would be something that reminds us of the way other cultures have interacted with the world —aboriginal cultures or Native American peoples. There is a land wisdom there—a way of doing things and growing crops that has worked in the past, but which we have lost through our emphasis on mechanism—that would be part of this. And part of this new wisdom would be—

sg: Synthetic in character, then? It would be drawn from many different sources: the best of technology and the best of the older traditions. Is that what you're trying to say?

CM: Yes, except it's not like going around the world and picking this or that thing and trying to paste it together—not appropriating it, but coming to it ourselves.

SG: You feel it would be more like an emergent thing, something that will rise up in and of itself, with us and through us, rather than that we go out to try and find it.

CM: Exactly. It will arise out of our attempts to get away from the betrayals of the past, to see what has not worked and to try to make something else work. It will be something that comes out of our own cultural conditions and predicament of the moment; it may draw inspiration from other places, but these ideas will have to work in a context that is uniquely our own.

SG: Since you're talking about creativity here, I'm wondering if you have personally encountered any art that speaks to you from these new emerging principles?

CM: We have in California a project called "Reinventing Nature," which in a way sounds arrogant, but it really means that there are overlays of changing constructions of nature that people make all through history. "Reinventing" suggests that there is a deep cultural construction that goes on and that can change. One dimension of that is art in the landscape. Specifically, in San Diego, Newton and Helen Harrison are looking at whole watersheds, and thinking about how those watersheds—

SG: Can be restored to health.

CM: Yes! They think of the world as a giant conversation in which everybody is involved, not only people, but trees and rocks and landscapes and rivers. So it's seeing things on a regional basis, and in artistic terms at the same time. And also seeing it in participatory terms, in which many people are engaged in a conversation together, people of all cultures, who are connected to, or living in, a place or a wider region or watershed.

SG: Before we fold our tent here, it strikes me that your own writing—and I bracket what I'm about to say with the statement that I'm in awe of your books— is done in a kind of old paradigm mode of distanced, objective scholarship, and I'm wondering if there is any sense in which you feel that perhaps even your own work needs to undergo transformation in relation to the notion of a process paradigm?

CM: Yes, that would be a good idea! My recent book on *Radical Ecology* [1992], which is meant for a general audience and for classroom use, tries to give examples and to set scenes and places in the community that help draw us into a problem, so we can talk about some of the contradictions in that problem. I think in that book I did try to use a style that comes less out of the academy and involves people more as participant readers. But, it's still a book, and it's still the written word, and I'm still an academic, so I am not, in that sense, a creative artist trying to create new forms of writing. And I'm not sure that I'm capable of doing that. I mean, I have my own creativity, it shows up in certain ways that I put ideas together, and synthesize things, and try to search for new examples, but I'm not sure that it's my role, really, to invent new creative art forms.

SG: I totally understand that. My own gift is in the same sphere, it's basically that of a synthesizer, taking information from lots of places and integrating it. But I have found a need to personalize what I do more, to leave behind, in a sense—and it may be easier to do this in aesthetic philosophy than in scientific philosophy—the scholarly mode, with elaborate footnotes, and so forth. Of course, one runs into other problems then, where your work may be considered not serious or intellectual enough.

CM: I guess I've been trying to do it more in terms of teaching, because I do see young people as the hope for change, and personalizing, I think, is very important. And so, in my environmental history class, I ask people to start by thinking about their personal environmental histories—the environments that they identified with most closely as they grew up; what environments their parents lived in, and their grandparents; and how their parents' and grandparents' values about the environment may be very different from the values they may have developed or feel now. Trying to understand what it was like in their own immediate family history connects people to places and to change over time. It asks them to involve themselves in history in a personal way, and to understand things that they had never really thought about before. So I think of my teaching as the way in which I can bring this creativity forward.

Breaking Out of the White Cube

RICHARD SHUSTERMAN

To pass beyond the modern framework, it seems as if we must be willing to surrender the ideology of aesthetic autonomy—the compartmental conception of fine art that segregates it to the separate realm of the museum. Art, life and popular culture have all suffered from these entrenched divisions and from the consequently narrow identification of art with elitist fine art. There is a fundamental passivity that underlies our established appreciation of high art, which is

*heightened by the traditional aesthetic attitude of disin-
terested, distanced contemplation, and which discourages
communal interaction or deeply embodied participatory
involvement. If any social function can be ascribed to autonomous art at all, it is the function to have no function. The
aesthetic attitude implies a break with the world and the
concerns of ordinary life; its premise is that art and real life
are, and should be, strictly separated. There is, however, no
compelling reason at this point to accept the narrow aesthetic limits imposed by the established ideology of autonomous art, an ideology that is no longer profitable, or even
creditable. The emancipatory enlargement of the aesthetic
involves reconceiving art in more liberal terms, freeing
it from its exalted cloister, where it is isolated from life
and differentiated from more popular forms of cultural
expression.*

*Imagine my surprise at finding in the mail one morning
a book whose bristling, provocative contents can be summed
up roughly by the philosophy delineated above.* Pragmatist
Aesthetics: Living Beauty, Rethinking Art *argues from start
to finish for an aesthetic of vigorously active and communally impassioned engagement, and for art that is neither
purposeless nor disinterested. Written by Richard Shusterman, an associate professor of philosophy at Temple University, the book was sent to me by the organizer of a*

symposium at Swarthmore College, at which the author and I were both invited to speak. The topic, inspired by the title of Paul Gauguin's famous painting Where Do We Come From? What Are We? Where Are We Going?, is a subject very much on people's minds today. Of course I was delighted and intrigued to discover a fellow-traveler, someone else who was challenging "the frame" by asking uncomfortable questions about the privileging of isolated and independent objects over process-oriented models, and who believed philosophy should not restrict itself to abstract arguments, but should actively engage in reshaping our aesthetic concepts and theories so they can serve us better. Shusterman definitely feels that we need to infuse our criticism of art with a wider awareness of its social role.

Shusterman expounds on how we can enlarge our conception of the aesthetic by embracing the practical, the social and the political, an aesthetic that builds on that of his intellectual mentor, John Dewey, who was one of pragmatism's founding fathers. Art would be richer, Dewey thought, and more satisfying to people, if it was integrated into their lives rather than being set "upon a far-off pedestal." Like Dewey, Shusterman claims that the compartmentalizing of art in museums has impoverished the aesthetic quality of our lives, a theme already introduced by Satish Kumar and reflected on by James Hillman. Dewey went *much farther than merely advocating the integration of art and life; he proposed that the rift between the practical and the aesthetic was a historic catastrophe that has produced "specimens of fine art and nothing else." According to Shusterman, art objects are aimed for sale in the market like other commodities in capitalist society, thus depriving art of its intimate social connection. Shusterman writes: "It is perhaps Dewey's most important aesthetic theme: the privileging of dynamic aesthetic experience over the fixed material object which our conventional thinking identifies—and then commodifies and fetishizes—as the work of art." For Dewey, as well as for Shusterman, the essence and value of art are not in the mere artifacts we typically regard as art, but in the dynamic and developing experiential activity through which they are created and perceived. The point is not a rejection of discrete, static objects, as Shusterman says, nor to close or destroy art's museums, but rather to expand them, and to show that aesthetic experience clearly exceeds the limits of fine art and its objects. "My defense of the aesthetic legitimacy of popular art and my account of ethics as an art of living," he states, "both aim at a more expansive and democratic reconception of art."*

An attractive man with an incisive, sophisticated intelligence, Shusterman seemed eager to talk with me about his ideas, which are in many ways analogous to my own. The following conversation was taped on April 16, 1993, at seven o'clock in the morning at Ashton House on the Swarthmore campus. We were both gulping down cups of tea before I rushed off in a taxi to the airport.

SUZI GABLIK: One of the running themes that has emerged from these conversations, Richard, is the notion that in other cultures, art has never been restricted to pictures on the wall, but has always been something much more integrated with life. When I read your book *Pragmatist Aesthetics,* I was struck by how much your views frequently go counter to a lot of current aesthetic ideology which asserts that art and real life are, and should be kept, separate. You pose a challenge to the aesthetic attitude that demands a break with the world and with the concerns of ordinary life and ordinary people—an idea you claim is no longer useful. Do you want to expound on this a bit more?

RICHARD SHUSTERMAN: Art's separation from life and the aesthetic attitude's break with the world and practical concerns are closely related, but I think it's important to distinguish them historically. Because there was art a long time before there was the aesthetic attitude. Throughout the ancient world and well into the Renaissance, we had art without an explicitly aesthetic attitude, art having the dual purpose of enjoyment and instruction, or *dolce* and *utile,* as Horace described it. The aesthetic attitude, like the term "aesthetic," is the product of the eighteenth and nineteenth centuries. It's only in more modern times that we start to have this greater differentiation of cultural spheres and greater specialization. Art becomes defined by the aesthetic attitude—that is, by the idea of a disinterested, distanced, formal contemplation of the world and of the art work. But the point here is a hidden elitism: only certain people can take that disinterested, formal perspective, and they are people whose practical world is already well taken care of. Their well-being is secure, so they are free to devote leisure time and energy to the more demanding pleasures of pure form. Someone who can look at a landscape in a disinterested and disembodied way in terms of its formal properties alone, and in terms of its sensual and emotional satisfactions, rather than in terms of what it means for one's life practically, is someone who doesn't have to worry about her needs and who can demonstrate great intellectual control. Thus, for all its purity, the aesthetic attitude implies a sort of social and intellectual distinction, and even serves as a marker of such distinction.

SG: In a previous conversation with Carolyn Merchant, who is a philosopher and historian of science, she talked about the evolution of the disembodied eye in science, which emerged along with the mechanization of the world picture around the same time that you're talking about. At that point, man began to chart and map, to schematize the world, and in a sense, his role was reduced to that of the eye which surveys, and which surveys at a distance. This disembodied, objectifying eye became the essence of the scientific attitude and, in a sense, of the aesthetic attitude as well. In your book, you talk about how the aesthetic attitude privileges product over process, and results in the "museum conception of art" that defines art exclusively in terms of autonomous objects, masterpieces quarantined to the separate realm of the museum. This pure aesthetic realm of distanced contemplation is intended to imply a break with the real world and its problems.

RS: I think that's largely true, but I'd like to make some qualifications. We must remember that the idea of objectifying art precedes the modern scientific revolution. It goes back as far as Aristotle—that is, the idea of thinking of art as external making, as the making of an object, rather than the performing and experiencing of an action or a process. The reasons for this externalizing objectification are, I think, very deep and very interesting. As I said last night, art was defined by philosophers in order to establish philosophy's superiority. Art can be incredibly potent, and Plato recognized this, which is why he wanted to ban the artist from the Republic. He saw art as some kind of divine possession or madness, which, even if it was divine, wasn't rational and therefore had to be feared. Aristotle also tried to reconceive art in a way that would tame its magical, experiential power by construing it as some kind of skill in making external objects. So Aristotle defined art as *poesis,* i.e., making, which he distinguished sharply from *praxis,* or doing. Thus, he was able to detach art effectively from the realm of action and ethics. In other words, for Aristotle, what you *do* affects who you are: the purpose of a virtuous act is connected with the kind of person that you are, which is expressed in doing that act. With art, on the other hand, conceived merely as the making of an object, the end is that external object itself. So it really doesn't matter who you are as a person; what you're doing is producing an object through a special skill but not through your essential character. This distinction between making and doing allows us to think of art as the production of objects that are altogether separate from who we ethically are and how we act. Aristotelian aestheticians, like Jacques Maritain, insist explicitly on this difference; it means that you can be a great artist and a horrible person. And certainly, this idea of art's separation from character and *praxis* has become a commonplace in our own aesthetic understanding. There is also the corollary idea that since what you make is purely external to you, it doesn't at all affect who you are, which seems quite false, from what I know of practicing artists.

SG: But it does fit with our understanding in the world of Cartesian thinking, which adopts a strict division between mind and body, and makes it extremely difficult to understand how they interact with each other. In the world of Descartes, subjects and objects, self and world, mind and body, belong to fundamentally different realms.

RS: Yes, and that's why I wanted to say that this kind of thinking goes back even further than Descartes, even if in earlier times it wasn't as powerful. I think the difference is that in modern times, we have this modern world picture—you called it "mechanistic," but we could also call it abstract and mathematical —where modern science advanced by separating itself from what's called the life world. In other words, the commonsense world that we see and experience is not the world of science. Galileo said that the world of nature is written in mathematics.

SG: It makes nature into a bunch of concepts.

RS: Yes, but concepts are always involved in our understanding of the world. The important thing about modern mechanistic science was that its concepts were seen as value-neutral, mathematical and abstracted from the practices of ordinary living.

SG: In a curious way, art has patterned itself on a similar model of separation from the life world; and this social isolation, as you've pointed out, has marginalized and disempowered the artist. In our minds, we tend to think of art and science as opposites. We think that art belongs to the "inner" world of imagination, which is not part of the rationalized, conceptual and objectified world of science, and yet the aesthetic attitude has framed our notion of art in a manner that parallels totally the scientific attitude.

RS: I think that's true. Actually, you could say aesthetic subjectivism is the flip side of scientific objectivism. And if you want to go even deeper, you can see both art and science as emerging from the general logic of modernity, which is concerned with liberating the individual subject from the oppressive bond of tradition and the harsh limitations of nature. But, I don't think that modernity has been such a horrible thing. I think, on the whole, it has been good for the West.

SG: Except that modern individualism has run wild, without the balance of any communal thinking.

RS: Yes, but think how much the idea of individualism was important in gaining social and political freedom for the subject: liberation from feudal lords, the right to vote, the right to privacy, the liberation from church constraints, and so on. One of the more positive aspects of individualism and this new privileging of subjectivity—which has as its correlative an objectified nature—is the growth in personal freedom that Western subjects have had. It's not a complete emancipation, however, as Foucault and Adorno have pointed out. Though in one sense the subject has been liberated from external authorities and from the ravages of nature, on the other hand, the subject is incarcerated by other kinds of logics, or regimens, that are more subtly introduced into the subject's own mind through modern society— for instance, the ruthless domination of human nature and desire by crudely instrumental, utilitarian thinking. But however we choose to evaluate this, I think the aesthetic and the scientific do have parallels that can be traced back to this general privileging of the subject and the rationalization of experience associated with modernity.

SG: The other crucial thing they have in common is the ideology of autonomy, meaning that ethics and moral imperatives are considered alien to the situation. Many people are horrified by the idea that art should embody any kind of moral imperative. Ditto science. And even criticism, as both you and I can attest, if it undertakes a moral position, will often engender a lot of resistance.

RS: There's another connection I want to make about science and art that relates to the economic regime of modernity—capitalism. In both art and science we see the need for radical new discoveries. Part of the impulse of modernity—and this has come with us into the postmodern—is the demand for change, new discoveries, new movements in art. It's like you're not a real scientist, or a real artist, unless you're making something new, or pioneering a novel discovery. I don't want to suggest that there's a simple, reductive, economic explanation to this common demand, but it's part of a whole Zeitgeist of always seeking innovations instead of using older forms that may still have good use-value. It dovetails very nicely, and is certainly in the spirit of a capitalist economy, which depends for its survival on constant innovation, because if there aren't new products, there won't be new profits. New products, new markets and new needs—the demand for novelty is something that runs throughout modernity. It has its scientific expression, and it has its aesthetic expression. There is a kind of artificial demand for novelty that keeps us breathless, unsatisfied and neurotic. I can even see it in the world of academic publishing, where there's so much pressure to come up with something new all the time, even when it's only superficially new. Autonomous art may resist straightforward moral engagement, but one of the major ethical injunctions for modern art has been the idea of "making it new." In other words, you weren't a serious artist if you weren't trying to make a radically new statement. Not to attempt this, for an artist, was a moral failure, not merely an aesthetic one.

SG: Postmodernism, of course, has done a pretty efficient job of dismantling that entire ideology.

RS: It has and it hasn't. It has, in the sense that this idea of pure innovation is completely unacceptable. We all now know that everything is a simulation of another simulation, and that we're all recycling, quoting and appropriating—we know about that. But there's still a very strong emphasis on the individual who has this particularly novel way of recycling, or this new way of showing that there is nothing new. Of course, there are people who work outside the institutions and whose primary aim is not trying to be original in terms of the art world's game of originality.

SG: One of the predictably regular responses to such work is that it isn't art. It's something else, something ephemeral, which may be interesting enough at the time, but is without the enduring quality we expect from high art.

RS: For me, one of the interesting questions is to ask at that juncture, what are the stakes in calling something art? Sometimes you can debate with people: Is it art? Isn't it art? And you get into an empty stalemate or into silly circular bickering. Then it's worth asking: In calling this art, what is at stake? That you take the work seriously? Again, what does that mean? That you ascribe an eternal transcendent value to it? I think that we put too large an emphasis on the permanent. It may be part of our theological tradition; for us secular people, art has come to represent the realm of the spiritual in a world that's been disenchanted from religion. And so, we expect from works of art some sort of permanent power, some kind of divine endurance. That kind of demand is, I think, excessive, because it's possible to appreciate lots of things that are ephemeral, like fireworks, or sunsets, or improvisational performances. Lots of beautiful and meaningful things are ephemeral, and part of their value is in the fact that they come and go. To deny that art can be ephemeral is to lock ourselves into an antiquated theological aesthetic.

sg: In the emerging ecological age, ephemerality is a blue-chip notion, because it means not adding to the world's already superabounding burden of stuff.

rs: I think there's a reason, which once again is historical, why we don't like the ephemeral, and why we don't want to associate art with things that don't last. When our world was much more difficult in terms of daily survival, life seemed very precarious, and people needed security and certainty, which is why a lot of the world's philosophies and religions have identified reality with what is unchanging. There's the changing world of appearances, but then there's this final, ultimate reality—people want to believe in something that is eternally real. It's the same thing with the demand for artistic permanence; in an uncertain world, you want to be able to bank on something. You want something you can read or look at forever, so you can always enjoy it. And now, I think, in contemporary times we've solved a lot of technological problems, and even though the solving of those technological problems has led to other problems, there is, at least in the rich Western civilizations, not much fear of immediate survival.

SG: Hey now, wait a minute!

RS: We can manage our pleasures more easily, and so there isn't a problem about investing in things that come, but may not stay. We can appreciate the ephemeral more, because we have security that new pleasures will take their place.

SG: Richard, I have to radically disagree with you here! The running theme of this book concerns the survival of Western industrial civilization. You used the word "precarious," but it was to suggest that the world is less precarious than it used to be. My sense of things is that we are verging on a level of precariousness that extends exponentially beyond anything the world has ever known before. A subtheme of all these conversations is whether or not you consider that we are living in apocalyptic times—and if so, what the role of art should be. Do you want to address that?

RS: I do, and I also want to clarify something. In the global, objective sense, we do live in precarious times, more than before. But the individual's sense of precariousness in her daily life has been greatly diminished. One's particular life feels less precarious, in the sense that it doesn't depend on whether one has a successful hunt today, or not. There's a kind of abundance and insurance—again, I'm only talking here about the rich Western countries where this kind of lifestyle exists. In such a situation, there's less of a need to get spiritual satisfaction and consolation from a belief in something eternal. There is less of a need to insist on art's value as existing in a transcendental, eternal form, because in our cultural life, as in our markets, there is a ready supply of satisfying items. However, I do agree with you about the fragility of the whole world scene.

SG: Do you think that this affects the role of art in the world today?

RS: I don't know whether it does—but I think it should. I think it should in at least two ways. One is that I have a great deal of sympathy with your ecological aesthetic agenda. I think that's a place where national boundaries can be overcome, because these are problems that go beyond particular national chauvinisms and political frontiers. Connected with this idea is the second direction where I think art can help, and that's in international and multicultural understanding. Even though I don't really have very definite and clear ideas about how this can happen, I'm convinced that the goal of an international, multicultural community has to be one of the targets of thinking for the new century. I wouldn't want to legislate this twofold agenda for all art. But I do think the sense of being in touch with the ground, with the earth, is important, not forgetting where we live and where we come from. However great humanity is, it shouldn't lose its contact with its natural local ground. But then, we shouldn't read that particular place in narrow, sectarian terms; we should try and reach out and also understand other cultures and people, who aren't in our particular locale.

SG: Can you give any examples of what you're talking about?

RS: One of the interesting international aesthetic movements that I see is hip-hop, the rap world, which came out of the inner city ghettos in New York, the Bronx, Brooklyn and Harlem. Now it has an international following, where it gets adapted into each different locale. Rap is a big thing in England and France. It is even a hit in South America and Japan. Afrika Bambaataa, who was one of the first great artists in that genre, went to Paris pretty early on and introduced his movement, the Zulu nation, into France. The interesting thing about rap is that although it's black music and it maintains its deep connection with African-American culture, when it travels, it gets inflected by the local culture and deals with that local culture's problems. I guess what I'm talking about are two needs that are different, and might even seem conflictual, but perhaps could be brought together—though they don't have to be. One is just the sense of renewed appreciation of where we are on the planet, and that can be ecological. But it doesn't have to be "green," because it's also important for artists to recognize other kinds of local ecologies that aren't "green," like the concrete inner cities, and not to just condemn all that as beyond aesthetic concern. The other need is a renewed appreciation of belonging to a complex multicultural planet, where we need to reach beyond our local geographical and cultural boundaries so as to nourish this richness and to enrich our lives through it.

SG: What you're saying is that we mustn't act as if only nature matters.

RS: Yes, and one reason not to do so is because that is objectifying and externalizing nature.

SG: I suppose it would be like a reversal of our present cultural story—the one in which only culture and Man matter.

RS: That's right. The point is that humanity is part of the natural world. We fall into Cartesianism if we deny that we are part of nature, and regard nature as only external grass and trees and lakes. The failure to recognize that we're part of nature has led to our ravishing of nature, but in ravishing nature, we've also ravished ourselves. So I think we need to work for aesthetic improvement in asphalt as well as green environments. There's always room for aestheticizing in a positive sense—for improving where we are, attending to the local environment, whatever it may be. You know, at the end of my book, I talk about ethics as an art of living, because life is something that you can aesthetically shape. Politics and ethics, at the time of the Greeks, constituted a form of art. Not in Oscar Wilde's aestheticist sense of "art for art's sake," but as something that intelligent people wanted to shape in a way that they thought was honorable, admirable and beautiful. Beauty, in Greece, was linked with the good, and both were considered aesthetic and ethical terms. There wasn't the strict divide that we have between the beautiful and the good.

SG: I totally agree. And before we finish, I'd just like to say how much I admire the comment in your book that "There is no compelling reason to accept the narrow aesthetic limits imposed by the established ideology of autonomous art." You go on to say— and it's a view I happen to share—that this approach has outlived its usefulness.

RS: Yes. Again, I think that autonomous art had its moment. It was good for freeing us from certain things that were on our backs, and on art's back; but now, we've got rid of those old limitations, and this freedom of isolated and purist autonomy can itself become a limitation. There's so much room for art in the practice of living, in how we organize our lives and how we improve them, that the idea of confining art to what we hang on walls is a pathetic failure of theoretical as well as artistic imagination.

Richard Shusterman • 265

Searching For the Essence of Art

ARTHUR C. DANTO

*C*ontemporary modern life will sometimes produce
those stupendous shifts in perception and parallel
worlds that sorcerers in Carlos Castaneda's books claim to
achieve by moving the assemblage point to a different position. For instance, yesterday I was covered with mud after
planting a crape myrtle and some paprika yarrow in my
garden in Blacksburg. Today, I am drinking café con leche
in a hotel in Barcelona, waiting for the critic Arthur C.

Danto to appear so we can have a conversation. Danto is a professor of philosophy at Columbia University, and has been the art critic for the Nation since 1984. We have never met, but both of us have been invited to speak at an international conference called "Crossing Cultures," organized by independent curator Mary Jane Jacob in collaboration with Arts International, that is being held at La Caixa Cultural Center in Barcelona. One hundred people from twenty-nine countries, including artists, critics and museum administrators, are here to investigate the changes in art that have taken place over the last decade, and to consider how these changes may affect its long-term practice.

There are interesting questions on the agenda: Can art build community or bring about social change? Does the artist have a role in shaping society? Has multiculturalism's recognition of cultural difference led to greater global dialogue, or to an ethnocentrism that reinforces separatism? How can audiences take the role of participant rather than spectator? When art has a social or political agenda or takes an activist stance, is its aesthetic quality or integrity compromised? This last question in particular generated a lot of heat in the mainstream press's coverage of the 1993 Whitney Biennial; it quickly became a vortex of seething intolerance, animosity and culture-bashing. Time magazine described the show as "a saturnalia of political correctness" and "one big fiesta of whining agitprop," while New York Times *art critic Michael Kimmelman wrote in no uncertain terms, "I hate this show."* A columnist for the Boston Globe *admonished visitors to the Whitney not to forget to pick up an airsickness bag at the information desk. "Why go to a museum,"* he asked, *"when the same aesthetic experience can be had peering into a toilet bowl, gaping at road kills . . . or visiting a landfill in mid-August?"* A reporter from the Christian Science Monitor *described the whole experience as being "like a waiting room at the Immigration and Naturalization Service." And in a comment book that the curators had put on the fourth floor for visitors to write in, one person stated, "This is the most alienating, depressing, horrifying show I have ever seen." In one of the few unhysterical, nondismissive reviews that appeared, critic Jerry Saltz wrote in* Galleries *magazine: "From the fire storm of reaction that broke out during the opening weeks of the show you would have thought the museum had been selling arms to Iraq." It's OK, he went on to say, not to like a show, but such hatred suggests an intolerance that in itself is disturbing and should be questioned. As far as I could tell, he was the only writer to say something like this publicly.*

I mention the critical response to the Whitney Biennial at some length, because it sets the scene for what the "Crossing Cultures" conference was about, since many key players from the Whitney extravaganza were present. Once there, I had a distinct feeling of having left my front porch in rural Virginia for the front lines of the contemporary culture war. Good questions can act as lenses, and certainly in this case, they served to focus the wide range of issues being disputed, not only about what art is and what it has been in the past, but also about who decides and who has the power and moral authority to determine whether something is good or bad, acceptable or unacceptable. The contours of today's debates seem to parallel many of the debates from the past, but it is clear that the problem has become much deeper and more extensive than the old philosophical disputes about the nature of art. The stakes are much higher now—underlying the contemporary culture war is a struggle about power and privilege. The emerging paradigm of cultural interdependence is exacting an awareness that the hegemonic model of white Western history, which has acted as a justification for imperialism and colonialism, is no longer adequate or even acceptable.

Given the urgency and shrillness that tends to surround multicultural debates, the choice of Arthur C. Danto as keynote speaker for the conference seemed more flamingo than flamethrower, since his self-declared detachment places him elegantly above the fray. Danto's philosophy of art is not a very combustible one, nor is it intended to be. As he would himself admit, he intentionally pitches his writing at a level that is sufficiently abstract that it can apply to everything. "I'm not the kind of critic who carries an agenda around," he has stated. What interests Danto above all is an equivocal border that exists between works of art and what he calls "mere real things," a border he feels has been most successfully tested by Marcel Duchamp's ready-mades and Andy Warhol's Brillo boxes; exhibiting an object in a museum or gallery is usually the "enfranchising maneuver" that confers artistic status on something that might otherwise be construed as merely an ordinary object (such as a urinal). When he was writing about the Whitney show in the Nation, *Danto felt he had encountered significant exceptions to this view. "There is* something *that evidently resists being turned into a work of art," he stated. This was the cautionary lesson of the 1993 Biennial, and, according to Danto, the Whitney deserved credit for showing us these exceptions. It brought that limit to light. On the whole, Danto found the works at the Whitney "mawkish, frivolous, whining, foolish, feckless, awful and thin"; they never rose above the level of bumper-sticker and T-shirt one-liners. Much of the work had only been included, he claimed, because it was representative of some group the curators felt was important to bring into the museum. "I can't imagine ever wanting to have had anything to do with the 1993 Whitney Biennial," he concluded.*

Before his lecture we were sitting together and chatting comfortably at La Caixa. At that point, I was unaware of the review he had written—I hadn't read it. I asked him if he was nervous. "When you talk in the art world," he replied, "you just don't know what you'll get into, especially when feelings run as high as they do here. The philosophy world is much safer." On the podium, Danto set up a polarity between the museum, where one is only a viewer, and the merengue, a Latino dance that is more participatory and sensually engaging. Why, he wondered, would a Latino child ever want to give up the merengue for art in a museum, for sight-dominant work? When all is said and done, even a medieval altarpiece was used for more than viewing: one prayed before it, seeking an intervention. It was made for a user rather than a viewer. In our culture, art has been defined in visual terms by museums; maybe, Danto speculated, the merengue is a better model? (It was hard to gauge the spirit in which this proposition was offered.) We even lack a word for any alternative position to that of viewer, he observed.

Danto passionately espouses an ethos of pluralism, in which "there won't be any more narratives, or stylistic imperatives" and no more of the structured kind of art history that puts forth mandates about the next thing to do. He has also seriously questioned the neutralizing of art's social role in his book The Philosophical Disenfranchisement of Art.

But Danto has no revisionary orientation himself. When I queried him about this in our conversation, he claimed he was stalking a different sort of analysis that would allow him to put his finger on the substantive essence of art. In light of all that was being contested at the conference, it was interesting to meet Danto in the midst of a situation whose stated intention was the revisioning of artistic practice, and the redrawing of ideological boundaries. In that setting, his moral detachment was both reassuring, and at the same time, unnerving.

Richard Shusterman has taken Danto to task for his neutral stance. Albeit with much respect, in an essay entitled "On Not Putting Art in a Box," he chides him for leaving art's reenfranchisement incomplete, and not taking the liberation he has so carefully prepared and prophesied far enough. It is almost as if Danto has been transfixed by Warhol's Brillo box—the avowed inspiration for much of his theorizing—to the point where, Shusterman points out, it has become almost as intoxicating for him as the burning bush was for Moses. Danto never quite manages to get beyond it—that is to say, he never makes the leap of incorporating more aspects of real life or participatory forms of cultural expression into his vision of what art is. The art he writes about is to be found, very reliably, in museums. But, if Danto categorically refuses the task of reconstruction, claiming, as he does in our conversation, that it is not his job, Shusterman maintains that philosophy betrays its mission if it merely looks on with abandoning neutrality at art's evolving history, without joining in the struggle to improve its future.

This conversation was taped at the Condes de Barcelona Hotel on June 12, 1993.

SUZI GABLIK: Arthur, I was hoping we could discuss what you mean by "the disenfranchisement of art." You've begun, more recently, to use the word "re-enfranchisement," and I'm wondering, for instance, if your use of these two words has any correlation with the terms "disenchantment" and "reenchantment" that I use.

ARTHUR DANTO: What I tried to do in that essay, *The Philosophical Disenfranchisement of Art,* was to trace through what philosophers in the great tradition have had to say about art. I mainly talked about Plato and Hegel, and the thought was either you're going to try and show that art is something secondary, derivative and ephemeral, or that it really is trying to do what philosophy does, but philosophy does so much better. Whatever the case, you get these vast systems, the point and purpose of which, I thought, was in some way to disempower art. Why philosophers felt art was dangerous and wanted to remove its power, I have no clear idea, historically speaking, but it's been an ongoing motif of philosophy, and it has tended to construct the whole form of philosophical aesthetics in that way.

SG: Richard Shusterman says, in a previous conversation, that Plato's rejection of art had to do with wanting only rational modes of thinking in his Republic, and not the less predictable or less controllable modes of imagination.

AD: It's conceivable. But it's hard to know. I do know that in Greek times, people did look to poets for moral guidance. I think that Plato probably thought philosophers could do a better job. And so, in a certain sense, there was a contest of powers there, for purposes of education. At any rate, by the time the eighteenth century came around, art got put on some kind of pedestal outside of life.

SG: So there's a certain equation, would you say, between art's autonomy and its disenfranchisement?

AD: Yes, but it's a kind of false autonomy, really. That is to say, I began that essay with a line by Auden that poetry "makes nothing happen," and so, in a certain sense, what disenfranchisement does is to get art to internalize the idea that it's not supposed to do anything. It doesn't make anything happen. Anyway, after I published the essay, people said, "Isn't it time to reenfranchise art?" And I said, "Well, it's not my job."

SG: I was going to ask—who's in charge of *that?*

AD: Who's in charge of that? Right! You know, the moment artists say to philosophers, "Reenfranchise us," they're in a bad way, it seems to me.

SG: In a sense, my own word, "reenchantment," involves the reenfranchisement of art, but there's a lot of hostility around, still, to the kind of art that is socially engaged, or active and participatory in the world, especially when it leads to the blurring of that boundary which philosophical aesthetics so carefully makes between art and real life. Many people would argue that a lot of art being made today has no aesthetic component—it was a big issue with this year's Whitney Biennial. The art that interests me is more like an intervention, or interaction, in a real life situation, but it doesn't have the quality of social protest or political hectoring. It consists of qualities more like those we're addressing at this conference: it's made with a specific audience in mind, or with the audience as part of the creative process. Interactive art can often actually build community, I think. In your writing, I don't find you talking much about that kind of art at all.

AD: No, I don't, not very much. It just hasn't come up. I don't have any special agendas.

SG: I realize that, and it's something I wanted to discuss with you, actually. The critic Robert Pincus-Witten once made an interesting distinction between what he calls "advocacy" criticism, and "stroller" criticism, which I expect is a reference to Baudelaire's *flâneur*. It's clear to me from some of your comments in *Beyond the Brillo Box*—like this one, for instance: "I look forward to an art world in which . . . the animating style of the West wanes, leaving just the individual styles and the lives of the artists as a plural biography"—that your mode of pluralistic . . . I suppose you could call it permissiveness—

AD: Yeah.

SG: Is the very opposite of advocacy. Unless, of course, you would want to say that what you're advocating is pluralism.

AD: That's right. I don't see any grounds for excluding anything, and that makes it, at least for me, a very interesting time to be writing criticism.

SG: It's particularly compelling for me to talk with you, because your approach is so different from mine. For better or worse, my writing tends to take a strong stand.

AD: Well, I'm not against taking stands; I think I've taken some. But as far as having an agenda as a critic, no. I don't see things like that. After all, what's different about me and most other people who write criticism is that I come at it from the direction of professional philosophy. My philosophical concerns with art have been just to provide some kind of definition, to discover an essence, if you like. But whatever I would discover in that way, in the way of philosophical analysis, would have to be compatible with everything; it doesn't entail any stylistic injunctions. So let's say the difference between myself and somebody like Clement Greenberg is that Greenberg identified the essence of what was in the end nothing but a style, and thought that he was grounding in philosophy what was just a stylistic imperative. I think philosophy can't generate any imperatives as far as style; it's got to be compatible with everything. It only describes. It only says what's there invariantly as to the kind of art it is.

SG: Many people take the position that art shouldn't generate imperatives either. But to put myself forward, for just a moment, as somebody whose critical writing does generate imperatives, I want to say that these imperatives don't come so much from within the art arena, but rather from my sense of the perilous state of the world. The imperatives in my work come from a sense of social and environmental unraveling that I feel, and from the crumbling of the Western industrial paradigm, although I realize not everyone shares these feelings. Perhaps we're experiencing not only the end of art history as you've described it; perhaps we're also presiding over the end of Western civilization itself. That's been a major thrust of these conversations—wanting to see how people feel about such matters, and whether it affects their view of what art should be doing.

AD: Oh, I think art's quite powerless to solve any of the serious problems of the world. I think everything's a bit powerless to solve those problems. A lot of them, I think, are just going to run their course, at this point. I'm thinking particularly of the terrible factionalism in the world—that seems to me like the worst problem that we have.

SG: It's something that we see being lived out even in the art world.

AD: Probably it is reflected there, but in a fairly civilized way, by comparison with Bosnia, Sri Lanka, and maybe thirty other places around the world.

SG: Of course there aren't any literal deaths or dramatic enslavements, but I think a lot of people would have liked to murder the curators of the Whitney for putting on that show. I mean, there was a kind of ritual slaughter of the whole event in the press, wouldn't you say?

AD: If what we could do would be to carry out ritual slaughter in place of real slaughter, then we would have made immense progress. I mean, that's in the nature of criticism, to be the moral equivalent of war—it's not such a terrible thing. And there was a consensus, a lot of people who thought there was something that they didn't like, let's say, about the Whitney show, and they responded. But nobody was killed. Everybody's still able to walk around afterward, and so as I say, if we could find a solution to our problems that's more like that, we would have made, I think, the most immense headway. After all, there's always going to be real differences. What I think is the problem is that people haven't learned to live with differences. I mean, differences have been repressed for a very long time, and now, all of a sudden, differences are coming out. They've been there all along, and so what are you going to do? Well, you get the sense—taking Bosnia as a paradigm—that the only solution is to erase them, to extirpate them, to purge, to cleanse, to kill. I think what one's probably got to learn to do is to handle difference in a civilized way. But whether it's the end of civilization, I don't know. That's hard for anybody to say. I mean, how many examples of a real civilization coming to an end do we have?

SG: Oh, quite a few, I think.

AD: You do? The Roman Empire came to an end, and we went into a kind of Dark Age, probably not so different from what we've got right now.

SG: The difference with what we have right now is surely the global scale of the ecocatastrophe. There may have been infringements, in the past, on individual locales, having to do with the way that cultures impacted on the environment, but now there is a massive debilitation that is totally locked in with our particular world view and way of being in the world. Add to that the complexities of overpopulation, et cetera, and you've got a recipe for disaster.

AD: Well, I think there's a lot to that. It's like everybody's trying to kill everybody else off while the ship is sinking in some way.

SG: You do have a sense, then, that the ship is sinking?

AD: That's what I honestly don't know. Nor, I think, do a lot of people—I don't think anybody knows the answer. But it is a way of presenting a genuine concern in a vivid way, the concern being what's happening to the planet, and how long it can endure. But, as I say, I think nobody knows answers to questions of that sort.

SG: Does your understanding of the reenfranchisement of art involve any consideration of art taking a more active role in the world?

AD: I wouldn't rule anything out at all. It would take a more active role if, in fact, it took a more active role. I mean, if somebody did it, it would be done.

SG: In other words, you feel it isn't up to you. It's not a vision of things that you are promoting or would especially care to see happen?

AD: No! After all, people also expect things to be done by philosophers, and I know everybody in the world of philosophy, and I have no confidence in anybody much to take those positions. [Laughter]

SG: Do you have more confidence in artists?

AD: No, I don't! I know a lot of artists, too!

SG: Do you have confidence in politicians?

AD: No, I don't. That's why I think the problems are really bigger than any group, or any particular individual.

SG: Does it follow that you think we are ultimately doomed, then, if there's some gigantic flaw in human consciousness?

AD: If there is, indeed we are, yes—but that's what nobody, in fact, knows. I do think that this incapacity to tolerate difference, which is at the moment our besetting moral crisis—if we could solve that, maybe we could get together and think about these larger issues.

SG: One of the people who has influenced me to shift my work into the mode of dialogue is Arnold

Mindell, who works in the area of conflict resolution, an undertaking that he calls "world work." It involves getting the conflicted parties to share their viewpoints by listening to each other, and letting a transformation of the field occur through the interpenetration and exchange of these energies, rather than through one of them trying to knock the other off the board, so to speak.

AD: I think that's commendable.

SG: Also, the quantum physicist David Bohm, before he died, was writing a lot about dialogue, because he believed that learning how to talk and really listen to each other, rather than trying to win points relentlessly and put the other guy out of business, was the only way anything would change.

AD: I think that's a beginning. I don't think the way people are presently handling conflicts is ever going to be productive of very much except more conflicts. But I do think it ought to be possible to resolve conflicts through discussion, and this should be institutionalized as widely as possible, because if people accepted those institutions, I think the problem would already be solved.

SG: Do you feel there are radical realignments and reassessments going on in the world of art at this particular moment in time?

AD: Yeah.

SG: Are they changes that interest you very much?

AD: Sure they do. I think a lot is happening. On the other hand, I do think there are certain demands that it's unrealistic to make of art, or of artists to make of themselves. That is to say, there's only so much you can do as a human being, or as an artist. I can't think of any cases—though maybe there are some—in the past where art solved any real problems. I may be wrong.

SG: Well, I think an obvious case in point would be the ecological projects of Helen and Newton Harrison in San Diego, restoring life to polluted rivers, for instance.

AD: They're very interesting artists. I like what they do, and I think that they do show ways that certain problems could be solved.

SG: But they also collaborate with other people to actually solve the problem, to transform the condition of a river, for instance.

AD: I quite agree. I think that the Harrisons are a good model for something, and I think there are probably other examples. In a slightly frivolous way, I think Christo's pretty good at that sort of thing—getting people to join together for a certain kind of project, which they believe in. Of course, it doesn't usually penetrate very deeply into the world, the way the Harrisons' solutions would.

SG: Another example of how artists can solve problems is John Malpede and his theater group with the homeless, LAPD. Or Tim Rollins and K.O.S.

AD: Well, Tim Rollins I know quite well, and have written about. And he is a visionary. He does see his role as almost the rescue of the culture. He's involved in Hawthorne, and Melville and H. G. Wells—he's rescuing their books. He's trying to revive literacy. Tim works with these kids and gets them to collaborate on projects which, when they're good, are amazingly good, like the *Amerika* series. I thought less well of the others. But even that is only a kind of confirmation for him. I think what he's trying to do is feel his way toward some larger, transformative institution. He's had a hard time, too; but I admire him a great deal. He's got a quality of genius about him. I don't know that anybody else would be able to do what he's doing. And I think that in many ways, until something can be institutionalized, you haven't really got a solution. Too much depends upon charismatic and imaginative individuals.

SG: This whole question of the ending of history, the ending of narratives, and particularly the ending of art history as a story about masters and masterpieces —you've been one of the pivotal people to signal not only that this has happened, but also that it's probably a good thing to have occurred. You seem to feel personally almost more comfortable in a sort of free-floating plasma of no stories.

AD: I felt very comfortable with the other situation, too, I must say, and I feel a nostalgia for it. I wish I could think that way still. I thought that was wonderful.

SG: You mean, with styles overthrowing one another, muscling each other in and out of the picture!

AD: Yes, and the sense of things driving forward. But I think, on the balance, it was pernicious, particularly in our century.

SG: It was certainly exclusionary.

AD: It was exclusionary, but theories in their nature are exclusionary. I mean, you've got to exclude something. You can't have a story if you don't leave something out.

SG: The problem is that when you're totally inclusionary and pluralistic, and you don't have a story, then it's much harder to make distinctions, there's a process of democratization that seems to kick in.

AD: It's still possible to make distinctions, but it's just that you're no longer thinking that what history demands is of great importance.

SG: I think the problem with a pluralist agenda, or philosophy, is that it invites yet more individualism, when for me, the need is for a new paradigm of interrelatedness and interconnection and community.

AD: Well, I think maybe that's too raw a disjunction.

SG: You don't see pluralism, then, as just another extension of individualism?

AD: I don't believe so, no. Because I don't think anybody in the art world is able to function without other people being involved—other artists, critics, people who pay the bills, people who use the work. I feel we're in a structure in which it's as though there are a great many conversations going on. And you can't have a conversation all by yourself—it's not individualistic in that way. On the other hand, it's a much looser notion than a community. I'm always a little scared of notions of community anyway. I don't like the invasive ideal of a community.

SG: What scares you about community?

AD: Other people. I'd just as soon not be told what I have to do. It bothers me.

SG: Community doesn't work that way, though. It's a consensual, not an authoritarian, structure.

AD: Mostly it does work that way, I think. Personally, I've always loved universities, because that's been my milieu my entire life. I like the philosophy world, and up to a point, I like the art world. Again, it's not invasive in any way. You have a group of people who have some common interests and who work together to promote those interests. When I think of the word "community," it feels like something more is being demanded of me.

SG: What's in the picture there that you're resisting?

AD: I want to be able to drop out of it whenever I feel like it, and I don't want to have the sense that it's always there, watching over me, keeping check and registering what I do. But as I say, I think that in between this kind of communitarian picture and this highly individualistic picture is what really does take place—which are temporary, ad hoc, single-purpose organizations and engagements of various sorts. And I think that the art world's a lot like that.

SG: You've said that your field is primarily philosophy. Is it aesthetic philosophy?

AD: No, I did analytic philosophy when I was exclusively in philosophy. It was primarily a philosophy of language and logic.

SG: Did you publish books about this?

AD: Oh, a great many, but probably you only know the stuff on art. I did three books: *Analytical Philosophy of History* [1965], *Analytical Philosophy of Knowledge* [1968], and *Analytical Philosophy of Action* [1972].

SG: Are those books still in print?

AD: Yeah. Cambridge University Press published them. Those books have been widely translated and continue to be discussed. They were major works.

SG: Would you say that your renown in the world of straight philosophy equals your renown in the art world, which is pretty formidable?

AD: Yeah, it was large.

SG: Has it diminished somewhat since you've taken up writing about art?

AD: Oh, no. I keep the two up. To tell you the truth, Suzi, I was very happy as a philosopher. I felt, as it were, in community with the world of professional philosophers. It's a wonderful world.

SG: But you also feel at home in the art world, don't you?

AD: Less. I have a sense of belonging, but it's a different world. Nobody pays any attention to the world of professional philosophy except other philosophers. You're only writing for one another. And you know everybody, pretty much, who's productive. However, I do think professional philosophy is a little stagnant right at the moment.

SG: But not art?

AD: No, I think art theory is very lively indeed—and I take a bit of the credit for having started some of that.

SG: When you write essays for the *Nation,* do you feel like you're enacting the role of a critic more than a philosopher?

AD: Sure. But there's a lot of philosophy in those pieces. I probably can't write about something unless I find a philosophical way of doing it.

Removing the Frame

MARY JANE JACOB

"Within the modernist aesthetic," Arthur C. Danto has written, "all art stands outside life, in a space of its own, metaphorically embodied in the Plexiglas display case, the bare white gallery, the aluminum frame. When one seeks a deeper connection between art and life than this, Modernism is over." While Danto may be cautious about closing the gap between art and life, Mary Jane Jacob is not: she has taken the plunge, damned the consequences and climbed on the back of the tiger. Frustrated by the cramped ideology and practical limitations of working in a museum, she decided several years ago to abandon her job as chief curator at the Museum of Contemporary Art in Los Angeles and strike out on her own to see if, indeed, there wasn't a better way to bring art closer to life. She returned to Chicago, where previously she had been chief curator at Chicago's Museum of Contemporary Art from 1980 to 1986. "Going out into the real world to find a place for art," she says, "enlivened what was seen as the institutional white-box vacuum."

Jacob has since become the orchestrator of a new genre of public art, which takes the form of interactive, community-based projects inspired by social issues. The idea is to encourage a mode of artmaking that transcends the notion of sculpture plunked down in a public park or plaza, the kind of art in public places that Krzysztof Wodiczko calls "liberal urban decoration" and "happy self-exhibition," which, he suggests, is not a form of social practice but is instead a pretentious form of environmental pollution. Jacob's first big undertaking as a free-lance curator was the series of site-specific installations for "Places with a Past," part of the 1991 Spoleto Festival in Charleston, South Carolina. Artists participating in "Places with a Past" were invited to seek out nontraditional exhibition spaces that ranged from the city's Old Jail to the slave quarters of the governor's mansion, and to include disenfranchised groups, through dealing with issues that would also be of interest to the local community.

Jacob's next big endeavor was "Culture in Action," a citywide program of art works in which eight artists (or artists' groups) were commissioned to create projects during May to September of 1993 by Sculpture Chicago, an independent public art agency. At this point, the focus for Jacob shifted again, from site-specific installations toward a more interactive kind of participation with local communities over an extended period of time. The program's self-declared goal was social interaction, not only as a means of engaging new audiences for art, but also as a way of transforming the audience's role from spectator to participant. Involving and collaborating with local individuals will often, over time, create a sense of community where there was none. For instance, one of the "Culture in Action" artists, Mark Dion, met each Saturday with a group of inner city high school students (who called themselves the Chicago Urban Ecology Action Group) to examine issues related to the rain forest ecosystem, a study that culminated in a two-week journey to an ecological research station in Belize, Central America. Once back in Chicago, the group reassembled to become a resource pool of volunteers for a variety of environmental projects in the city.

If the question that is facing us in the 1990s is "where do we go from here," then it is a question that applies not just to artists, but to critics, curators and museum organizers as well. This is something Jacob understands and tried to address in our conversation. Museums are among the most conspicuous fields of conflict in the contemporary culture war. They are under scrutiny for their assumptions, biases and practices of selection. It is not difficult to see why they are so strategic in the current debates, because of their crucial role in forging the system and its canons. As events surrounding the Whitney Biennial demonstrated, in a world that is already out of balance, even a temple of contemplation can be transformed into an explosive battleground of controversy. One influential commentator on multiculturalism puts it like this: "I think the job of democracy, in the field of art, is to make the world safe for elitism. Not an elitism based on money or social position, but on skill and imagination." These comments, made by Time *magazine critic Robert Hughes, at a conference at M.I.T. on the role of the federal government in the arts, were obviously not meant to make him soar in the multicultural ratings. Even more so, since he then went on to label cultural diversity as a "sentimental" philosophy entailing pious gestures of support while actually producing little that might, in aesthetic terms, challenge or add anything to the thinking of the status quo.*

Mary Jane Jacob • 293

Museums are crucial to the definition of what consti-tutes art in our society. Despite their alleged neutrality, they act as powerful agents in the construction of cultural iden-tity, and as Hughes's comments make demonstrably clear, those who have had no voice may continue to be defined as insignificant, and their interests deemed irrelevant. As the ratifying institution chiefly responsible for what gets exhib-ited and preserved, museums play a major part in determin-ing what will count as art and what is "worthy" of recognition. At issue with the Whitney show was something more than a conflict over aesthetic quality, which is what appeared to be the focus of everyone's wrath. At issue, really, was a power struggle over whose definition of culture gets accepted. We have witnessed, over the last decade or so, an unprecedented collapse of the hegemonic story that posits "quality" as the unique basis for evaluating art's identity and worth in the cultural order. The narrative of masters and masterpieces, which represents the white Western cul-tural canon and thus chronicles a certain national identity, has been derailed by other coalitions, who speak with a different moral vocabulary and operate within a different constellation of values, interests and assumptions. The his-torical tendency has been for one voice, one cultural narra-tive, to dominate, virtually eclipsing those of other communities. In the controversial 1993 Whitney Biennial, the curators generated an institutional melt-down by giving others a voice and an opportunity to impose other standards for evaluation than the attribution of "quality," taken as a definable, transhistorical measure of value applicable for all time and for a universal model of history. The very term "quality," especially when it takes itself for granted as an objective absolute, belongs to a specific historical paradigm that has organized the Western practice of artmaking.

If the symbolic significance of art is that it is a microcosm of the larger society, then the task of defining art's value, meaning and purpose becomes integral to the right to define the way things are and the way things should be. It means, in other words, to have a voice in how public culture should be shaped. The politics of culture may be changing, but we should note that parity has not yet been reached. Any dissenting practice must still run the gauntlet on the battlefield of Western dominance and power relations. As Australian curator Bernice Murphy commented at the conference in Barcelona, "The center still adjudicates discourses and never quite concedes its power to circulate meaning about their works to the periphery."

This conversation took place at the Condes de Barcelona Hotel on June 13, 1993.

SUZI GABLIK: Let's start with the reasons you became an independent curator, Mary Jane. What, exactly, does that particular profession involve for you?

MARY JANE JACOB: You know, that's a significant question, I can see! [Laughter] My decision to become an independent curator at the end of 1989 was quite personal, but it was also related in some ways to the times that we had been through in that decade. The last show that I did under formal circumstances as chief curator at the Museum of Contemporary Art in Los Angeles was called "A Forest of Signs: Art and the Crisis of Representation," and it was quite a catharsis for me. I was dealing with work that had a very interesting and exciting energy, and that brought about a new focus on contemporary art. That was very invigorating. But my personal discomfort at that juncture involved several things: one was the increasing consumerist focus of that art, whose meaning was being evaporated by a system of collectors and museums vying for power to be obtained through the possession of those art objects.

SG: Did it seem to you, since these were objects through which artists were trying, in some sense, to be critical of that system, that the consumerist focus was even more embarrassing than usual?

MJJ: And more ironic, yes. I remember presenting the subject of that exhibition, which I was struggling with in terms of its point of view in critiquing consumerist culture, and finding the trustees of the museum just wholly embracing it all. And I remember thinking to myself, "But, you don't get it. You're the butt of the joke. This is a critique of your lives."

SG: Do you really think they didn't get it, or were they just enjoying the irony?

MJJ: I think they loved the idea of having an exhibition that would bring in a lot of art stars, like Cindy Sherman and Barbara Kruger and Mike Kelly. They were very excited, because they read it all through names, and not through the critique of culture that the artists were dealing with. My other problem was with the artists themselves and the complicity of the work, which was straddling that line as well; there was a critical edge that was very fragile and could easily be lost in a system which would end up devaluing the meaning of the work.

SG: Did you feel that this complicity—and cooptation —was somehow linked to the whole museum conception of art? In other words, when you finally decided to become an independent curator, was it the museum itself you were leaving behind, or was it the kind of art that goes into museums?

MJJ: It was what happens to the art when it goes into the museum. I think the same art, in and outside of the museum, can have a different life. It was about what happens within that process of institutionalization. And, I think it was also about the changes that were happening around that time to art itself, a shift from being less a personal expression to being more a cultural expression in a Western postmodern world. This new kind of "Pop Art," that reflected and commented on contemporary culture, became highly problematic when viewed within the institutions that it critiqued, because they became partners in a way that led, you might say, to the depoliticization of political art. It diffused the critical edge of what the artist was doing through the great seduction of success in the established art world. Having gone to Los Angeles in 1986, I felt I was in the perfect situation to observe that era of consumerism, because L.A. is a great consumer capital. What I got from the conversations I had with trustees and collectors was their keenness to be a part of something that was hot, to buy into names that were current. They also had that investment-oriented perception of art, which was not my feeling at all.

SG: How do you feel about the "PC" Whitney Biennial of 1993, which was heavily political, but was presented in a museum? Did that show manage to bypass any of the pitfalls you've been talking about?

MJJ: I think it's problematic, because on the one hand, we have people saying, almost universally, "This show is no good. It has no aesthetic value. Why are we doing this?" On the other hand, like any Whitney Biennial, if it's about looking at the trends of the moment, then it's really quite accurate, because this kind of art is about something that is happening on a broad base. You know, if Color Field painting were "in," and that's what artists were doing, that would be what they would present. But art with a social or cultural edge is the art of the day. So, for those who are part of the conventional art world to be saying, "Why is this in the museum?" is rather shortsighted, because it is a timely show. The problem for me, from a different point of view, is that putting such art into the museum in fairly conventional terms points up the difficulty of placing work with that kind of subject matter within existing institutional practice.

SG: At least it didn't lead to the consumerism and manic inflation you were talking about before. Nobody wanted anything to do with this art.

MJJ: The extreme negative reaction may also be the result of a general critical, or curatorial shift, which, after focusing on work with a social or cultural message, has led critics to cry "enough." In addition, the widespread practice of such art has also given us mediocre examples as well as great ones, and it runs the risk of becoming just another style of the moment, soon to be passed over as we look again for something new. On this point of working independently, I think that even though there was an accelerated consumerism during the 1980s, we also saw an invigorated discourse—which, for my personal taste, became a bit too theoretical, but which also brought a very interesting, broader cultural point of view to art. I saw it as perhaps our own era's way of contending with that juncture between art and life, which is what I'm interested in.

SG: So your shift in curatorial projects does entail a specific move away from the museum. And it's not just a move away from authoritarian structures, like having to answer to a board of trustees and so on, it's also to be free of the space itself, in order to work more directly in life situations and non-art spaces.

MJJ: Yes, not only physically, but also conceptually, because really the center of my work is the artist's practice, and trying to make it possible for projects to happen, by intervening appropriately between the artist and the audience. Institutions have another agenda, which doesn't always have the flexibility that's necessary for the individual artist's vision. That's the other part of what I was finding problematic in working within institutions.

SG: Can you talk about some alternative situations you've been involved with, or that you're trying to make happen?

MJJ: I think the space within which we view art, the frame, is very important to our perception of it. Having grown up with a Western attitude about the "progress" of art and the importance of continual innovation, at a certain point it was no longer enough to see styles changing, as one saw a succession of different things on the walls of the museum. It also seemed important to change what was inherent in that frame of the museum itself. And part of that was about extending some exhibitions into spaces that were complementary to the museum, but which often were non-art spaces—doing things outside of the walls. It was a matter of starting to see that, from the artist's point of view, and for the reading of the art, we could really understand art's meaning better within the context of the real world, as opposed to that artificial world that the museum creates. I guess I believe in art being less about artifice and more about life. The museum is yet another artificial box that separates art from its existence in the world, and it becomes a world unto itself. The museum, I feel, has contributed to what Arthur Danto calls the disenfranchisement of art. I became interested in returning art to a premuseum state by looking to the human impulses and expressions that gave cause to art at its origins. But there were other problems that came up, as well, with the kinds of questions that were being put to me as chief curator, and in the form of mandates that came from various funding and other administrative agendas. These were posed as "problem-solving" questions, but were not considered essential institutional agendas. They were questions such as, "We need to address multiculturalism. Therefore, let us look at the exhibition schedule. Now, do we have a woman artist? OK, we have a woman's show. Now, how many blacks do we have?" This kind of statistical analysis would create a certain demographics for the exhibition calendar, but it became merely a numbers game, which is why we also have the same problem in criticism, which says: "This exhibition is good or bad because it doesn't have any Latinos in it," or whatever. Talking in terms of numbers is a way of quantifying the problem, but it doesn't really get to the heart of it. The same thing happened with issues like needing certain kinds of representation on our board, and the thinking there was: "OK, we'll find one such-and-such kind of person, and we'll solve that problem."

SG: The tokenism approach.

MJJ: Yeah, so how many numbers make it OK? Internationalism was another issue: how many shows are we doing of Europeans? Another was education: OK, so we've got our curatorial agenda resolved, now what are the educational aspects of it? It wasn't discussed in an integrated way, assuming that all our practice is about art and education at once, but rather stayed within a kind of hierarchy that I perceived as being quite at odds with my personal perception of the teachings of modernism that were to have gotten us beyond conventional hierarchical categories. But instead, those categories were acting as roadblocks.

SG: Is it your sense that any of these problems can be comfortably transcended within the institutional structures themselves? What needs to take place before that can happen?

MJJ: I think it's a problem particularly in places or parts of the world where there hasn't been that possibility for the institution to be there. The question is, do we need to always first build up, and then tear down, the institution to get somewhere else? Do we have to go through that whole process, or can it be short-circuited? For instance, I find my own work, and artists that I'm working with, coming closer to certain more primal, if you will, cultural expressions, such as parades, that have gone full circle, back to where art existed in a preinstitutional form. So can we only arrive at that after we've had institutions?

SG: Many other cultures that have been influenced by the West think getting their own museum of modern art is the most desirable thing that can happen. They think it will put them on the map somehow.

MJJ: Exactly. They want that prestige and validation, and so what is indigenous to the culture becomes lost; it might be put aside, or even wiped away, while they're adopting another culture's forms. And do they arrive at the same point where we are now, only later? Or are there things about our practice that they can avoid in order to take their institutions to a different level? For instance, in our models, the artist becomes a product within the institution, rather than a driving force; the artist does not get integrated into the institution as a thinker. The artist functions as somebody whose objects are consumed, appropriated, purchased, preserved.

SG: Of course, for most artists, that seems like the ultimate goal, the final aim of their deepest ambitions, doesn't it?

MJJ: Not for a large number of the most interesting artists who are working today. And that's the focus, I suppose, that has contributed to my own distancing from those institutions: the work that I find most vital is work that doesn't philosophically or physically fit in there. So these things that have become buzzwords in the United States right now—like multiculturalism or education—were things that we would sit around the table and struggle with in a very hermetic and impossible-to-resolve way within the institution, to the point where I was internalizing those roadblocks and feeling this dead-endedness of art. It was losing its vitality for me. So the possibility of working outside the museum structure—which first happened when I was offered the chance to curate "Places with a Past" in Charleston—immediately became a way of working out some of those old problems, uniquely providing a solution. For instance, this notion of multiculturalism that within the institution became a statistical game, took on an actuality in "Places with a Past," when we found ourselves in this place that had been the capital of slavery in North America, and from which there is a heritage of a racial divide. To bring African-American artists to Charleston to do works became a meaningful reason as to why African-American artists were there—not because we needed to fill quotas, but because they brought something to that experience, and that experience also shaped and changed them in essential ways.

SG: Did the artists make their work specifically in relationship to the context there?

MJJ: Totally. All of the work was commissioned, and it was new, and it was also work that was created out of a dialogue between the artists and the curator. Personally, this was extremely satisfying for me, because it wasn't a relationship based on curatorial approval or choice, but a real dialogue between artist and curator that contributed to the final result, the completed work of art.

SG: What was so compelling for you in these more interactive, collaborative situations?

MJJ: For an artist like Lorna Simpson, for instance, who had grown up in New York and was somewhat removed from her own heritage as an African-American, being in Charleston was a new experience. Her photographs of black women had all previously been kept within the frame of the object, and this request to come and create an intervention in Charleston gave her a chance not only to get in touch with a part of her own world that had not been personal before, but also to extend her art into an installation mode. Ultimately, she chose to work in a dependency, an out-building of a mansion that had previously been occupied by slaves, and had been their sleeping rooms, laundry room and dining room. What she created out of that situation was a five-room installation, which became a dialogue between images of agriculture and anger, both respecting and commemorating these people who had come from West Africa—people who brought to this area a centuries-old tradition of rice cultivation that their English owners did not have. What was really important about the whole exhibition and the way that it was put together was that it had no fee structure, it was free. And it was in places in and around town that one might happen on by chance, not knowing that this was an art exhibition, but becoming a part of it nonetheless. The controversial newspaper coverage and the general on-the-street conversations brought a lot of Charlestonians out to see what the fuss was about. But the number of people who came is not something that could be easily recorded, because there was no front door, and no one stationed with a clicker. When people not versed in high culture went out to see this work, they didn't laugh, because they recognized themselves very quickly, and it was very meaningful for them, even if it wasn't meaningful for Gian Carlo Menotti, the organizer of the Spoleto Festival. I'm interested, I guess, in the non-museumgoer, and in breaking down the traditional barriers between high and low culture.

SG: The word "low" is unfortunate, because it perpetuates the hierarchical view you're trying to undo. But the issue really is about trying to move beyond the elitism that has been the basic frame for what we know as "high" culture.

MJJ: All that's become even more clear with the Chicago program "Culture in Action" that followed the Charleston show. It takes off from where David Hammons's piece ended up in the earlier exhibition. Hammons wanted to collaborate with the community; his project gave some authorship and ownership to the community. It occupied two vacant lots in the black ghetto and included an unusually narrow house structure that, through the artist's intervention and dialogue with the community, was turned into a model-house museum that aimed to give the local youth pride in the homes in which they lived. He actually constructed the house with individuals from the neighborhood. That project became a turning point for me in taking these notions of site-specificity and the meanings that they can offer, and developing them into a genre, whose high level of interaction with the audience removes it still further from the museum situation. So, while we might call Charleston a museum exhibition outside the museum space—where you could visit a series of installations in a day's time, where you could still see a show—the current Chicago project is not a show at all. It's something that exists over time, and each project has multiple phases that exist in different places.

SG: There's no connection with a museum situation at all?

MJJ: No, everything but that. And from this situation has arisen the real significance of the Chicago project: a redefinition of the audience for contemporary conceptual art. In Charleston, it was the art tourist who came, and the Spoleto Festival operagoer, who was given a daytime alternative. And also the inhabitants of Charleston, who, because all this was intervening in their space, came to check it out. In Chicago, it's much more a lived experience—it doesn't ever have to be any of those art or city activities designed for tourists. In fact, it's less about seeing than about doing. The other shift that's happening is that the most privileged experience is not reserved for the richest patrons. So we're dealing not just with an ethnic diversity, but with a social and class diversity —we're shifting who gets access. Not just in the sense of who gets to go inside the museum, but who experiences the fullest impact of the work of art. This has proved to be extremely confrontational for the art world, which still maintains definite divisions between high and low, aesthetic and not, and which very much questions what these projects are about, and why this is art.

SG: Can you give an example of work that is being challenged as art?

MJJ: Mark Dion, an artist who deals with ecology and has himself moved out of the museum framework at times, set up a process of working with a hand-picked group of twelve students from different parts of the city, all high school juniors, who met on the west side on Saturday mornings and attended a class that Mark taught. The work exists somewhere between the practice of art, education and natural science. To see the class as part of the art work itself brings up that old sixties buzzword of "process," in the sense of Robert Morris or Barry Le Va—

SG: But their work had to do with the physical manipulation of materials: pouring, dropping, scattering.

MJJ: Or, we had process as it moved into time arts and performance, but here we have an artist who's dealing with process as interaction with the public. It not only involves engaging the students in conversation and actual work, but part of his piece also involved taking the students to the rain forest in Belize. But to get back to the question: why is this art? We can talk about how Mark Dion's piece relates to performance practice and installation, and even find precedents for how the two have been fused. And we can talk about the whole attitude we've had in the twentieth century of what art can be—of breaking down the boundaries, of not fitting within a single category, but multiple categories. Obviously, precedents for the genre of this art exist by way of explanation. But what I have found is most problematic about these projects for the art world really centers on who makes them, and for whom. That is, this work was made with the coparticipation of an artist, but also with a lot of decision-making happening on the part of constituent-collaborators who are not artists—like students, and, in the case of some of the other projects, factory workers, mothers in a public housing development, AIDS volunteers, gang youth, and so forth. The possibility that a nonartist can be a maker of high culture and art—that's problematic. And also the fact of "for whom," meaning that it isn't exclusive to those who possess a knowledge of art history, or the status of having taste. It's something that's shared with people of different backgrounds.

SG: The main point, then, is about stepping outside, and actually bypassing, the elitism of the whole professional sphere. But then, what about this embattled issue of aesthetic quality?

MJJ: It's totally about frame. When we take work that is physically constructed or crafted and put it in the museum, it is the museum that says it's art. It is not inherently in that material. When we start to take that contextual attitude of site-specificity—

SG: We take power away from the museum.

MJJ: It's when we start to integrate art into the process of living, and to not put it into designated art buildings—as with Mel Ziegler and Kate Ericson's paint charts that ended up in True Value hardware stores alongside standard commercial charts—that we really have taken the frame away. And this is the problem; it's not because the aesthetic has gone away.

SG: I guess the final question here is whether you think dialogue and interaction could stand up as art without some physical manifestation of an object, or monument, as well?

MJJ: Oh, I think it can, in terms of my broad definition of art. From an avant-garde way of thinking, art can certainly exist in many ways that are temporal, rather than spatial or physical. However, that decision isn't mine; that decision is the artist's. I think, generically, that art can be just an interaction, or it can be something physical like an object. What I found extremely interesting in undertaking "Culture in Action," is that for all the radical propositions offered—defending the idea that there may, in the end, be nothing to see—even with all that latitude and no gallery to fill, the artists and their collaborators still chose to make art works. And those art works embodied the whole process, and had something very beautiful about them. Meaning was shared through the object, and those works of art then went on to communicate the group's sentiments to others.

Two Undiscovered Aborigines
Dancing on the Wound of History

COCO FUSCO

In commemoration of five hundred years of practice that informs multiculturalism in the West, Coco Fusco and Guillermo Gómez-Peña, two performance artists who move fluidly back and forth between the worlds of both Western and non-Western cultures, staged an extraordinary performance work in which they lived in a gilded cage for several days and posed as aboriginal inhabitants from an undiscovered island in the Gulf of Mexico. They did this in a number of different settings around the world, including Columbus Plaza in Madrid during the 1992 quincentenary, with subsequent performances in Covent Garden in London, the Smithsonian Institution in Washington, D.C., the Australian Museum in Sydney, the Field Museum of Natural History in Chicago, and at the opening of the 1993 Whitney Biennial in New York. Gómez-Peña, the male "specimen," wore cowboy boots and a garish feather headdress, and for a dollar would tell stories in his "native" language. Fusco was also elaborately costumed, and with her face painted, danced to rap music on request. Surgical gloves could be obtained on request from the "guards" for use by any visitor who wanted to feed or touch them.

People had to figure out for themselves that the "natives" were not legitimate. And, given the racist stereotypes of the "savage" that inform much of Western understanding of so-called primitive cultures, they didn't always succeed. One visitor to the Field Museum, for instance, exclaimed in disbelief, "This isn't right! How can the Field Museum put these people in a cage?" Another called the humane society, who said that since no animals were involved, it was outside their jurisdiction. "As artists of color in the United States," writes Fusco, "whatever our aesthetic or political inclinations, Guillermo Gómez-Peña and I carry our bodies as markers of difference and reminders of the endlessly recycled colonial fantasies on which Western culture thrived."

"In Madrid," says Gómez-Peña, "mischievous teenagers tried to burn me with cigarettes while some handed me a beer bottle of urine." In England, some businessmen treated them as if they were monkeys, and made gorilla sounds.

Non-Western human beings have been exhibited in theaters, museums, zoos, circuses and world's fairs for the past five hundred years. In most cases the people who were exhibited did not choose to be on display, but, according to Fusco, "served as proof of the natural superiority of European civilization, of its ability to exert control over and extract knowledge from the 'primitive' world, and ultimately of the genetic inferiority of the non-European races." This is how Caucasians discovered the "other," by exhibiting them as fetish objects offered for inspection, or as trophies of imperial conquest. The first impresario of this sort, Fusco points out, was Christopher Columbus, who brought several Arawaks to the Spanish court in 1493, where he left one of them on display for two years. In 1906, a pygmy was brought to the United States and put on display in the primate cage at the Bronx Zoo. As part of her own and Gómez-Peña's "display," Fusco researched a chronology of every occasion that indigenous humans have been collected and exhibited as curios or exotic artifacts over the last five hundred years. Her chronological plaque hides a story—a story of racial hierarchy and objectification. Their performance, "Two Undiscovered Aborigines," is like a public exorcism of departed ghosts.

This morning as I was making my bed, a news item on National Public Radio grabbed my attention. It was a review of a new book by Ken Harper, called Give Me My Father's Body, about six Inuits who were brought from northern Greenland in 1898 to the American Museum of Natural History, and were put on display as "savages" in the basement, until they ended up in Bellevue, where four of them who died had their bodies dissected for medical research.

I met up with Fusco at the Barcelona conference. She is a very dynamic, charismatic individual and an intense speaker. In her presentation at the conference, she spoke in Spanish—since not all Americans, she explained, speak English. In the white Western intellectual tradition, the established order tends to be seen as the natural state of affairs, and multiculturalism is viewed as a dangerous infiltration and is euphemized as "political correctness" by the powers that be, who have an intense fear of any invasion into the dominant culture's world by the "other," which Fusco claims includes, at this historical point, the "multicultural barbarians" of the new urban jungles of America. "For many of us," she says, "this counter-quincentenary has be-

*come an occasion for redefining America's cultural identity
as multiple, heterogeneous, and multiracial—both Western
and non-Western at the same time." Whatever the avant-
garde might be today, Fusco points out (in her catalogue
essay for the 1993 Biennial) it "isn't about . . . tracing one's
bloodlines to Marcel Duchamp and Andy Warhol." One
thing it is about is reckoning with a history of colonialist
power relations. For the privileged purveyors of culture in
this country, she claims, confronting the limitations of one's
own knowledge and relinquishing authority can be seen
either as a challenge or a crushing blow.*

*The strong presence of alternative political communi-
ties at the Barcelona conference did seem like an optimistic
barometer registering the end of cultural monopoly. Certainly the new, postcolonial, cross-cultural dialogue that is
emerging is infinitely more alert to institutional issues of
racism and power, particularly in relation to the role of
museums and their privileged authority.*

*The following conversation was taped sitting in a noisy
corridor at La Caixa Cultural Center in Barcelona on June
14, 1993.*

SUZI GABLIK: Coco, you said a few minutes ago you thought
that somebody should blow the lid off this conference. What did you mean?

COCO FUSCO: I've participated in so many cultural events in the last couple of years in which the local versus the national, and the particular versus the general, and the regional versus the universal have been discussed. I've also heard many geographic paradigms bandied about to describe difference: centers and peripheries, or margins, et cetera. I feel that we are circling around a set of issues that are more politically vital, and much more emotionally charged, than people at the conference have wanted to deal with. I also think there are people here who are critical of multiculturalism, who are trying to express their criticisms in very veiled ways, and I personally would prefer it if they would just state their cases. For example, there is a museum director from Spain, who was talking today about how nobody in Barcelona went to see her Alfredo Jaar show, and nobody went to see her Francesc Torres show. The implication was that something's wrong if the museum doesn't get the audience it wants.

SG: Do you mean something like: how can a responsible museum director continue to put on certain shows if nobody wants to see them?

CF: Yes, but I would want to know what kind of audience she gets for other exhibits, to compare figures. I also feel that setting artists up to talk only about their own work is a very good recipe for blocking dialogue. Why couldn't they talk about each other's work, or about a historical moment that they're all participating in? I guess I'm hoping that between this afternoon and tomorrow something will happen so that the event has a more dynamic flow to it, instead of just consisting of these static presentations.

SG: But don't you feel this is a generic problem in all conferences? They have a style and a way of doing things that is hard to break out of and change. When you said something about blowing the lid off, what was your picture of how that might actually happen? If you were going to do it yourself, what would you do?

CF: First of all, I would have panelists direct their comments more at each other; also, I think some of the problem has to do with delivery, and with audience participation and involvement in the issues that are being discussed. I was at another conference last week in New York called "Cross-Talk" that was a multicultural feminist conference, and believe me, you could not get people to leave—there was so much engagement and involvement.

SG: Presumably everybody was speaking English.

CF: Yes. The conference was conducted in English, but I don't think that language is the barrier here. I think that there is a slightly more conservative way of dealing with public events in Europe than in the alternative art scene in the United States. I also think my recent experiences in different parts of Europe have indicated to me that these are issues that people in the art world understand are "current," but they are very skeptical about their role in the context of art. There's a tremendous amount of suspicion about "politicizing" the art debate.

SG: Is the suspicion and discomfort coming mostly from institutions in the art establishment, which is basically white, or is the suspicion and discomfort just as strong on the part of people who don't fit into that category?

CF: Of the people who are participating from Europe, there are very few who don't fit into the category you just described. But I don't think it's about an essential whiteness. I think the problem has to do with politics, and an attitude toward culture and toward artistic production that prevails in Europe, that is very class-based, and ultimately very elitist— and for me, very stultifying. I think some of the most interesting activity in the arts in the "New World" —versus the "Old World"—involves breaking down those very hierarchies.

SG: And institutional barriers. Can you give any specific examples of ways in which you think this is happening?

CF: I think that we're in a moment where some—not everybody, but many people—involved in making contemporary culture are really interested in transforming what we understand as art.

sg: Do you mean the meaning of artistic practice?

cf: Our practice, our audiences, our institutions: we're talking about a different relationship to notions of ownership and cultural property, about museums reflecting on their role in the colonial past of America, and America's imperialistic relationship to other cultures and peoples in other parts of the world. We're talking about projects of repatriation, or a redefinition of the relationship between museums and native peoples; we're talking about who's involved in making decisions about culture within museums and galleries; we're talking about changing hierarchies that put popular culture at one level and high culture at another. All those things are happening with a kind of fervor, at least in North America. I just find that the version of it that you get over here is much more distilled, much more rarefied, and it doesn't have the same kind of ferocity that it does in the States.

sg: Maybe that rawness is a particularly American characteristic—a willingness to jump into the fray and lock horns and grapple with each other.

cf: I think there is something American about it. There's also less of a fetish about class.

SG: Is it your sense that a kind of cultural war is going on in America right now?

CF: Absolutely. I think that it's more manifest than it has been in the past. I don't think the sentiments that people express, or the guardedness or defensiveness of those who want to protect their interests, is new. I think what's different is the way in which people who represent those different interests are interacting with each other. The access given those who didn't have access before to those debates changes the very character of the debates. It's very different to conduct a discussion about race and culture when you have a room where half, or close to half, of the participants are not white. In Germany, I spoke to a woman who attended a gathering of filmmakers and video artists from the African diaspora whom I was involved with. This woman told me she had never been to a cultural event with so many black people, and that this aspect was the most important thing about the whole experience for her. She couldn't even get to the work—the physical confrontation in itself made such an overwhelming impact.

SG: I'd be very interested to hear, from your point of view as a nonwhite person, how it feels to be on the other side of this opening up of the debate in your direction, and in your favor. Is it a wonderful and exciting thing, or is it full of snares and traps?

CF: I think it's both. I've been fortunate, myself, in the sense that I have an education that makes the rhetoric not alienating to me, so that's one distinct advantage. If I wanted to obscure all those differences and pretend that these things weren't issues, I suppose I could masquerade in a certain way. And I've gone through periods of really strong uneasiness, either because I've felt that I've been pushed into a certain kind of a corner, and forced to speak as a representative of a particular community, or because I've felt as though misconceptions about my interests, or my strength or talents, greatly outweighed my own capacity to counter those mythical perceptions. But I guess that with experience, I've gotten more comfortable with this situation and don't even dislike fighting anymore. I feel as if it's a better situation than not talking about these things. I also feel that maybe the backlash against these debates is a symptom of the reality that there *is* change taking place— there wouldn't be a need for a backlash if somebody hadn't made some headway. And that makes me feel very hopeful!

SG: Do you see any real shift happening in the power structure? Do you feel as if the hierarchies really are breaking down and that some of the power is beginning to be genuinely shared? Or is it just being talked about?

CF: I think that change is being talked about more than it is taking place in any real fundamental way. Still, I think there are incremental changes that have made differences in people's lives. I think we've become more sensitized to issues that maybe ten or fifteen years ago we weren't sensitive to. I think our ability to counter conservative arguments has become more sophisticated. I think many artists who didn't have the possibility of making a living from being artists might have that possibility now—and I know how much that means to people, because it means a great deal to me!

SG: I assume you're talking mostly about artists of color.

CF: Or women artists. Or gay and lesbian artists whose work deals specifically with their sexuality. Multiculturalism has made an enormous difference in that sense. I also think it's made more of a difference in contexts where the capitalist market is not so dominant, like in university settings, or the alternative art sector, than it has in the commercial art world. But I think there's some degree of dialogue and change in the commercial art world, too; I just think that the interests in that world are so powerful and so overriding that the economics involved make it very hard to change the fundamental conservatism in that part of the art world.

SG: Do you personally take a lot of interest in what goes on in the institutional art world?

CF: I can't not deal with it. I mean, to pretend that institutions don't exist, or that I could exist and that I could circulate in my environment as an artist or writer or thinker—a person involved in making a culture—and not have any interaction with institutions is totally absurd. I'm not a hermit, and I don't do the kind of work that has a really profound existence without a connection to the public. And you can't really get to the public in the world that we live in without some kind of institutional mediation. So I need to negotiate with institutions. Some institutions are easier to negotiate with than others.

SG: Is there any experience you could talk about that was particularly difficult for you?

CF: This cage performance project that Guillermo Gómez-Peña and I have worked on over the last year and a half has been really interesting, primarily because of interactions with institutions, and then also because of interactions with the public. Our idea for the project was to invent a fictional identity and present ourselves as "savages" from an undiscovered island that had never been touched by any Western explorer. We intended to exhibit ourselves as curiosities, parodying the practice of the ethnographic display, and trying to make the argument, in a playful way, that this is a kind of performance art that we need to take into account at least as part of the history of performance. So we said that we came from this island in the Gulf of Mexico that doesn't exist. We spoke a language that was a non-sensical language; we lived in Madrid, London, Sydney, Chicago, Washington, D.C., New York, Minneapolis—

SG: What do you mean by "lived"?

CF: We lived in a cage for two or three days in each of those cities. And in each place there were guards whose job was to interpret our actions for the public, feed us, take us to the bathroom on leashes, and attend to us because we were supposedly helpless.

SG: Were they real guards or performance artists?

CF: Sometimes they were performers and sometimes they were just people we got access to through friends who agreed to help us. But generally, they were people who had some experience dealing with the public in cultural institutions.

SG: Were your presentations all held in art museums, or were some of them in ethnographic museums as well?

CF: Actually, they were split more between outdoor public sites and natural history museums, like the Field Museum in Chicago. And then, we did three nights at the 1993 Whitney Biennial during its opening.

SG: What kind of responses did you have?

CF: What was sensitive about the piece changed from context to context. In Spain, for instance, we were doing it as part of the quincentenary, and so we chose to be in Columbus Plaza. We had to get per-

Coco Fusco • 325

mission from city officials, and for them, the importance—or the potential danger in the work—was the political damage we might have on the image of Spain in the year of the quincentenary. So their reading of the piece was limited to their own political concerns—they weren't interested in whether we really were who we said we were, or whether it was theater, or ethnography, or whatever.

sg: Only that it could spell trouble for them.

cf: It spelled political trouble, and so they kept on saying no, until we finally charmed them into saying yes. And then, when they found out what we were doing after they came to the site, they had some bad feelings about having gotten involved, but by that time, there was nothing much they could do.

sg: Did you lead them to believe you were doing something different from what you did?

cf: We gave them a very limited interpretation of what we would do, stressing the allegorical, romantic, fantastic, dreamlike quality of the little fiction that we created, and implying that it was street theater and all for fun.

sg: So you downplayed the political aspect of it?

cf: Right, because they were raising the stakes in that area. In Britain, the concern was more about the morality of fooling the public.

SG: Who might not realize that this was performance art rather than real human "specimens"?

CF: Right. And then, the British Museum, which was where we tried to get in originally, they just—it was too hot for them. They didn't want to deal with us.

SG: So did you try the Museum of Mankind after that?

CF: No, we didn't. We'd had such a good time in Columbus Plaza that we decided to go for Covent Garden, because it was a similarly over-trafficked, public site, where we knew that being juxtaposed with other kinds of street performers like jugglers and rappers would mean that nobody would know exactly what was going on, and this would add to the atmosphere and be conducive to creating a better piece.

SG: Being in a kind of noncontext, it would decontextualize the whole event?

CF: Right. And the way that we were interpreted by many people who believed us in that context fell within the history of British imperialism and its connections to anthropology and ethnography.

SG: Did people try to talk with you inside the cage?

CF: Some people tried, but the fact that they were constantly being told we didn't understand any language really created a kind of fear about us, and so not that many adults tried to communicate with us.

SG: Presumably they talked with each other, and you could hear what they said.

CF: We heard all kinds of reactions, from people who were morally outraged, to people who thought it was charming, to people who—

SG: Thought it was a hoax?

CF: Some people thought it was a hoax, others believed it. Some people wanted to know if we were married and if we mated in the cage. They wanted to know what kind of sex life we had, what we ate, and why we needed to be fed. Even people who knew it was a hoax enjoyed participating on that level, and at a certain point, the piece became about how well they could play the game. Some people knew that they were as much a part of the performance as we were. One guy said, "Oh, I get it—this is really about us. It's about what we think. It's not about them." Someone on ABC news in Chicago said, "I've been interested in Native Americans for a long time, but I've never seen this kind of tribe before. This is really weird." We got all kinds of things. There was an elder from a Pueblo reservation in Arizona who spoke about how important it was to have this happen at the National Museum of Natural History at the Smithsonian, so people could understand what had happened to native cultures by seeing us in a cage, and how moving it was for him to understand what we were trying to do by making a statement. He read the metaphorical level of the piece immediately. There were some people, on the other hand, in the natural history museum in Chicago and in the Smithsonian, who were worried about the image that foreign tourists would go away with of their museums, because we were not what we said we were. Their main concern was that we were inauthentic and did nothing to admit that. They thought we were damaging their institutions' reputations by suggesting that dissimulation takes place, not only in our cage, but in their exhibitions and their dioramas and their wall labels. There was all this concern about their own institutional investment and what they stand for, and the assumption was that it's fine to understand the mistakes of the past, but you can't flaunt it in a way that undermines the credibility of the museum. Natural history museums tend to be more didactic than art museums, anyway.

SG: Of course, there's another way of looking at this piece—not as lying, but as finally telling the truth about something.

CF: That's what I say! But that's not the way a lot of other people who represent the interests of certain institutions would see it. We've had to fight with bureaucracies in every natural history museum we've tried to work with, precisely around this issue.

sg: And you've had fewer problems with art museums? I suppose they're more familiar with your work and your reputation as serious artists.

cf: The only indoor art context we exhibited ourselves in was the Whitney. When we did it at the Walker Art Center in Minneapolis, we were outside in a sculpture park. But in the case of the Whitney, we were clearly part of the Biennial, and in that context, the issue was not whether people believed it or not, it was whether it was appropriate to put performance in a museum space devoted to visual art objects. We wanted very much to make a statement by putting ourselves in the museum—and not including our piece in the performance series that they did as part of the Biennial, but in another space. We didn't want to buy into the hierarchical privileging of art that doesn't move. And we wanted to make a statement, also, about how we had been objectified. The distance between being objectified and being an object is pretty small, you know, and that site was going to make our performance resonate in the way that we wanted it to. There was some resistance to putting us in the museum, so we ended up with the compromise of being in a tent next to the restaurant, but it was still the space of the Whitney.

sg: I find myself thinking of that singing sculpture, *Underneath the Arches,* that was done live by Gilbert and George, years ago. I expect they were allowed into a museum without any trouble—there was no political content to the work. I'd like to know what your opinion is about whether multiculturalism is leading to an active and compelling global dialogue, or whether you think it's leading to a more self-conscious ethnocentrism?

CF: I think that both things are happening at the same time. I think that there is a kind of distilled, rarefied, without-the-bite version of multiculturalism that you get in big art shows in Europe and in North America, and I think there's also been a process of transformation that's coming from below that has to do with who's involved in making culture, and who's paying attention to the making of different kinds of culture in different places. I think that more people are listening, watching and experiencing cultures that are not necessarily part of their daily lives all the time. It's almost as if what's gotten universalized is the local experience of colonialism—having other cultures dumped on you all the time. Now everybody's getting bombarded with everybody else's culture—maybe not in an equal way, but there's some kind of cultural interaction that we share, which has to be understood better, in order for us to understand how we're constructing ourselves, and our sense of who we are, all the time. I'm not pessimistic, and I'm not optimistic, I'm both. I think that there's a great deal of resistance from the top. I think there are many artists and bureaucrats and people with power who aren't used to sharing it, and don't like to have anything interfere with the absolute liberties that have been accorded to them up to now. And I think that they feel the pressure coming from all over. That's going to produce a backlash in any kind of situation, and we're living with that right now.

SG: Is it your view that Western industrial civilization is very much on the wane? Do you think there is any threat to the survival of the human species?

CF: I certainly think there are good reasons to worry about environmental issues. I think we don't care enough about the damage that we do to the earth every day, and I think there's a lot of environmental racism. Some populations of the world are suffering more than others because we're dumping our garbage on them in many, many ways, and that is threatening the lives of many people right now.

SG: I find myself quoting Guillermo frequently when I lecture, saying that we're living in a state of emergency, so it is not enough to make art any more. I presume you share that view, so I wonder if you would make a comment about it?

CF: I think that if you only think of art as making attractive objects, then yeah, I think that much more has come to be included in our understanding of what artmaking is. For myself, I like to think of a productive relationship to society and to creating culture as being a back-and-forth kind of movement between going out into the world and learning about people, places and situations, and then going back and reflecting on them in the work that I do. To replenish my energy I have to go out into the world and have experiences that aren't art-specific. Maybe that's where Guillermo's and my thinking dovetails the most: we both really like to be out there in the world, and then come back and do something with those experiences.

A Few Beautifully Made Things

THEODORE ROSZAK

W*hen I found out that Theodore Roszak would be giving a lecture on his new book,* The Voice of the Earth, *at the Open Center in New York City, I decided to go there and hear it. Roszak is someone who has been taking the bit between his teeth about issues related to the urban-industrial world ever since his ground-breaking book of the 1960s,* The Making of a Counter Culture, *which was nominated for a National Book Award in 1969. We had already* discussed and agreed to do a conversation together, and I was hoping to seize the day this time, since a previous arrangement to meet in Berkeley during the spring had gone awry when I had had to cancel the trip.

Roszak's lecture proved to be truly remarkable, not least for being delivered in a room with no air-conditioning during a monstrous heat wave that was lashing the whole eastern seaboard with temperatures that broke records in several cities. Roszak, however, spoke with shattering clarity above the vibratory whirr of giant floor fans strategically placed around the room. He began by stating that because we have broken the biosphere and now think we must "fix" it, we are constantly asking ourselves, "What are we going to do about the environmental crisis?" But perhaps, he proposed, the way that question is phrased is not the real question. Perhaps the real question is: what is the environmental crisis going to do about us? It could be that the earth knows how to adjust itself—knows how to defend itself against the human experiment. Perhaps the earth is not a casualty, as we imagine it to be, but is a key player, who will have the last word.

That week, the New York Times reported, something unimaginable had happened: the Mississippi River was running wild. No one had ever seen it so high or so wide. Rain had been falling in biblical proportions for weeks and weeks,

Theodore Roszak • 335

and the country's system of levees and dams, stretching from Minnesota to Missouri, from Kansas to Illinois, was helpless to stop the swollen river and its tributaries. Everything in its path was being submerged or invaded. Snakes floated in the contaminated water, and the stench of dead worms was overpowering. As the slow, inexorable onslaught continued, the rivers washed out highways and railroads and flowed over entire towns, which had to be evacuated. A spokesman for the Army Corps of Engineers in Missouri was quoted as saying, "We really don't know what's going to happen. Nobody has ever seen anything like this before."

In the same week, thirteen-foot tidal waves were reported in the Sea of Japan, monsoon floods of epic intensity tore through Bangladesh, and the temperature in Barrow, the northernmost city in Alaska, reached a record high of seventy-nine degrees. (A normal summer day is usually around forty-five degrees.) It was inevitable, after hearing Roszak, to wonder if nature wasn't speaking back. Has nature got its own ways of getting rid of us?

If we trained our perceptions in the right way, according to Roszak, we would be able to hear the voice of the earth. Then maybe we would listen to, and begin to heed, her message of distress. But we have a long history of screening out intention and purpose in nature. The fact that we don't listen, he feels, is a reason to question the sanity of *urban-industrial society. To believe we have no ethical obligation to our planetary home, he claims, is "the epidemic psychosis of our time." Make no mistake: "A culture that can do so much to damage the planetary fabric that sustains it, yet continues along its course unimpeded, is mad with the madness of a deadly compulsion."*

Why, we may ask, are we doing this? How did we stop seeing ourselves as deeply embedded in the evolutionary cycle of things and begin seeing ourselves, instead, as alien strangers in the cosmos? This is a question that continues to haunt Roszak, a long-time philosopher in the sociology of alienation. In his conviction that every environmental issue has a psychological component, he found himself turning to psychotherapy for answers—where, he claims, he found nothing. Like Hillman, Roszak finds himself critical of modern therapy for being too private and nonpolitical; its current practice, based on the solitary psyche, is deeply flawed by its failure to include the greater ecological realities that surround us—as if the individual soul might somehow be saved while the biosphere itself crumbles. Given our present rate of planetary loss, Roszak believes that further disintegration is in the cards, and he suggests that many of our illnesses, both physical and psychological, may be symptoms of a biospheric emergency registering at the most intimate levels of life. For this reason, he advocates a new "ecopsychology" in

*which the fields of psychotherapy and ecology combine forces
to develop ecological awareness and to find ways of dealing
with our compulsion to damage the planetary fabric. The
goal is to lift the repression of our connectedness with the
natural environment, and to evolve a mature "ecological
ego," one that is aware of its ethical responsibility to nature.
We need to see the needs of the planet and the needs of the
individual as a continuum.*

*Roszak and I met, for the first time, a few hours before
his lecture, in a conference room at the National Audubon
Society in Soho that had been kindly offered to us by a
friend of his. We were both suffering extreme discomfort
from the claustrophobic heat outside. The dialogue was
taped there on July 7, 1993.*

SUZI GABLIK: What's your considered opinion, Ted, can
the earth afford us?

THEODORE ROSZAK: Rather than "us," I think it's important to say it's the high industrial societies of the
world that are proving biospherically unaffordable.
I've become much more discriminating in the way I
use the word "we," since there are surviving indigenous people who are not part of that "us." "We,"
the high industrial civilizations, are living way beyond what the earth can afford, in such a way that,

for example, population problems can no longer be calculated just by counting heads; you've got to count appetites. If you take into account the appetite for resources of high-industrial societies, then we are many times the size of the Third World countries. By that calculation, our society is living far beyond what the earth can afford. While that sounds like a condemnation, it is not meant to be, at least on my part: it's meant to be a wake-up call to the need for very deep changes. My current interest is how to bring about those changes as gracefully as possible.

SG: There are two things you wrote about in *The Voice of the Earth* that were particularly compelling to me. One is that we need something more than knowledge to get out of this mess—we need humility, a willingness to admit that what we're doing is incorrect. But you also allude to the tendency of the dominator society to follow its technocratic rule as a "deadly compulsion." How do you reconcile these two statements? If what we need is humility and a willingness to think again, how are we going to manage that, in the face of the systemic addiction our society has to its way of life?

TR: You use the word "addiction," and addiction is something I've come to focus on more and more in the work I'm doing with ecopsychologists. It is entirely possible that a large number of environmental problems that we can track with facts and figures are far more than simple moral problems. We usually think of moral problems as simply a direct choice between doing the right thing and the wrong thing. Where addiction is involved, you're dealing with people who clearly know what the right thing is, but they can't do it; they know what the wrong thing is, but they can't *stop* doing it. It's been interesting to me how psychotherapists deal with addiction. They do not deal with it by trying to make people feel more ashamed or more frightened, because if you do that, you lose the patient. They simply fall back on defensiveness, or they desert you. The way in which psychotherapists deal with addiction is usually to take it as an opportunity for self-knowledge—you dig deeper and deeper into the addiction. You work *with* the guilt, not against it. The addictive condition is characterized by an enormous amount of guilt; it's not as if the addict needs more of it. What the addict is often doing, in effect, is crying out for help because of the shame. So the question is, what binds the addict to self-destructive and shameful behavior? There may be many answers to that, but the important point is that this now becomes a psychological problem, not simply an ethical or political or economic problem. The essence of ecopsychology is to identify those issues that are psychological in character, and to turn to the people who might be able to help us most with those. I think psychotherapists can do that, especially if they themselves share some concern for the environment. What I've discovered is that a very large number of them do. A lot of the therapists I've been dealing with are as much part of the environmental movement as they are part of psychotherapy. They sincerely care about the fate of the planet, and indeed identify our relations with the planet as crazy and self-destructive. They want to do what they can to cure that condition. This is a distinctly new approach, because environmentalists have never thought they needed that kind of skill, or support. They've usually behaved as if they could simply force people to change their habits by sheer guilt-tripping or scare tactics.

SG: It seems to me as if we have two separate considerations here. One is the Hillman approach of turning away from our inward focus and the exclusive attention to healing our own souls, toward a concern with the *anima mundi* and the state of the world. Then we also have the issue of addiction—the addiction of a whole society to a way of life. I know it's possible for therapists to work with the addictive process in individuals and to change their behavior, but how do you get a whole society to give up a way of life that has become destructive?

TR: I want to reject the distinction between the outer and the inner; this is really part of the problem and not the solution. Ecopsychologists make the following assumption: if we are a species that has evolved out of the womb of this planet—as all other species have—then there is something in us that is bonded to the planet and that responds to the needs of the planet as directly and as strongly as we respond to the needs of people we love, as with parents and children. If that bond exists, then the role of psychotherapy is to find it and to understand how to awaken it. Now, if you don't look for it, or if you don't think it's there, then you're never going to find it. But if you begin looking for it, what you may discover is that it is indeed there, and that once you've found it within people, it takes on political and social dimensions. What I've discovered in just run-of-the-mill workshops is that there's an enormous desire on the part of people to talk about their environmental habits, and to talk very candidly about them, with a plea for help. "I'm doing things I don't like doing—I feel trapped in bad habits" is one of the most frequent confessions people make. Sometimes they'll say they feel addicted to those habits, and that they're not happy consuming and wasting. They're not happy with their whole way of life, but they don't know how to get out of it. The very fact that people can be so candid about that is important. It means that there's something there to work with. It's not as if they haven't heard the message of the environmental movement. They have heard that message. They know that what they're doing is ill-advised, maybe even lethal, as the facts and figures tell them. What they need is for someone to listen to their story, to ask why they're behaving the way they're behaving. If you listen to them, they begin to tell you things that are very instructive—to you and to them. For example, they recognize that a number of their environmental habits are linked to fears or to aspirations that might be dealt with in some other way. Many people will tell you that they go shopping when they're depressed. It's not that they want to buy more things—they're not greedy. The core problem is the depression, and to get them to focus on why they're depressed actually turns out to be a way of dealing with an environmental issue: overconsumption. Many people go to shopping malls because they find some diversion from their own inner problems, or they seek to prove themselves through acquisition. Yet they're aware of the fact, I discovered, that these are very feeble, ill-considered ways of trying to meet needs in their lives. The ability to talk about it to other people seems immediately to bring the sort of self-knowledge that therapists think has an effect on changing conduct. If I think about it, then I can change it; but if I never think about it, if I never talk about it, I just keep on behaving that way. If you delve into the psychological foundations, you often find that the bad environmental habits of people are connected to thoroughly legitimate, understandable human aspirations, but they've all been diverted into the marketplace, into getting and spending, into production and consumption. It's remarkable to me how aware people are of this if you simply give them a chance to talk about it.

SG: How would you define the primary aim of ecopsychology, then?

TR: In the long run, the goal of ecopsychology is to redefine sanity, in a major public way. Changing the meaning of a great word in society—whether it be "justice" or "freedom" or, in this case, "sanity"—is a way to change society. Changing the meaning of sanity is a major project, but once it's been changed, it is more than simply a private matter. So while therapy is usually thought of as a small face-to-face relationship that goes on in an office, the outgrowth of changing the definition of sanity can be an enormous change in society and culture.

SG: What looms as a major problem for me—and it's something I can't seem to get past—is that even as an environmentally aware person, I still find myself inextricably hooked into all the lethal aspects of modern life. It's pretty hard to figure out a way to give up many of these things, like cars and planes—unless, of course, you decide to live in a solar home and grow vegetables and never go anywhere.

TR: I don't know how you can change the world and have everybody do the right thing—I don't know the answer to that. What I'm aware of is that if you give people a chance to be heard on the stickiest environmental issues, they are more aware than many of us may realize and more eager to change things. Their sense of being trapped is strong, and the very fact that people recognize they're in a trap creates the desire to be free of the trap. The worst traps are those we don't know we're in. That awareness of being addicted, hooked, caught by a system that is environmentally unsound and lethal—that awareness is growing. The problem is so big that we sometimes lose track of the fact that progress does get made here and there, by fits and starts. That's why I would like to see the authority of psychotherapy come to include a sense that if we are not in balance with the natural environment, we will remain crazy in every aspect of our lives. Good personal relations cannot be achieved within an environmentally crazy society. The madness will show up somehow, somewhere, one way or another. If you had the authority of the psychotherapeutic community behind that idea, I think it would make a lot of difference socially. I don't think it would make *all* the difference, but it would make as much difference as I can imagine bringing about.

SG: You say in the book that within the framework of ecopsychology, we raise the question: "How did a psyche that was once symbiotically rooted in the planetary ecosystem produce the environmental crisis we now confront?" In other words, how did we lose our instinctual solidarity with nature? Have you come to any conclusions about that? Do you think the dissociation happened as an accidental side-effect of the industrial way of life? Could we really learn to retrieve it through something like ecopsychology?

TR: In every field of inquiry, you have great, imponderable questions, and I suppose this is the imponderable question in all studies of ecological philosophy:

where and why did the human race go wrong? It is clearly part of our human potentiality to go wrong. Now, that may mean a number of different things. It may mean that we are a profoundly flawed species —that is, the very capacity to do the wrong thing, which we seem to have done in the high industrial societies in an all-but-irreversible way, may indicate some flaw of the kind that gets brutally sorted out in evolution—meaning that this is the beginning of a form of extinction. I don't like to think that way, because it's just too grim, but that's one possibility. Just as other creatures were flawed in some way that made their survival impossible, so our species may be flawed in a way that has allowed it to create a culture that is environmentally not sustainable and which is bringing about our extinction. On the other hand, there are plenty of human beings in the indigenous cultures who don't share our bad habits, and so you might insist that, psychologically speaking, the human psycho-gene pool still includes all these other nonindustrial people who have not gone the way we've gone. Can we learn from people who have never taken much stock in industrial progress? Industrial progress has really been the ideological battle cry of a very small number of people, those who've had enough power to impress it on the rest of the society. It may be that there are a number of people who have never thought that's what they wanted. I think one of the main cards that's been played, collectively, in our society is that the only way we can feel secure in our lives is to have power over nature. The ability to dominate nature is what many believe to be the secret of security. I would characterize Western civilization as being the civilization that committed itself to that proposition about three or four centuries ago, as soon as we were able to invent machines. Through the use of that technology, we have sought to lord it over nature in the name of giving ourselves security. Now, there's one other great choice, and that is to trust nature and move with it, rather than against it, and to find in that harmony the secret of true civilization. Our civilization has not gone that way; it's gone in the other direction of saying security lies in domination. But the desire to feel secure, to have a decent chance to be healthy and have a long life—that desire is legitimate. The problem is that in the Western industrial societies, we seek to achieve it through domination rather than trust. And if I understand the real meaning of deep ecology and other environmental philosophies, they are summoning us back to a sense of trust, as the secret of security.

SG: I would say they're summoning us back—at least, in the more extreme versions like Earth First!—to a status quo that predates the industrial holocaust. Their view projects that nature will regain its ascendancy over the manmade world in due course. My own concern is that given the lifestyles we have, which are the only ones we've ever known, there are very few of us who would have the skills or the knowledge, much less the will or desire, to live without the comforts that Western industrial civilization has wrought.

TR: Part of what you say is true, but I'm just not sure about the breadth of the generalization. I don't think it's true of all of us, but I think it is true of some of us. You and I have spent the last few days here in this hideous city called New York. I'm not under the impression that I want to live here, or have anything that's in this city. Maybe New Yorkers would like to tell me that this is the way life's got to be at its highest pinnacle of achievement, but I don't believe that for a minute. I daresay a lot of people you see dragging around in the streets out there are sick to death of this city. They may not know how to get out of it, but they're not here because they think it's a great place to be. They're struggling with it every minute of the day. So even some of the things we're sure people will never give up on, like television, which fills people's lives—I'm meeting an increasing number of people who tell me they can't stand it and they don't watch it anymore.

SG: Is that likely to happen with computer technology, too?

TR: Yes. I think it's entirely possible that our history has been made up of waves of enthusiasms, and that what we've identified as progress has been one wave of enthusiasm after another, each of which has subsided and vanished. Let me give you an interesting example. I teach nineteenth-century British history, and it's impossible for my students to understand that there was once a time when railroads were considered so magnificent, such a manifestation of human genius, power and progress that there was a romance of the railroad. People wrote books and poems about the railroad. Now nobody sees the railroad that way; the railroad is looked upon as something clunky, old, defunct, and not the least bit interesting. I can remember in my own lifetime the romance of the airplane. In the 1940s and the fifties and sixties, when air travel was just coming into its own, it looked to many people, myself included, like something fabulously luxurious and efficient. I've lived to see air transport become a horror. The reason I don't move around very much these days is that I cannot stand airplanes—and I'm not alone. What we have here is still another example of such waves of technological enthusiasm, each one of which comes along with great hype telling us *this* is the pinnacle of progress. But within a certain period of time, the enthusiasm wanes, and it turns out to look like a horror, or a dead loss. It may be that industrial society has been buoyed up, not by steady progress, but by these waves of enthusiasm that keep telling us the next wave will be the one that really matters. Now it's "high tech": with a computer linked to your television and your telephone, you'll have heaven on earth. And I'm sure there are people who are willing to try that out. But I'll make a prediction that in another generation, this will look like a bunch of defunct old equipment. Nothing will work the way it was advertised, and at some point, people will be turned off by it.

SG: That would be great, in my opinion, if only it would also shut down the desire and the need and the search for ever more complicated equipment, but I fear that it won't.

TR: I agree. That's because so many of us are still hoping. It may be that after a certain number of these waves of enthusiasms have passed and left disappointment behind, people will finally get the point, that technology is never going to be what Francis Bacon thought it would be: the secret of immortality and salvation.

SG: But by that time, since our whole society is so interwoven with it, the inevitable result of any real retraction would be the collapse of society as we know it.

TR: Suzi, I spend fifty percent of my time feeling just as gloomy as you do. If I were feeling that gloomy today, we wouldn't be having a conversation. I have a closet at home filled about halfway up to the top with defunct electronic equipment that broke and cannot be repaired. Nobody will repair any of it— it's cheaper to buy a new one. I can find no one who wants to buy any of these things. Every time I open that closet, it's like a vision to me of the tremendous waste of high-tech junk. There's not even any way to recycle it. By the way, I suppose that closet could be an art work; maybe I could exhibit it as an installation somewhere.

SG: Are you saving it for a particular reason?

TR: I keep hoping somebody will find some way to use these materials. It is very difficult for me to take what still looks like a working piece of equipment and throw it out. I have no idea what to do with it all. To me, it's a vision of the way high-tech is going. I think that as the years go on, that closet will fill up with more and more of this stuff. The image I have is of technology becoming more and more monumentally disappointing. And that may take more of a toll on people than we realize.

SG: It sounds positively utopic to me, but it's not the way things look to be playing themselves out.

TR: I'm also strongly political, and I believe we need to make as much political change as possible. It seems to me that if you give people enough rewards for doing the right environmental thing, that you will motivate a lot of them to do it. But this has got to work in tandem with something deep in people, it's got to have a more personal dimension. It can't all be done at the level of law and policy.

SG: What about art, then? Do you see art as having a part to play in all of this?

TR: Art relates in two ways to this particular crisis. It is, first of all, one of the major sources we have of a different sensibility from the one that is orthodox in our society. Of course, it's not true of all art. You've made this very clear in your work—there's a lot of art that confabulates with urban angst and ephemeral urban values, and simply reflects the problems of the times in ways that are not the least bit critical and don't open up any new dimensions. On the other hand, there's the art that I respond to most strongly, which is a vision of something that is both new and old—organic, earth-based values that are as old as the human race and still available to us. Artists of that kind are one of the most important resources we have for ecopsychology, for changing our sensibilities and our tastes. They need all the support they can get, and they need as much exposure as possible. The other aspect of art that I have come to value is art as a new form of wealth: the more creative people become, the more opportunity they have to experience the joys of creativity, the less they will be consumers, especially of mass-produced culture, and the more time they will embed themselves in that form of richness. I see that as a kind of new wealth that counts for more than owning and having material things.

SG: Is this linked to the breaking down of the professional elitism of modern art?

TR: Yes. I'm talking about art as something people do rather than consume, and do as a normal part of their lives: creative endeavor as a form of profound spiritual satisfaction. I don't think that creative experience is restricted, inherently, to a small group of professionals. It's something you can find in any child. If you awakened it in people so that creativity was an integral part of their lives—if we thought, for example, that creativity was as important for children as computer literacy—they would grow up assuming that a certain amount of their life needed to be spent at music, art, theater, writing, poetry, dance, or whatever the art form might be. This would be a part of their life that was not spent consuming, destroying, watching television, doing the things the world now tells them they should be doing with their leisure time. Incidentally, all this is an echo of William Morris in the nineteenth century. In his *News from Nowhere,* he created a utopia in which people integrated art into their lives, and among the benefits was low consumption—in his utopia, people valued having a beautiful few things more than an ugly many things. I've always felt that this was an extremely important insight, that the aesthetic dimension, the more it is developed, has a role to play in people's daily lives that we often don't realize. It could very well be the case that good taste would settle for a few beautifully made things and not need a lot of miserably bad things that were cheap and ephemeral. Morris thought that this was the alternative to mass production. How you bring it about is another question, but it's interesting to have that as a goal, as a standard. The idea that mass production has to be there because people want so many things overlooks the possibility that these wants are extremely artificial, and can be met in an environmentally sustainable way by using better taste.

Our Students Need the City

CAROL BECKER

In 1994, Carol Becker was appointed dean and vice-president for academic affairs of the School of the Art Institute of Chicago, having been a former chair of the graduate division before that. She received her Ph.D. in literature at the University of San Diego, where she was a protégée of Herbert Marcuse. One of my first encounters with Becker was through reading her book The Invisible Drama: Women and the Anxiety of Change *several years ago. A precursor to Gloria Steinem's more recent bestseller,* Revolution from Within, *Becker's book questioned why so many "successful" women were suffering symptoms of anxiety at a time (during the mid-eighties) when opportunities for women seemed to be increasing and they should have been feeling "the exhilaration of possibility." The anxiety experienced by individuals who have been adventurous enough to break the rules in order to bring new ones into existence is inevitable, according to Becker. "Breakthroughs," she writes, "bring anxiety with them." They tend to destroy what people believe is essential to their intellectual and spiritual world. People who cause breakthroughs know that they have unsettled the foundation upon which the culture is constructed, and that the rest of the community may take out their own anxiety about change on those who have had the courage to shake up the concepts upon which the collective has structured its reality. Without such people, Becker says, the species would wither and die.*

As I've come to know her better, it seems accurate to describe Becker herself as just such a ground-breaking person. A lecturer in women's studies since the late 1960s, and a writer on psychoanalytic theory and cultural politics, she has been mulling over the obsolete attitudes and strategies of the art world for a long time, particularly the issue of the artist's responsibility to society, which she claims is a sensi-

tive issue that makes everyone uncomfortable, defensive and insecure. Becker feels that many artists simply refuse to address the issue at all. Artists often choose rebellion, which alienates them from their audience, and then become angry at the degree to which they are unappreciated. In part this is a consequence of the way we educate students in art schools, envisioning the artist as a marginalized and romantic figure who, she claims, operates "out of what Freud calls the Pleasure Principle while the rest of us struggle within the Reality Principle." Students need to think about their work, she feels, not in isolation, but in relationship with an audience and a larger societal context. The artist's relationship to the public and to an audience has not been addressed in art-school pedagogical situations. American art students, like most American college students, Becker claims, have not been trained to think globally or politically about their position in society. In a sense, art has seceded from American culture so completely that it has lost its effectiveness and become a subsidized bureaucracy of self-serving specialists. The mutual alienation between artists and audience is a matter with serious consequences for society, but in the nineties this is beginning to change, and Becker feels the goals of the art world will eventually change as well. Many artists in this country now appear to be refusing the place of isolation and marginality they have been given, which they themselves romantically have often confused with freedom. In the current wave of reaction against traditional structures like mainstream galleries, which have disempowered artists by regarding them as mere producers of commodities, Becker is skeptical about whether artists who attempt to make strong political statements, even against the art world itself, can successfully refuse the dynamics of capitalism and keep from becoming the darlings of the world they seek to critique.

Our own cultural system is so pervasive that we tend to mistake its attitudes, practices and beliefs as a fact of life and the way things necessarily are; we would have a hard time imagining life without these institutional practices. Yet the assumption that the artist has always lived in a marginalized or antagonistic relationship to society is not accurate, says Becker. "Because history reveals that this is not the case, there needs to be a way to expand our analysis so that other possibilities are allowed to influence this paradigm," she writes in her new book, The Subversive Imagination: Artists, Society, and Social Responsibility, *an anthology of essays by artists, writers and intellectuals from all over the world, which she commissioned and edited. The book is a direct challenge to Eurocentric assumptions "which have long held artists to be without responsibility or impact," and addresses the need to break the paradigms that perpetuate this mutual alienation between artists and society and keep art from having an impact. Becker poses the issue of responsibility "not so much as a constraint but rather as a condition for freedom and as a mark of the culture's maturity."*

In our conversation, Becker talks about the need to incorporate into the teaching process a fundamental concern for the particularities of audience and the placement of art within a larger societal context. "I am committed to the notion that the traditional expectations for the place of art in society must be challenged," she states. Along with many others in this book, Becker feels that traditional structures, such as mainstream galleries and museums, have disenfranchised artists, regarding them as mere producers of commodities.

It is unusual for someone in as centralized a position of authority as Becker to be so receptive to ideas of change. The necessary overhauling of basic assumptions that is currently ripping apart the fabric of our culture will often seem too drastic to be taken seriously by individuals who are comfortably embedded in the status quo. But perhaps Philip Slater's comment in his book about authoritarianism in American democracy, A Dream Deferred, *is correct, and "the most important social innovations of the next century will come from women, who are free from the male-dominated agendas and patterns of the present era." This is how I think of Carol Becker: urbane and street-smart, impassioned and intense, with many talismanic, colored glass hearts swinging insolently from her neck as she speaks.*

The following conversation took place in Becker's office at the School of the Art Institute on Friday, October 8, 1993.

SUZI GABLIK: Your current big subject, Carol, seems to center upon the place and function of art and artists in contemporary society, which you claim has never really been sufficiently articulated. You've said that, in many cases, artists themselves have actually refused to look at this issue. You state, and I'd like to quote you directly here, "In part the serious debates artists are now engaged in, in their work, remain hidden to those still caught within conventional notions of what art will do, what it will be, how far it can go, what subject matter it should address." I think that's a very good starting point for us, and I wonder if you could address the ways you think this may now be changing. Maybe you'd like to talk a bit about how you think this indifference to the social role of art came about in the first place. What is prompting these chaotic streams of change that we seem to be undergoing in our field?

CAROL BECKER: Lots of things. I think American society in particular is fundamentally an antiintellectual society, and always has been. There hasn't really been an articulated place where people of ideas, like artists and writers, are welcomed. I was in Spain, for instance, during part of the Gulf War, and every day in the newspaper, they would quote artists and poets, asking them what they thought about the war. They were actually asking creative people what they thought about the world, what they thought about the political arena. That's never the case in America —I mean, what artist ever gets quoted in the *New York Times* on major issues about the society? The populist image in America seems to mean the lowest common denominator, as if the American public could only handle the simplest, most banal and one-dimensional kinds of statements, or films, or books. So there really hasn't ever been a place established, and that's made it difficult, I think, for writers or artists to actually take a stand and be present in the culture.

SG: But in a sense, we've also created a certain conception of art that suggests it isn't supposed to be engaged in those areas anyway, what Arthur Danto refers to as the "disenfranchisement" of art. Now, suddenly, we have a situation where many artists are rejecting that notion, while at the same time, others are complaining that the more politicized approach isn't art at all. All this attention to political, social and environmental matters, they claim, isn't what art is about.

CB: I think what I was saying was that American society hasn't encouraged artists to be part of the dialogue

—not just to talk about politics, but to talk about life. There hasn't been any attempt to pull out from people who are really creative, ideas about how things work or should work. But I think you're right that now artists are beginning to question the fact that they have also isolated themselves.

SG: You're one of the people who has pointed out that this is an effect of the way we train artists. We teach them to remain autonomous, to stay in the studio and make art. So, if a situation now exists such as the one you describe, where our culture doesn't look to its artists as a creative resource, isn't it also the case that artists have not been trained to take on that kind of role?

CB: I've written about this. I think art schools in general have perpetuated the problem. I don't think we've helped it. And I think that artists had become, for a long time, quite comfortable in their role as disenfranchised and infantilized beings, left on the periphery, tangential in the society. Everybody was comfortable with that.

SG: It's the trade-off for aesthetic freedom, right? Disenfranchisement is linked with capitalist notions of autonomy and freedom and exercising one's individuality.

CB: But the truth is, this is a very bourgeois notion of freedom that we've encouraged, which is a freedom for the individual *apart* from society, not a freedom for the individual *within* society. It used to be, when you came to Chicago, that you could recognize Art Institute students from a mile away, because they were the only ones dressed in black; they were the only ones with green hair. You'd see them on the subways. Now the city's become more hip, and there are whole other populations of people who look that way. But I think the image of the school in the city was this sort of bohemian place over there by Grant Park, and the students really bought into that. It was a kind of cultivated separateness. But, it was also self-preservation, because this was the only way they could define themselves against the visual and cultural mediocrity of mainstream American society. It was the only way they could really say to their families, "We're not going to live these kinds of lives; we're going to pursue a whole other track and follow our creative desires." Some of that was a necessary and healthy thing, the way bohemian, avant-garde movements have always been, but some of it was sad and lonely, especially when they couldn't find a way back into the society. And we couldn't figure out how to get them back. A lot of faculty were quite content with that state of affairs, because they also felt alienated and separated themselves. So we had a whole perpetuation of this notion that freedom is to be found outside of society.

SG: It's what you've called the paradigm of alienation. But is this what's changing now? How much of it do you feel is actually changing? Take your questions, for instance—the ones you say need to be asked, like what is the responsibility of the artist to society? And what is the responsibility of society to the artist? What kind of answers have you personally come up with about how this relationship needs to be understood?

CB: Well, I think the tension of maintaining a position of alienation like that is becoming very great, although many students continue to believe that's what freedom is—to do whatever they want, wherever they want, whenever they want. We certainly have taken tremendous blows as an institution, because of the American flag, for instance, that Scott Tyler, a student, exhibited on the floor, and because of the painting depicting the late Chicago mayor, Harold Washington, in women's underwear, that was removed by city aldermen. Responses to things the school has been involved with have really challenged our notion that we're separate. We really are an urban-based school, and if we ever want to be part of this city—which I personally very much want us to be—then we also have to think about how we project ourselves into the city. Our students need the city. They need to get right inside the life-force of the city and the community. They need not to be separate, because as long as they're separate, the only thing they can generate work about is themselves. And they're really often too young to have articulated yet what they are; besides, how does one ever figure out who one is except by pitting oneself against the world in some way? I don't mean to say that everyone should make "political" art—I have no one image of what art should be. I just know that everything in society exists within society. I want our students to think about where they are in relation to the society.

SG: As the dean of a very important art school, have you found any ways to implement some of these changes? Or are they already happening quite naturally?

CB: Both. There are a lot of students and quite a few members of our faculty who really want to be working outside of the school They want to bring the school into the city. You know, we've just started this cable-access show; we have a program of art in the libraries, and during the summer months we do classes at Navy Pier for kids. We've always had a Young Artists' Program for children. We have lots of things that bring us into the city, but I think the mindset has only really shifted in particular instances. We still often look at these activities as bringing art into "impoverished" locales, instead of realizing that we're often going into communities that have a strong cultural base of their own that we can also learn something from. I think traditionally when art schools have ventured forth, it's been seen as a kind of social work, and I think there's a similar confusion in the art world as well that has to be thought through. For example, what's the difference between certain kinds of community-based art and social work, and do those distinctions matter at all? These are the kinds of questions I think our students need to be thinking about, like, what makes sense to do? Does one go into a place as an artist and do whatever one wants there, or how much do you actually need to do your work in relationship with others? Several of our faculty are helping students to think through these complex issues.

SG: Do you see the conflict around these issues as you're experiencing them right here, in your institution, as a kind of culture war? Or isn't it that dramatic?

CB: I think it's dramatic, but I see it more as a shift of paradigms. I think we're trying to shift a very old paradigm, and that's not easy for people to do.

SG: You've described it as the paradigm of the romantic and alienated artist, who functions only on the fringes of society, without any substantive role.

CB: I guess that's what's going to shift. I was just at a foundation think-tank for two days, and a lot of the discussion was about community: What is community? et cetera. I have a lot of resistance myself toward extremes of either-or in any way, and I think it would be a tremendous mistake if everyone now felt that the only art that mattered is art that is out there in a very socially conscious way. Because we all know that we've gotten great joy and pleasure from things that were made from a very personal vision of the world. I wouldn't want us to condemn painting, for instance, or to categorically lop off whole disciplines because we've decided they're bourgeois. I think that's very reactionary. I want to see it *all* exist, and what I really would like for our students is for them to know the whole range of possibilities—and within that, to choose who they're going to be. And to know that this definition of themselves can evolve and change, and that they can start in one place and end up in another. But they've got to see models of people who've made those transitions.

SG: Most of all they need to understand that there's more than one model for being an artist. You make that point so well in your comment questioning our assumption that the historical role of the artist has remained unchanged—as if freedom of expression has always been the central artistic concern. We also tend to assume that artists have always lived in a marginalized or antagonistic relationship to society, but they haven't.

CB: One of the reasons my new book is very international is because I thought that, in order to find new models, I would have to look outside of this culture. American society tends to implode on itself, and the American art world, which is a small part of the American society, implodes even further. It becomes very dogmatic and very judgmental about who, this year, is doing the correct thing. I think any of those trends is very limiting, and that creative people should be expansive people, they shouldn't be limiting of other people's creativity. So, in the last few years I've been to South Africa twice, and both times I've been invited to speak. And when I was there, I had a tremendous opportunity to talk to people who were involved in debates about where art is going in this transition of the ANC [African National Congress]. What will be the place of art in this new society? They're having to rethink their whole society from the ground up, so even things like what will be the function of museums, what will be the function of art schools, who will get to go to school, what kind of work will be shown—all of this is under scrutiny. How do you create environments that truly represent the panoply of South African society, which is incredibly complex and racially diverse?

SG: And in that sense, comparable to our own society.

CB: Very comparable. I think Americans who go to South Africa often fall in love with it, because what you see in South Africa are the same issues pushed to their limits. People say, "Oh, isn't there terrible racism there?", but it's not that different from here —it's just much more overt. You cannot avoid your race there; it's with you everywhere you go. Racism isn't hidden, the way it is in America. In every encounter you have with people, they immediately talk to you about politics. If you're not a political person, I think you'd hate South Africa. South Africans live at such a pitch that if you're an intense person, you feel like, oh, this is home. Nobody thinks I talk too fast there; nobody thinks I worry about society too much, because that's what they worry about. So if you like political discussions, then you love South Africa. But you realize that for these people, the discussions are not just theoretical. They're really making policy. There's a National Arts Initiative, for instance, which is pushing against the ANC and saying, "You're going to establish a cultural policy as the ANC becomes the government, so what's it going to be? How much freedom are artists really going to have, or is it going to become a country of social realism? Is it going to look like the Russian revolution? Is it going to be like Cuba, or China?" There are lots of models now for what hasn't worked very well for artists. So artists want to be sure that they're going to have freedom and a range of possibilities—and not just be asked to make political art. And this is coming from very political artists, many of whom have been in the ANC for many years.

SG: So basically the tenor of these debates would feel quite different, if you were actually to attend one, from a similar kind of conference or debate in this country about what the future direction of art should be.

CB: The big difference is that they're talking about really making policy. We don't get to make policy as artists, or writers, in this country. But we're ahead of places like South Africa in other ways—for instance, the kinds of community-based projects that are happening here aren't being done yet in South Africa.

SG: Is there something similar going on in South Africa to what I experienced years ago when I was in India, which is that the local artists go abroad to study and then come back with some kind of watered-down version of modernism?

CB: Yeah, there is that problem. But you have to realize that South Africa has had a cultural boycott for so many years that no one has allowed a show of art to go there, either to the museums or to the galleries. So all the international art that South African artists have seen, unless they travel, has come from issues of *Artforum* and *Art in America.* They've been cut off for so long that when they do do a version of postmodernism or modernism, it looks very out-of-date to Americans. I think the most exciting work happening there is when you have the really indigenous art mixing with the Western traditions. All South Africans who are in any way progressive are also connected to black culture and are involved in it in some way. And they're influenced by it. Black artists are also influenced by "Western" art and popular culture. So where it's hybrid is where it gets interesting.

SG: Let's go back, for a bit, to these issues about education. I'd like to know how you would envision re-training, or redirecting the standard university art department programs in this country, so that they are more in tune with what you called the paradigm shift. Do you have specific suggestions that might be helpful to somebody, say, who is reading this book? Somebody who might be trying to restructure an art department? Where should they start?

CB: I think there are many things. First of all, the notion that anybody, at the age of eighteen, is ready to delve into their soul and pull out a universe is, at best, totally naive. What students need, fundamentally, is a very good education, because one of the things artists aren't given—and it disempowers them terribly in the world—is good reading skills. And it's the same with writing. Very often young artists can't write well, and they're told not to worry about it, because they're artists. Artists need good language skills—I think that's crucial. But there's been this idea that if you verbalize, or intellectualize, it'll destroy the spontaneous, intuitive qualities of artmaking. I think that's crazy—it's developing only half a person. I want our students to have a good, solid, historical education, so that they know the culture they're living in and are curious about the rest of the world.

SG: One of the things that has always struck me about training to be an artist in our society is that, unlike educational training for medicine or law or most other professions, where you go through years of learning about everything that's ever happened in your field, and you have to take in an immense amount of information, the way that art is taught, the student produces work for a diploma show. That means they spend those crucial learning years putting out rather than taking in. Many of them take hardly any art history or contemporary issues courses.

CB: That's a very good way to put it.

SG: So perhaps what you're saying is that we need to reverse this process, or at least get it into better balance, so that students will be taking in at least as much as they're putting out.

CB: It's interesting, because what we're doing is training people how to see. We're training people how to make things, and we're training them how to have vision. And so, what do you need for this? When you think about other cultures, and what spiritual people have to go through in their training, let's say, to become visionaries, it's a lifetime's process. We don't even tell our students that it's going to take their whole lives to become artists. We don't tell them that, because art stars make it in their twenties, so our students think this could happen to them. Often students complain that they have to do all these other courses in humanities and art history, but what they don't realize is that they're really developing themselves, and that without that, there's little to make art about.

sg: Some of the retraining that needs to go on, wouldn't you say, is with teachers, because of their direct influence on the students? Teachers need to frame these issues as being important for the students.

cb: I think sometimes the way that people themselves were trained is how they train other people, and it's very hard to shift that. My sense, in building institutions, is that what you need to do is bring in new people, young people, or older people who have kept up with new ideas and have changed and grown and evolved. You can have a whole spectrum of kinds of instructors, but the students need to understand that every person they encounter is just one piece of the puzzle, there isn't just one view. I remember when Baudrillard came to the Art Institute—it was right after he'd been on the cover of *Art in America,* or somewhere like that—and he was the theoretical hero of the moment. And I thought, our students really have no idea where he comes from. They think that this guy is magic—you know, that he fell out of the sky. They've never read Marx or Hegel; they've never read the Frankfurt School. They have no idea whose shoulders he's standing on. And unless they understand where the arguments have come from, they can't even make a decision about whether they think he's right, or wrong, or anything. Because he's fashionable in the art world, that's what the students respond to. But because they often don't have the critical tools, and aren't given them, they can't make decisions for themselves. You only get *that* courage by having developed your own sense of what's important.

sg: What was the student response to Baudrillard?

cb: Well, what was most hilarious was that he read a wonderful paper in English. However, he pronounced every word with the emphasis on the wrong syllable, so I don't think anybody really understood what he said. I'm not sure what the students thought—I think that, often, with those kinds of events, it's mostly spectacle. But the fact is, the students here are very intelligent and original. They haven't bought into any one world view, ideologically. But I also think what really has to happen, and it's going to take a long time before people are willing to do it, because it risks a lot, is that the whole way schools have been structured around separate disciplines, like sculpture or painting, has to be demolished. It doesn't make sense any more. People don't work that way any more.

sg: You mean, there are no separate disciplines any longer?

cb: I think people are working through ideas, and then they look for the medium that best actualizes their idea, or they combine five different media. So I think art schools should be structured around ideas, not around physical matter or what tools you're going to use. Maybe they should be more like departments of narration, departments of political art, figurative art, abstraction, and so on—and then, whoever wants to work in whatever medium would think about the ideas first, and then find the medium at any given moment through which they could fulfill them. But it would be the ideas that would frame the school. And the ideas could change and we'd reconfigure the departments accordingly. Now, to do this you would have to knock down every art school that has been physically built to accommodate and separate all these media. You'd have to start from scratch. It's not happening tomorrow. In fact, we have a whole new building on Michigan Avenue, and one of my colleagues just said the other day, "You realize we have solidified ourselves into these disciplines with all those thick walls, and that means that we're inflexible." And he's absolutely right, because the twenty-first century, I am convinced, is not going to be about the exclusivity of forms any more; it's going to be about ideas. And the way that we've all structured our institutions is already obsolete. The students are beyond us, they work across disciplines and we can't really accommodate them. So that's a big problem.

SG: Well, this is quite an astonishing set of statements! [Laughter]

CB: I'll never get a job again. No one will ever hire me, they'll think, "Oh my God, she's going to come in and demolish the buildings." But I do understand, dialectically, that this is the tension we're in right now. Our students have a different mindset. They are truly post-postmodern people. They don't see the world the same way we do. We need to explore this, to speculate about what it signifies.

SG: What do you mean by that? What's a post-postmodern person?

CB: It just means that they're conscious of what postmodernism is, and they're self-consciously not postmodern. But they're beyond it, in that they understand it.

SG: So if you come out somewhere beyond postmodernism, then where are you?

CB: I don't think they know yet. But I think that all this emphasis on political art and community-based art is a response, in some ways, to postmodernism. I think the radical thing that postmodernism achieved is that it smashed the categories and let people begin to work across them. That's why I'd hate to see any movement of political art or community-based art become dogmatic, because I think it would just reinstate another category, and we're potentially beyond that now. What I wanted to say about my students was that last semester, it was clear to me when I was teaching that they did not understand concepts like transcendence, or hope. They don't structure their lives as if they are moving toward a goal.

SG: You mean they don't have the usual professional career goals, or what?

CB: Not just that, but even personal goals. As modernists, when we were growing up, there was always the feeling that one was ever moving toward perfecting oneself, to greater and greater levels. Or that one was always trying to transcend the philosophical system that one came out of, to move to the next thing. These students don't frame their life with that sense of movement or progress. They live much more in a moment-to-moment way that isn't necessarily based on progression. It may not be going anywhere, and they can *live* with that.

SG: Do you think this has to do with the endgame, apocalyptic atmosphere of our times? Maybe you can't have grand plans and big schemes for your life when the future of life on the planet is open to question.

CB: I'm not sure that's the explanation, because I think we felt that, too, because we had the bomb. I think we also had an apocalyptic sense of things—an imminence that everything could just go, at any moment—but for different reasons. I don't know why this has evolved, but I think the computer is no small part of it. The computer is a very nonmaterial, nonphysically based form in which things happen electronically. They don't happen on the physical plane.

SG: It's Baudrillard's world of hyperreality and cyberspace.

CB: I think we're moving out of the physical plane as a species. I don't know if it's good or bad.

SG: It scares the shit out of me.

CB: I see the students in this strange purgatory; they don't want to give up the physical, but they've already moved beyond it, in some way. They're already working in forms that don't have a physical base. And that's new, too. I don't know what it means, but I find it very interesting. I don't know if this generation will develop a tremendous longing for the natural physical world, or if it just won't matter to them anymore, because the physical plane isn't where people will want to be living anyway. But I do know that they're in a different mindset than I am, and I feel this difference very much. I feel more and more that I will always be pushing toward this sense of transcendence, and they won't. There's definitely a gap, and we spend half our lives here bridging that gap. But I think not to admit that we're different would be a mistake.

SG: What you're talking about is obviously much more far-reaching than the traditional generation gap.

CB: I don't think anybody's really written enough about what this individual absorption with terminals and machines means—you know, people's obsession with their computers and InterNet and E-mail and all these things.

SG: Because I don't think anybody knows for sure. The people who have written about it, like Jerry Mander, claim that we are being affected dramatically, in ways that we don't understand, and one of the problems is that we never have the chance to discuss, debate or decide whether we even want these changes.

CB: That's right. We're already in them—there's no going back. And we're moving so fast we don't even have time to reflect on where we're going.

SG: One of the reasons it's scary for me is that I guess I've made a choice not to go.

CB: I think a lot of people will make that choice in one way or another.

SG: My instincts tell me not only that this is a direction in which I, personally, don't want to go, but also that it's a dubious direction for the whole human race. I guess I'm very attached to the physical, sensual world, and I'm not interested in a life lived plugged into machines—in fact, it's abhorrent to me.

Carol Becker • 379

CB: You have to mention that for our students, their sensuality and physicality is mediated by the presence of AIDS, in a way that ours wasn't. I think it's hard to imagine what that would have been like—to be twenty years old and not to have freedom in that arena, to have friends who are ill and to lose people who are so young.

SG: It could even make the physical world seem repellent.

CB: It could. So I think that the world of AIDS is a whole new paradigm, too, that has to be thought about also. In the midst of this, we're trying to run this gigantic art school, and figure out how to prepare our students—we're not even sure for what. Because we're not sure what any of it will look like for them in twenty years. I know that the art world as it existed in the 1980s may never return. The students may never see that kind of boom again in their lifetimes. I think this is probably good for them, liberating, because it's forcing them to search for a route that is more interesting and has more integrity. None of them really believes anymore that they're going to be art stars—well, maybe some of them do, but most of them know better. They're trying to think about what's really meaningful, and so this is also our chance to say something to them about what's really meaningful.

The Liminal Zones of Soul

THOMAS MOORE

*T*homas Moore is a psychotherapist best known for his work in the field of archetypal and Jungian psychology. He also holds advanced degrees in theology, music, art and philosophy. As a young man Moore lived for twelve years as a monk in a Catholic religious order; he now describes himself as a "self-employed, poetic-minded, independent scholar who was also a former cleric." When his book Care of the Soul appeared in 1992, it unexpectedly brought the house down. I say "unexpectedly," because although he had published several other books, only a few people had read them, and Moore mistakenly assumed that few would read this one as well. When Care of the Soul *began its slow-motion ascent on the bestseller charts, no one was more stunned by the intensity of the response than the author himself. "I'm used to writing books that no one reads," he says. The book certainly caused many of the smarter coyotes I know to walk on their toes from sheer excitement. We soon found ourselves huddling over his every word as if we had found a secret grove full of lady's slipper orchids.*

Our estrangement from the world, according to Moore, is a result of our depersonalizing philosophies and the culture we have made. If we truly wish to care for the soul, we cannot continue to live the life we are living. Care of the soul involves a fundamental reorientation to what's going on. What we need is to become more artful about our lives instead of mechanical. The soul is not amenable to mechanical and structural thinking, it works alchemically. When a radio MC, who was commenting on Moore's extensive travels, said to him, "Your battery must be running down," Moore replied: "I have no battery." In the modern world, we tend to see everything as if it were a machine, and our use of language reflects this. A better metaphor, according to Moore, would be to imagine ourselves as huge, deep, *mysterious and awe-inspiring as the night sky. Seeing one-self as a universe, and not as a machine that needs fixing, takes us closer to the mystery of soul.*

The soul loves the labyrinth rather than the ladder (which symbolizes "getting somewhere"), and it prefers relatedness to distancing. Paradox, mystery, being sick, failures, foolishness, blank spaces, not knowing where one is going, are all good for the soul, which is ripened by making mistakes. Magic, not reason and will, accomplishes what the soul needs, allowing its eccentricity to emerge. The soul does not have an urgent need for understanding or achievement; rather, it loves intimacy. According to Moore, conversation is one of the "technologies of intimacy," an inherently soulful activity that gives us an appreciation for unresolved complexity. Care of the soul is more a process of listening and following than of hanging on fiercely to our own interpretations and programs. Soul has little to do with our intentions, expectations or moral requirements, and slight shifts in imagination, Moore claims, have more impact on living than major efforts at change. With his friend and mentor James Hillman, Moore argues for a new soul ecology: a responsibility to the things of the world based on appreciation, affection and relatedness rather than on obligation or abstract principle. Ultimately this is where the fields of psychology, ecology and art overlap.

For Moore, the arts are central to finding ways to nourish the soul. Art gets us away from problem-solving and into the mystery. But we forfeit opportunities for soul when we leave art only to the accomplished painter and the museum. Moore feels that professionalism can be lofty and remote, while soul is ordinary, daily, communal, felt, intimate, attached, engaged, involved and poetic. In a world where soul is neglected, beauty is placed last on its list of priorities. The implication is that the arts are dispensable: we can't live without technology, but we can live without beauty. To begin building a culture that is sensitive to matters of the heart, says Moore, and to care for the soul, we will have to expose ourselves to beauty, risking "the interference it can place in the way of our march toward technological progress. We may have to give up many projects that seem important to modern life, in the name of sacred nature and the need for beautiful things." All this is part of our effort to replace modernist psychology with care of the soul.

A personal encounter with Thomas Moore is a bit like finding oneself in air rich from the aroma of marigolds, climbing roses and pollen, with maybe a rare whooping crane cruising overhead. There is no doubt that he stimulates, in me, a propensity for extravagance, arabesques and flashes of soul. We met, for the first time, at the thirteenth annual "Common Boundary" conference of transpersonal psychologists, attended by several thousand therapists, artists and social workers and organized every year by the editors of Common Boundary *magazine*. Moore was offering an all-day workshop on "Care of the Soul Through Art," and I signed up for it. I also wrote him a letter asking if he would have a conversation with me. He agreed. The conference was held at the Hyatt Regency Hotel in Crystal City, just outside Washington's National Airport—a polished steel and glass environment in which there are no hills, no stones, no soul. From my room, you could peer down through the picture window at a snarl of railroad tracks, which, under the melancholy November sky, was pure de Chirico. That humdrum hotel room was slowly transformed, during the hour in which we spoke, into a place where many rivers converged.

In Moore's company, one enjoys precisely that kind of discussion that is never complete, and that leaves one hankering for further talk. You can't not be taken with the druid look in his eye, the convivial grin. In his new book, Soul Mates, *which came out a couple of months after we met,* Moore describes conversation as one of the chief conduits of soul—different from discussion and argument. People trying to win an argument, make a point, preach a sermon, hold forth on a theory, are not engaged in conversation, he claims, because these agendas are burdened with narcissism and offer little room for soul. Meaning, according to Moore, is overrated, but conversation is "the sex act of the soul"; it helps us in living together and enjoying our differences, and as such it is supremely conducive to the cultivation of intimacy. Through listening to other people, we find ourselves.

During the workshop he jokes about his favorite fantasy: to open up a chain of slow-food restaurants: "Only five people served in the last two years!" The orientation of Moore's whole philosophy is Epicurean, framed by beauty and by pleasure. He would make our lives more artful by an intensification of color, sound, texture, food, and by taking lots of time to be with something, letting things have their impact. Moore seems to share a sense, with Satish Kumar, that art's raison d'être is to give us an artful, beautiful life that appreciates the sacred everywhere.

I almost did, but couldn't quite, drop everything in order to accompany Moore on a ten-day sojourn he was leading to Tuscany, called "Renaissance of the Imagination" and sponsored by the Center for Advanced Studies in Depth Psychology. The purpose of the trip was to "travel to the place of the Renaissance and bring it to life via the imagination." Seminars were held in an ancient medieval castle near the town of Anghiari. The castle houses a renowned medieval culinary arts school, and lunches for the group *were prepared daily by a chef. "All of my work," says Moore, who studies the writings of fifteenth-century philosopher Marsilio Ficino in the original Latin with the same passion that a commodities trader studies the financial markets, "has been inspired directly by Renaissance Italy, and I look forward to further explorations of Renaissance art as magic." Were he ever to go back to school, Moore says, he would study the religions of the world and become an iconographic theologian.*

The following conversation took place on Friday, November 12, 1993.

SUZI GABLIK: Tom, you've said that the great malady of the twentieth century, implicated in all our troubles, and affecting us individually and socially, is loss of soul. It seems as if you've taken on as your primary work to think about how we can bring soul back into life, back into the world. It's a subject that is very close to my own heart, and I was particularly struck with your comment in this regard that "care of the soul is a step outside the paradigm of modernism and into something entirely different." What is it that's so entirely different?

THOMAS MOORE: The first thing I might say—a very simple thing—is that care of the soul as I am presenting it is not something that you do within the present cultural system, or paradigm, or habits that we have now. It seems like a lot of people would like to be able to find some way to keep what we have, the life that we live, and make some adjustments so we'll all be happy. That's not what I'm trying to suggest at all. What I'm suggesting is something deeper: we have to get rid of certain things. To bring soul in means other things go out.

SG: What things have got to go?

TM: I guess when you think about modernism and about the modern world, there are obvious dimensions of it that make it difficult to live a soulful life. One of the primary things is trying to get along in this world relying on reason, on mind. Even today, I read the brightest, most interesting people, full of imagination, talking about the mind-body paradigm, and to me, that just doesn't do it. That's the old world; it's still a dualistic way of looking at the world. It still relies on mind—in fact, there's a lot of brain talk in all of it—and I think there's no room in that for soul.

SG: So you're saying that even the people who are trying to change the old Cartesian body-mind split are still trapped in it in some way?

TM: Yes.

SG: Because the new body-mind paradigm that they're talking about still doesn't address issues of soul?

TM: Exactly. I wish I could have said it that way myself. It's an interesting problem, because if you look at certain religious traditions—the most obvious one would be Zen—it seems to me that in certain schools of Zen, there's an insight that the only way you can really find a solution to the questions that you have is to reach a point where your questions dissolve. There's a personality dimension there that has to break apart, and that I think is being bolstered, actually, in that other response.

SG: When you talk about needing to let certain things go, surely part of that must include the way we frame issues to ourselves, and the way that we talk and think about things.

TM: Yes: the language that we use, the style of our talking, the way in which we do things. To be a little more specific, I think with this mind-body talk in medicine, what happens is that we try to get out of the split by making mind more attractive—like, OK, let's have a higher form of consciousness. Let's be more imaginative in our mental life. In other words, we're digging the hole deeper by making it more attractive.

SG: So what is the mysterious element, or component, called "soul" that is somehow absent from this picture? And how could we better put it there?

TM: I have actually learned a lot of things since this book has come out. I didn't know what it was about when it first appeared, really. Just now, after a year and a half, I'm beginning to get a better picture of what it is.

SG: Is this through the feedback you've had, and the many interpretations others have laid on your work?

TM: Yes, and also having to speak about it so much. Over and over again I've had to simplify, and I've had to realize, very concretely, especially when speaking on an AM radio station, that you can't be too subtle about things. You have to try to convey, in a few minutes before they announce the sports scores, what soul is all about and what care of the soul is. So I've had to really hone this down, and one of the things I've learned that pertains to the question is, we have to find ways of talking that are not in that split place of mind and body, or in that rationalism. And so, I'm very interested in talking to people who don't have any education around these philosophies of modernism and postmodernism. For example, I do not see my book *Care of the Soul* as a popularization of these questions, even though it has sold a lot of copies. Some people might look at it and say, "You're trying to be accessible." I often hear that. I'm really not trying to be accessible, that's not one of my purposes. What I am interested in is finding a language that in itself is not stuck in this dualism, and avoiding situations where the language itself becomes so removed from even my own daily experience that I have to figure out how to pull it down and apply it to my life.

SG: One of the qualities of the book that I experienced most strongly when I read it did have to do with language, and the use of language in it. What I experienced was almost like a physical alteration in my body, a kind of cellular realignment, or direct transmission, which might be comparable, say, to the effect of listening to certain types of music. I felt as if the words were making me know something through my body while I was reading them. Is that anything you consciously worked for?

TM: Well, not too consciously. Maybe artfully. You know, I try to see myself as a writer, and as I said at the beginning of the book, "this is fiction," at a certain level.

SG: It certainly has an alchemical quality. Maybe it's because you're so steeped in those traditions from the Renaissance that you're able to bring an alchemical force into the way you write.

TM: I'm actually surprised how much the studies of alchemy and astrology, world religions and music, have affected my work—it's not terribly conscious, though. I do notice, looking back on it and hearing people respond to me, that yes, I guess there is a lot of that in there.

SG: We never really got to the heart of what it is in the modern paradigm that needs to be left behind if we're going to have a more soulful existence.

TM: One of the things that needs to be left behind, as I suggested, is too much reliance on reason and mind, especially on what my Renaissance sources would call a schizoid, or split-off, mind—not having soul. When our reasoning and our education and teaching have soul, they have more imagination; they're more poetic in style. They're not going toward solutions to problems. They're not objectified, or quantified. And also, technology is not divorced from other dimensions. You see, the one thing about soul that's very interesting—it's in this new book of mine, *Soul Mates*—is that soul is *convivial*. That's the word I'm using for it: it's convivial in itself. So, let's say with technology: as long as technology is convivial with the arts, and with other dimensions of our experience, then I see no difficulty with technology. But to make technology convivial in the sense I'm thinking about would mean to leave modernism, because modernism has been built around a monotheism of technology. It's a little like James Hillman's idea of "psychological polytheism," only I'm emphasizing the erotic aspect of multiplicity. I don't want to speak at all against technology—it's crazy to do that.

SG: What would make for a convivial technology that was somehow linked with the arts?

TM: I think we can learn from our ancestors that it's possible to be a technologist while at the same time being a poet. Emerson writes about this when he says that only the poet knows astronomy.

SG: It sounds as if you're suggesting a model like that of the Renaissance person.

TM: I think that idea of the Renaissance individual as being someone who can do a little bit of everything has been misunderstood to some extent. What it really means, I think, is that this Renaissance person is living in a world where all the arts, and all the activities we do, are convivial with each other. They're distinct, but they have a relationship where one acknowledges and supports the other, and they do not allow any of them to become so dominant that the others go into eclipse.

SG: It seems that we're moving, culturally speaking, into a more interdisciplinary, interdependent, multicultural kind of environment right now.

TM: Well, that's a good move, but I think that this idea has got to be deeper, even, than that.

SG: I think what makes all this relevant to the struggles art is going through at this point is how modernism made art into a highly specialized pursuit, practiced only by trained professionals. As I understand your sense of the soulful life, it would mean bringing art back into a more vernacular, everyday world, and taking it out of the more rarefied sphere of professionalism. You mentioned in the letter you wrote to me that you are very interested in the role of the arts in the world today. Do you see art as being an important vehicle for the return of soul?

TM: Probably its most important vehicle.

SG: Do you want to elaborate on this?

TM: Yes, there's so much to say here. First, though, I'd like to pick up on this point of yours about everyday life. There are a number of ways in which we could bring the artist back into everyday life, so that we don't just have this fringe art world that doesn't really touch on the values of the way we live, essentially. One way would be for the artist truly to feel a sense of—here's that word again—conviviality in the society, in being part of that community, so that there's a responsibility, and a pleasure, in going into the world and being part of, say, actually designing the city. I agree with someone like Ficino from the Renaissance that architecture is probably, from a certain point of view, our most important art, because it creates the space we live in and work in every day. And it is part of ordinary life. We have allowed people who see life as primarily functional to create our buildings, so our buildings are very much like our psychology. Everyone now talks about dysfunctional families, and it's so much like the way we build our buildings: they're either functional or dysfunctional. It's a terrible way to talk about family, I think, and it's an awful way to build buildings. Now, as long as we live in a world where we're building buildings as functions—with a little trim around them—we're going to be talking about dysfunctional families, because there's a direct relationship between our lives and the world we live in, whether it has imagination, whether it's artful, or not. We can't suddenly begin living a more artful life, which is the avenue to soul, if in the public life around us, and in everything we see and inhabit, like this building we're in now, art is invisible.

SG: And so, in your thinking, that could be a whole new paradigm for a socially relevant kind of art—not precisely in the sense that's being talked about in the art world now of "political correctness" and social critique, but rather a kind of art that celebrates and participates robustly in the life-world.

TM: Exactly. And does so with pleasure. Here's another point about soul. A whole tradition about soul is Epicurean, in the West. The philosophers and poets who write about soul, like the Renaissance Neo-Platonists, and like John Keats and Oscar Wilde and Emily Dickinson, people like this recognize that soul enters life through pleasure. It's an erotic activity: psyche and eros going together, rather than principle and responsibility. Responsibility suggests a kind of outward superego coming in and saying, "You know, this is what you should be doing." Again, that is not a new paradigm; we're not moving out of the modernistic world then. We're just feeling we should do something different and more responsible.

SG: "If we are going to care for the soul," you say in the book, "and if we know that the soul is nurtured by beauty, then we will have to understand beauty more deeply and give it a more relevant place in life." It's not only pleasure and conviviality, but also beauty that is necessary for the return of soul. This is something Hillman talks about, too. It's interesting, don't you think, that archetypal psychologists are the ones who seem to be taking the lead for a renaissance of beauty in our lives, even more than artists or aestheticians?

TM: Isn't it true that many artists are not terribly interested in talking about philosophy and psychology?

SG: Do you think they're interested in talking about beauty?

TM: No.

SG: Why do you suppose that's true?

TM: It's possible that some artists, at least, have bought into the modernist philosophy of the time very unconsciously, and in buying into that world, they think that doing their art is a matter of self-expression. I hear that a lot from many artists, though they're not necessarily the most accomplished ones.

SG: The notion of self-expression has certainly been a prominent feature of the world view of individualism, and is a theme I take up a lot in my own work. One of the things that's happening in our culture right now, I believe, is this moving beyond the world view of individualism in many spheres. Art in modern society has had almost no communal dimension. Do your ideas about care of the soul have any relationship with the more interdependent and communal world view that seems to be overtaking our radically individualistic society?

TM: I think my ideas relate to a different kind of individualism, a deeper kind of individualism. There's a paradox at work here. The traditions say that soul is in the community and in nature; but, it's also in the individual and in culture. Soul overlaps in all these areas. You can't really care for the soul totally as an individual. What happens, I think, is that as you care for the soul communally and also in relation to nature, then people are able to touch places in themselves that are less controlled, and have less ego. Whatever we are made of at a deep level is full of mystery that we can never really know, but it comes out then, and a certain individuality is increased in our expression of ourselves. But it's not something that's done consciously, it's not self-conscious individuality, where I am expressing my philosophy and my ideas—

SG: Imposing myself upon the world.

TM: It's not that at all. I think there's an even deeper and sharper individualism that comes through when you get away from that. The insistence on being an individual is a sign—this is Freudian talk—that we don't have it. You don't insist psychologically and emotionally on something if you've really got it in its fullness. You insist when you feel the lack. We insist on individualism and self-expression because we haven't touched deep enough roots of what it is to be an individual. And I suspect that as we get closer to it, we'll discover that it is not as remote from community as we now believe.

sG: Another paradox about all this is how the loss of the communal dimension in our particular culture has actually truncated our sense of individuality, because we have such a distorted experience of the world that comes to us exclusively through the limited ego-self. We know only about separateness; we know so little about interdependence. But returning soul to the world and leaving behind the modern paradigm seem to be linked, wouldn't you say, with a dismantling of patriarchal consciousness and lifting the repression of the feminine? Is this kind of terminology acceptable to you?

TM: It's not a question of whether it's acceptable—I don't use it. I'm not interested in it; I'm very suspicious of it and I don't like it.

sG: You don't feel, then, that the modern world view has been an overweeningly masculine framework?

TM: No, and I don't think we have yet discovered at all what wonderful things patriarchy can be. To blame patriarchy for all these things that are wrong I think is an awful simplification. I could go on and on about this.

SG: Please do.

TM: Well, starting at the bottom line, one of the problems is that there's no way all of that talk about patriarchy won't bleed into talk of men versus women and therefore increase the divisions, and I think that's a sad situation. That's not this new world we're talking about, to have men and women divided, almost to the point where I get the feeling sometimes that we could have another civil war here. It's that bad. The divisiveness of the genders is so difficult at the present moment.

SG: Has the men's movement not been helpful, then, from that point of view?

TM: I can't say that. No, I think that both the men's movement and the women's movement have been important in raising critical questions, but they have not been taken with nearly enough subtlety yet, as far as I can see. I don't think we need those metaphors of masculine and feminine, first of all—they're dualistic, like mind-body. Dichotomies don't work: right brain-left brain doesn't work.

SG: Have you found some other terminology that you like better?

TM: Well, you told me that you thought the language in *Care of the Soul* had more body to it. I'm trying to find language where the words are individual words. I'm not trying to create any system. For instance, I don't use the words conscious and unconscious; I use my own vocabulary.

SG: When I made that comment earlier about your writing, it didn't refer so much to the choice of words, although maybe that's part of it. I was thinking more about the pace, and how the slowness and deliberation and subtlety of the writing cause one's whole being to pause and take a breath, to decelerate. I once heard someone on NPR—it was on the "New Dimensions" program—say that the most important thing any of us can do for the planet right now is to slow our individual lives down. Of course, it's the very opposite of what's really happening. Just look at any of us. Even the people who most understand the need to slow things down, who are the most dedicated to this idea, don't seem able to achieve it. We're all in orbit. Do you feel hopeful that our present culture will succeed at any of this in an intentional kind of way, or are we going to be slammed before anything changes significantly?

TM: Oh, I think we're going to be slammed, we probably need that. There's no indication that we're listening to what's going on. We have an atrocious situation in our cities; our cities are unbelievable. One thing I've learned from traveling a lot is the terrible shape so many American cities are in, because of crime, businesses closing down, people not able to live in neighborhoods anymore.

SG: One of the triggers for these conversations was Michael Ventura's comment, in *We've Had a Hundred Years of Psychotherapy—And the World's Getting Worse,* that Western civilization is over and there's no way to stop the avalanche of its collapse. In that book, the question is posed as to what therapy should be doing in such a time, and I've presumed to pirate the question by asking the same thing about art. Do you share the perception that Western civilization is collapsing?

TM: Well, the question I think you're really asking is what is my fiction? What is my myth of this? You can see this through an apocalyptic myth, but I don't. I agree with people that things are pretty bad, and I do think that there's no place for hope. One of my favorite authors is Samuel Beckett. He was asked by someone once if there wasn't some glimmer of hope in one of his plays, and he said, "No, not the slightest."

SG: What does it mean for you that there's no place for hope?

TM: It means that we have to empty our thoughts about hope so that we can feel the hopelessness, really feel it. We have to allow ourselves, and have the courage, to feel our hopelessness, right to the bottom of it. And I don't think we're doing that: we're trying to find all these defenses against it. I think a lot of what we're doing in our optimism is trying to defend ourselves against the hopelessness.

SG: And to fall back on a belief in all those technological wonders and panaceas that will solve everything eventually. But if we were *not* on the path of denial —if we were truly on the path of experiencing our hopelessness and our despair—do you think this would change the course of things? What might be happening then?

TM: I want to say that my own style is not to speak from a hopeless place. I find myself trying to get out there and inspire people, getting up and saying, "Get out there and do something."

SG: It's the same for me. But is your personal sense of things that there's no hope for us?

TM: I think it works this way, that the deeper you get into the hopelessness, the more genuine your optimism is. These are paradoxes again, and we need to get beyond the opposites here—of hope and despair. And the only way to do that is to really deepen both sides. I have been going everywhere and quoting a line that someone in one of my audiences gave me from Yogi Berra. He said, "When you come to the fork in the road, take it." And that's what I've been trying to do. [Laughter] It's a tough thing to do. And so, when you ask me about hopelessness, I have to realize that, yes, I want to get down that road of hopelessness as far as I can, but I'm not going to give up the path of optimism.

SG: That's incredibly well put, the fork in the road signifying that you can go down two paths at once, simultaneously; and if you do that, at some point, perhaps even parallel lines may actually meet, right?

TM: Yes. You get to a point where, suddenly, you don't even see two paths anymore. You're in something else entirely. The something else is what soul is. This gets back to your first question, how do you bring soul into this culture? It's something else. It's beyond any divisions that we are perceiving at the moment. We don't know what it's like to have a soulful culture, because we're still trying to learn to stand out of the way so that what can be will manifest itself—and it will not be what we think now it could be, because we're thinking still in modernist terms, all of us. That's my huge complaint about this talk of patriarchy.

SG: Do you feel that other cultures, or civilizations, besides our modernist one, were soulful cultures, or not?

TM: No, I don't. I think this is an archetypal struggle that all cultures have to deal with. I also think it's a mistake to ask: how did we get into this mess, and who's responsible? No one's responsible: it's an ultimate issue. We're always trying to make soul; soul-making is a process that is always going on. And I don't think there's any culture that has ever been "soulful" with big capital letters.

SG: In another one of these conversations, Ellen Dissanayake, who is a Darwinist, suggests that we have somehow managed to create a society to which the human species is not adapted. I wonder a lot, myself, about whether the human race is a dysfunctional species and is on a track of destroying itself, not to mention the thousands of other species that we are destroying as well.

TM: See, I don't feel that. I was trained as a theologian, and I think theologically. More and more so every day—it shocks me.

SG: Does your spiritual sense of life keep you from feeling hopeless about the human race?

TM: Not exactly. What I meant was, I'm very conscious of the story of Adam and Eve, and of the Christian doctrine of original sin—meaning that there's something in the very nature of things, not just in human beings, but in the nature of *things,* that makes them not perfect. Life is full of holes and failure and incapacity, and is self-destructive and self-creative.

SG: Living with soul would be to fully acknowledge and embody that understanding.

TM: Yes, and the less literal that is, the more you see that this all makes some kind of sense. If we could own up to our destructiveness, and allow life to be destroyed more than we do, and not be so aimed toward "goodness" and "success" and living life without blemish, I think if we really could look and see these two sides more stereophonically, or whatever, then I think that we would not have a backlash from all this shadow material.

SG: What is your next book, *Soul Mates,* about?

TM: It applies the ideas in *Care of the Soul* to relationships: to marriage, family, friendship, community.

SG: Does it suggest that we need to conduct ourselves in those realms rather differently than we have been?

TM: Yes. This book is primarily about allowing ourselves to imagine relationship to be what it is, rather than trying to have some fantasy that relationships are only valuable if they're good, and work out and don't have pain. I'm trying to give a place to all those things that happen and suggest that relationship is very much like art, like an artist's canvas or an empty staff of notes. It's the field on which we can do our soul work. It's an alchemical vessel, you might say. I think relationship can be imagined as being terribly important and essential to a soulful life. Just the fact of having a family is a tradition that connects you to the past. A family provides some of the eternity the soul needs. Soul can't just live on this personal life, it needs a much bigger context.

SG: Talking about a bigger context, what do you see as the path for artists today who are seeking soul?

TM: One thing I get from Ficino in the Renaissance is that the soul needs a vacation, regularly. Now that can be taken lightly, but it means something much deeper than what we mean by vacation. It means that the soul, in order to thrive, needs to get out of this life, regularly, every day.

SG: You mean, out of humdrum chores and tasks?

TM: Out of the world.

SG: Where does it need to go?

TM: It needs to go somewhere—as long as it's not here. [Laughter] It needs to vacate, that's the first thing. I want to emphasize that, because we immediately want to think about what does it do, when the important thing is that it needs to be vacant. It needs to empty itself out, and go somewhere that's empty. One of the things that art does is to provide that: art arrests our attention. It stops us, so that the world is not going on for a few minutes. But you can see that this would be a problem with propagandistic art, or political art.

SG: What's an example of art that arrests our attention successfully?

TM: A Bach partita.

SG: Does any contemporary art do this?

TM: Oh, yes. Any art that arrests us, and does not lead us back into life with an opinion about it, is inviting us out and is performing a very important service. What it is giving us is an occasion for contemplation. We've lost the capacity, as a culture, for real contemplation. We do not contemplate easily—it feels like we're not accomplishing anything when we contemplate. Now if we don't have contemplation in our lives, we're probably going to be going after it symptomatically—a lot of our spectating is like this.

SG: Like couch-potato TV-watching.

TM: Couch-potato TV-watching is totally symptomatic, it seems to me. It's a real symptom, not that this person needs to get active and get off that couch. That person needs to get deeper into the couch. There's another point about soul and art that's very important to me: soul also thrives on mystery. The French Catholic philosopher Gabriel Marcel distinguished, many years ago, between a problem and a mystery. Today we seem to deal with every issue in our cultural life as a problem, and never take it as a mystery. A problem is there to be solved; mystery is there to be initiated into, or to be entered into fully. But I don't mean mystery in the sense of black hole. An example would be, say, the mystery of Annunciation. That's a positive, specific mystery that I think all of us live. All of us can, in our contemplation, be visited by an angel, an inspirer of some kind, a muse —and this is what that mystery is about. Another mystery from my Catholic background would be the Crucifixion of Jesus—a tremendous mystery that we all live. I think all of us get crucified, and that's a very real way to appreciate that mystery.

SG: Are any contemporary images able to match those?

TM: We have as much of a wealth of those things as people ever did. I believe that these mysteries are always present and show themselves according to the styles of the times.

SG: So it's really a matter of tapping into the collective unconscious and its store of images and then finding a way to bring that forward with new meaning for our time.

TM: I would never use that language, but yes. That's a structural way of looking at what's going on. I would rather say that there's a great profundity of what creates our human life, and what invites us into the various dimensions of our lives—toward pain, or happiness, or love, or death. All these things that we've invited into our lives are beyond us. I don't like to talk about that as the collective unconscious, though; it's too defined.

SG: Would you say that by being beyond us, these things also lure us toward them?

TM: They lure us toward our own fulfillment, and, in a way, toward who we are going to be. That's what I had in mind when I quoted Picasso in *Care of the Soul,* when he says that if he were to connect the dots of all the events of his life, then he would draw a minotaur. It's a very nice image to think about. Our lives are fashioned, not by our intentions, but by responding to these invitations that come from fate, and from other people and events, mysteriously. And I think that what art can do that reason can't do is provide us with images that help us contemplate these mysteries.

The Aesthetics of Everyday Life

BARBARA KIRSHENBLATT-GIMBLETT

When I met Barbara Kirshenblatt-Gimblett for the first time at the "Crossing Cultures" conference in Barcelona, I had no previous knowledge of her or her work, but I knew immediately when I heard her mind-spinning lecture that I wanted a representative taste of her pungent, firebomb intelligence in this book. We finally caught up with each other several months later in New York City, in the Soho apartment where she lives with her artist-husband,

Max Gimblett, surrounded by a quantity of books that would make Susan Sontag's library look positively Lilliputian. Kirshenblatt-Gimblett is a professor in the Performance Studies Department at New York University, where she teaches a course on "The Aesthetics of Everyday Life." In addition to her academic hat, Kirshenblatt-Gimblett describes herself as a "curator of vernacular practices," which, it turns out, includes things like the Easter Parade, conversational narrative, street life, gardens and even food. In fact, shortly after our conversation, Kirshenblatt-Gimblett was headed for Cardiff, Wales, to participate in a three-day international conference exploring the overlaps between performance, food and cooking. The program of events, which she helped to organize, sounded extraordinary: cooking demonstrations; workshops and performances involving food, cooking and eating; scholarly papers; films and illustrated talks; and highly provocative food events, such as a traditional Georgian banquet, in which participants performed theatrical toasts and songs they had been taught at a prior workshop. I had no idea such extravagant things went on in the normally cool-headed academic world, but after studying the brochure, I realized how ignorant I was about the subjects of Chinese noodle-pulling, the making of wedding cakes and the divine role of fasting.

My interest in Kirshenblatt-Gimblett was magnetized

by her philosophical grasp of how suspect Eurocentric as-
sumptions about popular culture and indigenous traditions
are entrenched in the politics of art theory and in museologi-
cal modes of display. There is a subtle marginalizing process
that has deep roots in colonialism and cuts to the heart of the
multicultural debates of today. According to Kirshenblatt-
Gimblett, for instance, objects in museums are examined
and framed by means of "long labels, charts and diagrams,
docents conducting tours, booklets and catalogues, educa-
tional programs, and lectures and performances." Such con-
ventions exert strong cognitive control over the objects
displayed, and in the case of primitive or ethnographic art,
may have little or no connection with the cultural meaning
or intention of the objects themselves, when they are not
being thus transposed and filtered into Western high-art
terms. Western categories and attitudes are regularly im-
posed on non-Western cultures, however, often distorting
their original meaning by decontextualizing the objects and
isolating them for display. Kirshenblatt-Gimblett claims that
under the guise of neutrality, their presentation in a museum
context actually becomes a litmus test that determines
whether or not such objects "hold up" as art, once they have
been stripped of their original context and reclassified within
Western terms and contexts.

Such works are then viewed as "universal," tran-

scending space and time, and their original context is deemed irrelevant. In Gone Primitive: Savage Intellects, Modern Lives, Marianna Torgovnick, a professor of English at Duke University, writes: "Within the dominant narrative as told by art historians, the 'elevation' of primitive objects into art is often implicitly seen as the aesthetic equivalent of decolonization, as bringing Others into the 'mainstream' in a way that ethnographic studies, by their very nature, could not. Yet that 'elevation' in a sense reproduces, in the aesthetic realm, the dynamics of colonialism, since Western standards control the flow of the 'mainstream' and can bestow or withhold the label 'art.'" Indeed, this is exactly what happened in relation to the 1993 Whitney Biennial.

Words like "folk," "ethnic," and "primitive" define a kind of art that, although it may exist in the present, is not necessarily of the present; Kirshenblatt-Gimblett would say such art is "contemporaneous," but it is not contemporary. This way of using time to mark and structure difference is a linchpin of Kirshenblatt-Gimblett's thinking, inspired by the work of Johannes Fabian. We talk a lot about space in relation to art, she claims, but we don't talk about time. Within the Western idea of the "primitive," time stands still and does not lead to a changing future. Whereas the idea of progress provides a distinct arrow of linear time and suggests evolution toward a state of greater complexity, the idea of eternal repetition leads to nondevelopment. Hidden in these distinctions is a concealed devaluing of art that is not progressive in the manner of Western art movements, and is not driven by an avant-garde sensibility. Such art is not "innovative."

"The hegemonic," declares Kirshenblatt-Gimblett, "does not represent itself as ethnic—or as multicultural." It believes it transcends cultural differences and that it is the relatively impregnable center, which has the power to not be defined as multicultural. Viewing itself as if it were a universal culture, the hegemonic never acknowledges how it marginalizes certain cultures and elevates others. Instead, it makes transcendent claims to speak for everyone—even while suggesting itself as distinct from all these Others. Regarding the current debates about decentering this curatorial authority, Kirshenblatt-Gimblett asks quite baldly: Are we ready for it? Are we ready to break out of the art world jails? In Barcelona, she described the challenge as one of "inreach"—not "outreach," in the sense of trying to get art out to "them" or to get "them" into museums—but rather of embracing artmaking that goes on outside the art world. Are we ready to see the audience, or public, or community as artists in their own right? (This was the provocation taken up by artists who participated in Mary Jane Jacob's "Culture in Action" program in Chicago.) Can we learn to come together in the same time? "Community," says Kirshenblatt-Gimblett, in another of her gnomic, challenging and in-a-nutshell pronouncements, "as I understand it, is not audience or public. I think it's a euphemism for the disenfranchised whom the museum does not serve very well."

The following conversation took place on Friday, December 3, 1993.

SUZI GABLIK: When we met at the conference in Barcelona last summer, Barbara, you described yourself to me as a "curator of the vernacular arts." I was very intrigued by that, even though I'm not exactly sure what it means. I know you teach a course at N.Y.U. on "the aesthetics of everyday life" and I'd love to know what that's about. One of the emerging themes of this book has been the notion that the locus for art may be shifting away from galleries and museums and into the life world. Does this relate at all to the work that you do?

BARBARA KIRSHENBLATT-GIMBLETT: I guess I start from the premise that the possibilities for art are something that everybody has—in other words, everybody has something inherently creative and artistic in them. And it's in the nature of social life that there are ways to realize those possibilities; in fact, those possibilities are what make the world a habitable place.

So this spring, for example, I'll teach my "Aesthetics of Everyday Life" course and we'll do a variety of things. One of the questions I ask is, how do people reclaim public space and how do they make it their own in a large city like New York, where so much is controlled by the powers-that-be, by the state, by governmental institutions, by big business? My interest is in the everyday practices that ordinary people engage in on a daily basis to contend with those kinds of organizations, structures and sources of power. For example, I'm interested in gardens—not the Brooklyn Botanic Garden, but gardens that are produced, let's say, by people who don't own any land, who do not live in the suburbs and have a yard or a patch of ground in which something can be grown. And so, what I see here is a form of improvisation that is, for me, a key to survival. Improvisation is really where I would start in thinking about an aesthetics of everyday life.

SG: Are these gardens, then, created for aesthetic reasons, or are they used for survival purposes, as in growing vegetables?

BK·G: I don't make that distinction. What I don't like about the distinction is the notion that to be art, something has to be strictly for beauty. The arts of everyday life are highly utilitarian arts: they give form to value. That, for me, is what an art of everyday life is, something that gives form to value. Let me try to talk about all this in terms of what it is not. It's not about bringing art back into the everyday world, because I don't believe it ever left. And it's not about discovering that what we normally consider as art in museums or galleries also occurs in the everyday world. It's neither of those. It is about the arts of living, by which I mean giving value meaningful form.

SG: When you refer to the arts of living, does this involve daily activities and actions and interactions more than it does objects?

BK-G: It involves everything. It includes domestic interiors, the table, food, language. It also includes the arts of sociability, conversation, etiquette and dress. On a larger scale, it's about gardens, parades, processions, all of which are very much alive in our time. So it's a mistake to think you have to go to rural Spain to find them. All you have to do is walk out on the Lower East Side on Good Friday to see Stations of the Cross processions that are extraordinary. They are performance art *par excellence*. That is where the action is.

SG: You've said that this art is not professional, but that it's not amateur either. In Barcelona, we talked about how this kind of art is contemporaneous with the contemporary—that is, happening at the same time—but that our basically white, Western elitist culture doesn't count any of this as art, because it isn't part of the art world.

BK-G: Correct.

SG: This is probably what we need to talk about: why it isn't considered art by the art world, and how your views on all this differ.

BK-G: Let me say this: I'm not worried about the art world catching it, or recognizing it. That doesn't interest me, because the difference between what I call the arts of living and the art world has to do with differences in their mode of exchange. There's a fundamental paradox in the art world, because the ultimate value of art is seen to lie in its immediate commercial value. Cut it any way you want, the art world is basically a commercial market, where the stakes are extremely high. I don't know of anything in the world of that physical size and weight that can command those kinds of prices, and I take that as a defining feature of the art world.

SG: Do you feel that this compromises the power of art, or does it serve to enhance its power?

BK-G: Oh, in my humble opinion, money has nothing to do with aesthetic power: it is about the market. In my view, aesthetic power has nothing to do with money. So art that is defined by the art world and all its institutions is not personally where my heart is and not where my interests are.

SG: If we take you as a case in point, then, it would seem as if there's no convincing argument to be made that these worlds may now be coming together.

BK-G: Let me pick up again on that notion of the work of artists who are not professionals but are not amateurs either, and of work that is truly "contemporary" and not just contemporaneous, because that's really an important issue. The amateur-professional distinction is, for me, largely an art-world distinction, and I don't want to import art-world categories and art-world values into this realm that I'm calling the vernacular, because I think what that does is prepare the ground for the art world to *absorb* that which is happening in everyday life, and I'm not interested in the art world absorbing it.

SG: You'd prefer to see it stay in its own context.

BK-G: Yes, in its own terms, and making its own way. To give you an example: the people who put on these Stations of the Cross processions: What does it mean to ask whether they're amateurs or professionals? That's not a meaningful distinction. Do you say of people who are pious and who venerate a saint— do you ask if they're amateurs or professionals? It's an irrelevant distinction.

SG: I'd like to talk about this distinction for a bit in relation to the responses that were triggered by the 1993 Whitney Biennial. So much of the criticism that was leveled at the show declared that this was art by amateurs, that it consisted of one-liners rather than masterpieces, and that it lacked aesthetic skill. Somehow I suspect that your take on all this may be very different from the vast body of critical reviews that quite effectively made mincemeat of it all.

BK·G: First of all, I would say that the amateur-professional distinction is a gatekeeping operation. It's a way to keep some people in and some people out: that's what the distinction is about.

SG: But the people who disagree with this and hated the show would say this isn't true. They'd say that we did let these artists in, only to find that they had nothing interesting to offer.

BK·G: Yes, but that's gatekeeping in retrospect—they never should have been let in in the first place. This distinction is upheld in the form of criticism, and the criticism will then govern future actions. So it's gatekeeping any way you want to count it.

SG: The heat of the arguments seem to focus on the politicization of art, and the claim that as soon as you let politics in the door, aesthetics goes out the window. Many people felt this show had little or no aesthetic value. Was that true for you?

BK·G: All these distinctions are meaningless to me. They're meaningless because all art is political. Some art makes political issues an overt subject, but don't tell me that formalism's not political. To suggest that some art is political and some art isn't—

SG: What about the notion that some art is aesthetic and some is not?

BK·G: Also bullshit, if you'll pardon me for saying so.

SG: No, please do. Be my guest.

BK·G: If by aesthetics one means beauty, virtuosity and skill—and when one says that, one is referring to materials and execution, and particularly to practices that are learned within a fine art tradition in an institutional setting with accreditation—that's a very specific definition of what "art" is. But if you take my approach, which has to do with giving value form, that form may or may not be beautiful; it may or may not be virtuosic; it may or may not be an exemplar of craft. But meaningful form and value for me are at the heart of what art is.

SG: So for you, the Whitney show was value-packed?

BK·G: Of course, and form-packed as well. And full of deep commitment. If that's not art, what is?

SG: Why do you suppose it soured people so much?

BK·G: Because I think there are vested interests, and this was a show that was in-your-face. In some ways the show was doomed from the outset because of a peculiar convergence between the artists that were chosen and the kind of work that was shown, which is to say that those who are normally excluded showed work that addressed the conditions of their exclusion. Now, it could have gone a different way. You could have had the same people doing work like what everybody always does, or you could have had the people who are normally here doing work that addresses political issues. Neither of these possibilities would have had the power of the convergence that we saw at the Whitney. But that convergence is essentially a no-win situation, because it's in-your-face, and it gets written off as being nothing more than a slap of a particular kind that says, "You excluded us, and now that we're here, we're going to remind you of all the reasons that you excluded us, and of all the repercussions of having excluded us, and of all the pain that you created by excluding us—and not just artistically, but also socially, economically, historically, culturally, et cetera."

SG: Do you think the artists who did this, and the curators who invited them in, were aware of the intense drama they would generate, or do you think they only realized how threatening it all was after it took off in such a negative and baleful way?

BK·G: I think that the Whitney tried to "do the right thing." I do believe it was utterly sincere. I personally think it was a wonderful show: it was challenging, interesting, troubling. I don't have to like everything I see in order to find it worthwhile. Liking it is not a measure of worth, of value. To be exposed to some artists I had not seen before, to see others in this context, to see these works in relationship to each other, to see a very strong curatorial hand pursuing a set of issues, themes and concerns was, for me, very valuable and very useful. I don't believe that this institution was itself adequately prepared for how to receive what it had produced, because its modes of aesthetic reception are not equipped for this. And so in some ways one could say that the show was ahead of the institution. And I don't know if the institution wants to catch up.

SG: Mary Jane Jacob made an interesting comment. She said that what the show really made clear was that an institutional setting like the Whitney isn't the right venue for this kind of art.

BK-G: Well, yes and no. Because the other side is that these are legitimate artists, serious artists, who deserve to have the "same" success, recognition, income and enduring impact as any other artist working in our society.

SG: How do you get around the neoconservative backlash, and their claim that we've run our culture very advantageously thus far as a meritocracy, and that these artists just don't measure up?

BK-G: To what standard?

SG: To the intellectual and aesthetic standards that are the basis of Western civilization—to the canon.

BK-G: Ah yes, but you see, "quality" is the new racism. It's a code word. "Not good enough" is a code word for the exclusion of parties that used to be excluded on a more candid basis.

SG: You mean that, previously, they weren't even part of the debate. Their work wasn't even discussed or shown.

BK-G: Once you cannot exclude individuals for the reasons that are now laid out—race, gender, sexual preference, physical appearance, age, disability, you name it—once those are no longer mentionable, what have you got left but merit? And that isn't to say that there aren't genuine standards, and that everybody shouldn't meet them. I'm completely for standards. I'm even a fiend for standards. But I'm also extremely aware and very sensitive to the use of a merit argument as a new weapon of exclusion.

SG: So what is the issue around standards, then? Is it that they need to be reconstituted to accommodate a different value structure and a different kind of art that doesn't lend itself to being measured by the existing standards, or what?

BK-G: The incredible thing about the art world—and what has been the European tradition of fine art and aesthetics—is that it has built into itself a survival mechanism. The survival mechanism is the idea of merit. All the language of universality, that art is a universal language, that standards are absolute and not relative, that the standards can be stated and that they can be used as a measuring stick for anyone or anything at any point in any time, that they are inherent, that they are not culturally or historically determined, that great art transcends time and place and outlasts all others, that great works are produced by great artists, the whole concept of masterpieces and the whole profession of connoisseurship, all of that is an architecture to sustain the status quo, in my humble opinion. And what happens is that all the absolutism, the totalism, the essentialism, the universalism—until that position is properly understood, it will continue to exclude and define in the way that it has always done. As long as that assurance, that confidence, in the unassailability of aesthetic values and standards continues, nothing will change.

SG: I've just been reading a collection of essays in *Partisan Review* on "The Politics of Political Correctness" and it seems to be the considered opinion of almost every one of the writers that in this dismantling of the basic principles of the meritocracy and the deconstructive assault on the canon, we have effectively sanctioned the death of Western civilization.

BK·G: Look, the canon is not the Tablets of the Law given by God to Moses on Mount Sinai. That view of the canon, that genius springs up unpredictably and when it springs up, its excellence is unassailable and will endure through the ages—what can I say? The position is doomed.

SG: What about all the great art in museums that everybody goes to see because it seems to fulfill that very notion?

BK-G: Yes, fine. But it's not the only thing that we do; it's not the only thing that we support; it's not the only thing that we're interested in. This discussion arose because of the question as to whether or not the Whitney is the right place for certain art. And the notion that the Whitney is only the right place for the canon, what is that saying? That we're going to have minority art institutions for the rest? That you have to give each constituency its own place to be second-rate? It's a strategy that we know: this is basically apartheid. It's aesthetic apartheid. It's a way to spatialize difference. It's a way of zoning difference and then saying, "You can have it all; just don't put it in the same building. Don't put it in my collection. You're going to sully the water. It doesn't merit. It's not good enough."

SG: It will bring the level of everything else down.

BK-G: Right. And here's what I don't understand. You tell me: after Duchamp's urinal, how can we have this conversation? After Dada, how can we have this conversation?

SG: It sounds to me like you've said the definitive words on that issue. Let's go back to the contemporary-contemporaneous notion. You've said that the difference between the contemporary and the contemporaneous is that the contemporary is avant-garde and progressive, and so that's the art that we're interested in. Then there's all this other stuff, like folk, ethnic, primitive—and now we can add Whitney Biennial—art, which is somehow contemporaneous with the contemporary, but we're less interested in it because it's not really the cutting edge.

BK·G: Correct. The avant-garde is the truly contemporary, "pushing the envelope," as they say in the art world. It's part of the history of the avant-garde to always be in tension with the institutions of the art world. It is inherent in the nature of the avant-garde for it to make an institutional attack. The paradox of the avant-garde is that it needs the institutions, and it hates the institutions. But formalism allowed it to live in relative peace, if not in a perfectly symbiotic relationship with the institutions, whereas the work in the Whitney is all about making the institutions very uncomfortable, and if it can do so in their very belly, all the better. That is both its success—because it is an irritant, it is a slap—and its failure. But it's certainly in that spirit of the avant-garde, which is to be resistant, to be abrasive. And the appropriate response is discomfort.

SG: And yet, it doesn't seem to have been recognized or acknowledged as belonging to that avant-garde

Barbara Kirshenblatt-Gimblett • 427

tradition that we grew up with, which didn't take itself to be radical or serious enough unless it made people uncomfortable.

BK-G: Yes, but you see, modern avant-gardism did all of that increasingly within the history of art itself. And this work is saying no to a kind of hermetic aesthetic sphere.

SG: I recently spoke with somebody who said that when he was told to wear Daniel J. Martinez's admission button ("I can't imagine ever wanting to be white") at the show, he refused to go in. He was unwilling to compromise his white male identity by wearing that message on his lapel.

BK-G: Well, then the button did its job! I would say it was a very successful work because, by and large, most of the art that's out there doesn't provoke a strong reaction. And since when is a strong reaction a sign of failure? But I'd still like to address this other idea of the contemporary, which is where my own work lies, and that has to do with the arts of everyday life —which I believe are *fully* contemporary, and not only contemporaneous. I'm always very wary of another stratagem, which is not unlike the meritocracy argument but uses *time* as a way of saying that some art is in the present moving forward, and other art is in time, holding a position that is basically static —a position of the past. That's another way of insulting, or misrepresenting, these other areas.

SG: In one of your essays you ask, "Is anything really possible now? Are art museums ready to take seriously art which is made outside the art world?" What is your answer to this question?

BK·G: Historically, the art world has taken very seriously art made outside itself—but not the artists. The modernism-primitivism show at the Museum of Modern Art a few years ago was a beautiful case in point. One of the defining features of the avant-garde is its refusal to confine itself to the products of a strictly fine-art world. Its interest in, and use of, aesthetic principles and ideas and sensibilities from other cultures—like Brecht confronting Chinese opera for the first time in Europe or Picasso confronting African sculpture—is a far cry from recognizing, or treating as on a par, or having a genuine relationship with, the artists that produced these works.

SG: But in many cases, the artists would have been long since dead, wouldn't they?

BK·G: But that's for me the unfortunate assumption. A lot of the work I'm talking about is not archaeological, and not only that, it's the dilemma, for example, of the Museum for African Art, when the general public wants to see the old African material. The museum also wants to deal with contemporary African artists. Otherwise, it's like saying these other parts of the world don't have their own indigenous modern art tradition. I think we need to scrap the distinctions and start all over again.

SG: Would you say the more radical versions of multiculturalism are taking us somewhere productive?

BK·G: I do believe that things are changing. I know this best from the academy, which is where I spend most of my time. The academy is not now what it was when I entered the university in the early sixties, and I can assure you it's not what it was in the 1920s, and the difference is finally coming to awareness that major institutional changes have to be made if inclusion is to become a reality. And inclusion cannot carry the price tag that it has carried, historically, which has been to leave *difference* behind. Inclusion, in the past, was not put forward as forcefully and as loudly and as eloquently as it is being put forward today. And it's being put forward by an intelligentsia arising from the ranks of those who have historically been excluded—that's a huge difference. It's absolutely huge.

SG: Rather than being put forward by the dominant culture, or the "oppressors" themselves.

BK·G: Correct. The process is much slower in some places than in others. I think the art world is especially slow to move, partly because it has what I would call a "large installed base," by which I mean so many institutions and so much money sewed up in the status quo. Its investment and capital outlay are so extraordinary that it will be slower to change, I think, than smaller, more nimble, less entrenched sectors.

SG: Would you say that there is a movement toward bringing art back into everyday life more than within modernism?

BK·G: My general feeling is this. I think my experience in the academy is reflective to some degree of what's happening in the art world, so let me start with that. I experience myself on ground in which tectonic plates are shifting, that's how I experience the world in which I live professionally. These tectonic plates are the historical disciplines—history, literature, art history—that are relatively recent disciplines from the late nineteenth century. Particularly in the academy, a hundred years of human history is nothing, it's a spit in the bucket. But because it's the hundred years that has defined our moment, it seems like it's been there forever. My sense is, within this ground of tectonic shifting, that disciplinary lines are blurring. As we become much more aware of the political formation of knowledge, and how it gets institutionalized in departments and programs, it becomes much harder to defend those arrangements. And so I consider my era a kind of postdisciplinary era. It's beyond disciplines—antidisciplinary. I'm not interested in upholding the boundaries of purity and integrity of whatever it might be—literature, history, art history, whatever. Interdisciplinary says the more disciplines the better, but postdisciplinary says, "Forget them." Who needs them? Take a problem and go anywhere you need for the material. So it's a very, very different orientation. I feel the same holds true for assumptions about culture. The university has organized its fields around a notion of culture that is an expression of nationalism. If you look at the organization of departments, they are all organized around the concept of a nation—I mean, what is English literature? Only recently does it include the colonies, and that's Empire. Any way you cut it, these disciplines are historically formed out of political arrangements. But that is now being challenged. And I believe that the kind of work that was in the Whitney, and what it represents, is being played out in the academy as well as in the arts. The fact of the matter is that for most of human history, and in most parts of the world *to this day,* no such disciplinary separations exist.

SG: But if we blur all those boundaries back to what they once were, won't that cause us to lose the integrity of the professional spheres?

BK-G: Once one forms these units, they have a life of their own, and they will perpetuate themselves indefinitely. So that's not my project. Unless something radical happens, the status quo has a fantastic ability to sustain itself. What I'm interested in is destabilizing the assurance that these divisions are the most meaningful ones and that the reasons normally given for sustaining that kind of specialization should go uncontested. For many years I chaired a department of performance studies where I now teach, and it stands for an integrated approach to the arts. It says that we will never succeed in truly coming to grips with artistic traditions outside of Europe as long as we insist on the divisions we've insisted upon. We will continue to have a curriculum structured in terms of "the West and the rest" as long as we have the arts parceled out in the way that we do.

SG: Because the divisions are a function of our particular world view, so the others will never really fit into it.

BK-G: You have to put them in with a shoe horn. In order to be able to fit these forms in, so much of what makes them what they are will be left behind. What I'm saying is that our disciplinary formations are part and parcel of the history of our subjects. That means that the history of the arts in the West is reflected in the departments that have been created to study them. There's a fit between their history and the institutionalization of the study of them. And that fit is so culturally and historically specific that it is extremely difficult to alter so that it can properly address the arts of the world that are not organized that way. Music departments offer a world music course: that takes care of that! A course on non-Western art in Art History: that takes care of that! A course on world literature: do we need more? It's the West and the rest—it's not a solution.

Adrift on the Fickle Seas
of the Art World

LAURIE ZUCKERMAN

L aurie Zuckerman and I first met in the spring of 1992, a short time after she settled in Blacksburg with her husband, Tom Mathies, who had come to Virginia Tech in order to do doctorate research on the reproductive habits of lizards. They had previously lived in Seattle, where Laurie had pursued a painting career and also worked as a graphic designer.

Laurie exemplifies, to me, the sizable number of talented, committed artists who pursue their careers outside the traditional power centers of the art world. Until recently she had always considered her art to be a purely self-centered effort; her need to express her soul and imagination provided her primary creative drive. Now, exposed to the many changes going on in the art world, Laurie has begun to question her identity as an artist.

"Until recently," she states, "I had always floated my dreams and aspirations upon the fickle seas of the art world. Often I was buoyant. But now this stormy art world controversy between public and private goals has sunk my ship. I am no longer cruising through my career. Previously, all I wanted was to be a good artist, a respected artist, maybe even a financially solvent artist. But now, it seems as if I also have to be politically correct, socially conscious and environmentally sensitive. Neither my education as an art student nor my experience as a professional artist has prepared me for these other complications. Like Alice passing through the looking glass, I find myself in an unknown realm. What has happened to just plain making art for the love of the materials, the sheer magic of transforming one's imagination into physical reality?"

Self-expression has been the primary paradigm for achievement and for self-definition for most artists in our culture, but now these presumptions are being challenged by another set of cultural practices that are more socially and less individualistically oriented. "Stuck in a stand-off with the canvas," while the traditional categories of art are collapsing and reforming, Laurie feels a certain affront to her personal ethos of creativity. Encountering some of the ideas in the conversations for this book did not make it easier. She found herself with even more questions and challenges on her mind. The problems she is grappling with are paradigmatic, I believe, of the uncertainty and confusion many artists are undergoing at this time about the meaning and purpose of their art. In this conversation she speaks from the point of view of a threatened traditional artist confronted with new ideas that force her to take a look at the old ones, and whose entire raison d'être at this point is up for grabs. Laurie's self-questioning ranges all the way from "the soul-nourishing advantages of making objects to the relevance and appropriateness of making objects at all in today's environmentally and politically threatened societies." Laurie's need to understand and grapple with these issues impelled her to question me as deeply as I questioned her. Toward the end of the conversation, I try to delve into the matrix of her confusion and to feel out the rough texture of her soul's turbulence.

Our talk took place at Laurie's house in Blacksburg on January 12, 1994, and this final version includes segments distilled from two earlier conversations.

LAURIE ZUCKERMAN: You have described to me the ballistic shock that you experienced when you received that letter from Rachel Dutton and Rob Olds [see Chapter 2]. When you read it to me it was probably an even greater shock to me. I felt completely hopeless, not just about the future of art, but also about the future of the world, because their message was so totally apocalyptic. If that is the force that propelled you to embark on these conversations, are you still feeling as much of that shock?

SUZI GABLIK: I think I'm not in shock anymore because I've been living very close to the rawness of this possibility for some time. A lot of changes are going on in the world these days that I don't remember from the past, in terms of natural disasters, for instance. The chance disruptions of nature have always been there, but there seems to be an intensification of this process, and I'm not sure what it means. But along with some of the people in this book, I feel that nature could be talking to us and—

LZ: Giving us our wake up call?

SG: Yes, and the more we don't listen, the louder she's going to talk.

LZ: When you started these conversations, were you discouraged about the future of art? It seems like when you were writing *The Reenchantment of Art*, you felt as though art and artists could help turn around these apocalyptic events in the world.

SG: At this point, Laurie, I myself am unclear as to what can and cannot be turned around. I do think that living in the reality and the truth of our situation is one small step toward some kind of mastery of it, and is preferable to living in the illusion that everything is fine, on the one hand, or in the total disillusion on the other, that it's all finished and there is nothing we can do. Living in the truth of our situation is related, I believe, to really contacting the grief that one would feel at the loss of this beautiful life that we have here on this planet, or the inability of the human race to sustain itself. Somehow or other that grief has to be experienced fully, devastatingly, before we will actually make the necessary changes.

LZ: I was really surprised by your response to Rachel's letter, when you said that it was hard for you to imagine destroying one's art or giving it away. I had assumed you didn't care that much about art objects —at least that's how I interpreted your last book, in which you seemed to promote doing away with those things.

SG: I don't see the issue in terms of whether there is an art object, or there isn't an art object. What concerns me much more is a kind of blind participation in the norms of an art world that is soul-destroying and abrasive. Most artists whom I know complain about this regularly, and are filled with horror at having to fit themselves into such an oppressive set of routines. Every artist I know struggles with this, but Rachel and Rob were the first artists I know who simply stopped dead in their tracks and said, "We can't do this anymore—something else is happening that is much more important."

LZ: Did it make you feel sad? Did you feel as if they were heralding the death of art—even the more socially interactive kinds of art that you talk about in *The Reenchantment of Art?*

SG: No, my concern was not for the death of art; my concern was for the possible death of our planet— which became even more vivid to me as a result of their actions. It was as if they were saying that you can't stick this concern on the back burner anymore, and simply continue on with business-as-usual. They were taking this apocalyptic reality so deeply into themselves, and were making such drastic changes, that I found it truly alarming.

LZ: So you see them more as leaders than as dropouts?

SG: Well, their moves are so shocking that they do force people to think about things. On the other hand, what they are doing is so far out that many people will simply dismiss them as being the lunatic fringe. Meanwhile, I don't know where they are going with all this now, because I've lost contact with them.

LZ: I think the thing that disturbed me the most was this feeling that art is frivolous, a useless activity in light of what is going on with the world environment. It reflected my sense that what you were saying in your last book was that art in modern times had become frivolous, and that was *definitely* an affront to my mode of living and thinking. I'm wondering if any of that has softened up for you? Do you see any way to incorporate traditional modernism into these new issues such as environmentalism or multiculturalism? Is there a way to have both and bring them together, or must it be a massive shift from one to the other?

SG: I do feel there is a massive paradigm shift happening in our whole culture at the present time, which is not something that any one person, or profession, or ideology, is legislating, but it's affecting all spheres. In this transitional phase, you will have some people still committed to the old ideas and the old ways, other people who are in the process of shifting their ground, and still others who are firmly planted in the new structures and ideas. Exactly how that process of transformation is going to shake down, I can't say. But the process is bigger than any of us. A whole cultural path is changing. Arnold Mindell says it isn't only oneself that needs to change, but that by changing yourself, you are helping the culture to change. And that's how I see it. The people who are making these changes are making them not only for themselves; they're also paving the way for the whole culture to change.

LZ: Has the situation in the art world changed much in these last few years since you wrote *The Reenchantment of Art?*

SG: I think the situation has passed through much more of a transformation than it had when I wrote *The Reenchantment of Art.* It feels like we are more in the thick of it. I'd like to see myself as a kind of midwife to the process—someone who is helping to mediate it. Mindell says that if someone isn't there to facilitate the tensions and changes, it's possible that they won't happen properly, that they will go wrong.

LZ: Or that they may go by unnoticed?

SG: No, that they actually go wrong. They abort. They don't come to fruition. Someone needs to mediate the process in such a way that everyone can understand and relate to what's happening, instead of getting caught in the anxiety of change.

LZ: In your introduction, I noticed you put no emphasis on art functioning as beauty, or contributing beauty to the world. Do you think it is still an important function for art? Does beauty have any relation to the current concerns in the art world?

SG: Personally I love and crave beautiful things, beautiful landscape, beautiful everything, as you well know. But one of the things that needs to shift, I think, is our limited notion of what beauty is. For me, there is great beauty in art that is compassionate and healing—art that reaches out to people who are normally left out of the process.

LZ: So you are talking about more subtle kinds of beauty?

SG: I think that beauty comes in more forms than what is apprehended by the disembodied eye. It doesn't only have to be something that you look at. Beauty can also be something that touches your heart, something that is moving. It may be an experience that comes primarily through vision, but it may also come through something else, like Mierle Ukeles shaking the hands of all those sanitation workers. Touching them was a message from the heart. In making contact with them, she was building a bridge to them. That seems very beautiful to me. But if one is hung up on the idea that beauty can only show up through form or color, or in the way something looks—I guess I don't accept that anymore.

LZ: But you're not pushing that aside, you're not saying that it isn't valid anymore, are you?

SG: No, I think I very much follow the views of people like Thomas Moore and James Hillman—I believe that we need to put beauty back into our world, big time. Everything we are surrounded by should be beautiful, soul-enhancing and deeply nourishing to us. We live in a sterile environment where only artists make "beautiful things," and they are to be found only in galleries and museums. We know now that this is a very distorted kind of environment. As Satish Kumar says, maybe we need to look at the fact that we have created a desert everywhere around us with just these oases—these palaces—of beauty. What about beauty on a daily basis?

LZ: It sounds like you're promoting each individual's—not just the artist's—ability to create beauty in their own lives.

SG: Definitely. Beauty is not a big feature in the rat race. People haven't got time or thought for it, with the result that they live lives bereft of beauty, and that's a great tragedy.

LZ: Do you think that these ideas could help empower every person to feel they have the ability to create beauty for themselves, instead of always looking to the artist to do it for them?

SG: I think the heart of the matter is the value system of this culture, which is based on professionalism. The whole idea of mastery is to do something better than someone else. And to get paid more than someone else, thereby proving that you do it better. These ideas are so invasive, and have so colored our view of what matters in life, that everything else has been thrown out the window. Beauty doesn't happen in our world on any kind of ordinary, day-to-day basis, because of this value system. People are on a tread-mill, and they don't know how to get off. Many of them don't even understand the need to get off. This is the destructive pattern that we're forced to live by.

LZ: So with artists reaching out to non-artist individuals and communities and bringing them into the dialogue of creativity, do you think that more people are going to learn how to be creative themselves and be purveyors of beauty? Is that the goal?

SG: I don't know if it's accurate to equate creativity with being a purveyor of beauty, because that may be too narrow a definition of creativity. But certainly when artists reach out to others, some form of beauty is being created, in my opinion; some form of good karma is being brought to the world. And I don't see anything detrimental in artists using their creativity socially in that way—indeed, I see it as a positive force for good.

LZ: Maybe you misunderstood my question? My idea was of a chain reaction caused by these artists who are working more interactively. First they go out and work with people, and then those people in turn develop their own creative powers and work with more people, so that eventually there are even more artists, because *everyone* now feels their own artistic potential.

SG: Yes, that process would certainly destabilize the professionalization of art according to capitalism. We would no longer have a cadre of specialists who form an elite body, and who are supposedly the only ones who know how to be creative and make money off of it. How do you feel, Laurie, about this vision of everyone becoming an artist and having a more aestheticized environment that we would create for ourselves?

LZ: It couldn't come too soon! I agree with you that we need a lot more aesthetics in our lives. We've lost touch with aesthetics, not only in our art, but particularly in our approach to the natural environment. We can't continue to bastardize it to suit our industrialized needs. We need to emphasize aesthetics in every aspect of our surroundings, not just in terms of preserving the environment, but with regard to our man-made environment, too.

SG: Do you see this as something that artists could be doing, or as something that everybody can do?

LZ: If one makes the assumption that artists have been the only ones trained to perceive, create, and teach aesthetics, then I think that it would be the artist's role to hand those skills down to the rest of the culture. But I'm not sure that the present generations of artists have been trained well in aesthetics. It seems that aesthetics have gone out the window and other concerns have replaced it, concerns such as the environmental and social issues you addressed in *The Reenchantment of Art*. I think that everybody, not just artists, needs to reinvent aesthetics and reinfuse aesthetics in our everyday lives.

SG: Do you have any yearning, yourself, for the art world these days?

LZ: If I thought that everything I produce from now on would be a fabulously beautiful object and would affect people emotionally, then I would keep on creating. But, I'm not so sure of that. Plus, I'm concerned about cluttering up the world with more stuff. Maybe part of my problem is just a lack of confidence in what I have been producing.

SG: Why do you think your confidence has faltered?

LZ: Because I believe the highest purpose that I had in my work was to make something beautiful. I wasn't trying to change the world with it. So the fact that there are people trying to do more socially relevant things with their work stopped me dead in my tracks. I was having a tough time just making a beautiful painting. That was my goal. And I never felt that I ever met that goal completely.

SG: So are you feeling deprived of your old aim to do this?

LZ: Definitely.

SG: Because you think that it's not what people are asking for now?

LZ: Yes, but I think it's still what people need. I would much rather see people be surrounded with beautiful objects than be inundated by hideous ones instead. But it seems as if people who share your slant on the art world don't care about that anymore. And it was the thing I cared about the most—just trying to be good, in the sense of trying to make something that worked so beautifully and had so much power.

SG: But why have the changes in the art world stopped you?

LZ: Because I got hung up on the unidimensionalism of my aim. I was only aiming toward my personal expression of beauty.

SG: You claim that you haven't actually changed your feeling that this is the most important thing; you haven't lost a sense of its value and significance to our culture, much less to yourself. So why wouldn't you continue to pursue it?

LZ: I think I would feel more comfortable if I could pursue a quantitative social or environmental goal along with the goal of making something beautiful. I've had to stop and rethink if I could do something that is aimed more forcefully at an educational goal.

SG: Have you figured anything out?

LZ: I have a lot of ideas, but since my primary environmental concerns are with the depletion of birds, and I have been dealing with bird imagery for years, this is most likely the place that I will start with again. People don't recognize and appreciate the natural resources we have. They think of birds generically rather than as individual species and individual entities which we risk losing if we don't arrest our environmental negligence. Frankly, I'm concerned that both nature and art are in danger of becoming extinct through our careless disregard for beautiful things. We are losing our personal involvement with nature as well as any personal involvement with our surroundings. We let others create our homes, decorate our houses, and tell us what is worthwhile or trendy to own—abandoning our own aesthetic confidence in favor of the mainstream's mundane tastes. Our souls are suffering as these qualities dwindle away. But ultimately, I am more concerned about losing our natural riches. This is even more my mission than saving art is. Nature is far more inspirational to me than art. Nature is irreplaceable. Art could be recreated—at least it didn't take millions of years to evolve each work of art. But Suzi, why do *you* care about the art world? What about it compels you to make it your mission to write about it?

SG: The art world is high drama, Laurie! It's a place where things are happening all the time. And even though I find many of its values problematic, it's still the world I live in. It's the world that I grew up with.

LZ: But you also chose to leave it?

SG: I would not say that I ever left it. A more accurate description of my relationship to the art world involves the paradigm shift that I wrote about in *The Reechantment of Art.* I think we're living in a transitional time, when the values and way of life we've been taught to live by in our culture have to be seen as toxic. That brings up issues of healing, and of transformation. It seems as if there is a spiritual and social obligation to participate in this process of healing our world, however one can.

LZ: So many people in our culture are totally oblivious to the art world—and may not even sense that anything is missing in their lives. What I'm wondering is, if you remove art from the equation altogether, what happens? Because of having done its ivory-tower thing for so long, art has already been removed from the average person's life.

SG: Carol Becker talks about how the modern artist made art in the mode of rebellion and was totally alienated from all but a very specialized, elite group. But in the new, more interactive and collaborative modes that are emerging now, the audience is often integrated into the work and becomes part of the process. This kind of audience has much more invested in the art, and may not be an exclusively art-world audience.

LZ: At some point in your own life, you made a transition from making art to not making art. I'm wondering whether something in your soul was responding to other aspects of your life that needed artistic concern. It seems as if you changed your primary focus from "what shall I paint today?" and put that creative, soulful energy more directly into your life. I mean, you left London, where you were living, and moved to the country; you started a garden for the first time; and when I met you, you said that your garden was like a living canvas that you were "painting" with flowers.

SG: Gardening answers to the part of me that still loves to work with form and color and texture. But I would say that the primary channel for my creativity at this point is writing.

LZ: So why did you give up making art?

SG: It's something that happened organically; painting simply phased itself out. It wasn't a conscious rejection or an ideological stance, but rather the fact that writing began to take me, like a train, somewhere else that I wanted to go. I think one reason I shifted from painting to writing was that I wanted to have a voice in the life of the world, which seemed more available to me through writing. I also experienced myself using the same mental processes when I wrote as I did when I was making my collages. In both situations, it is a matter of gathering together and mobilizing images or ideas from many disparate sources. Then there is the concentrated act of synthesis in how it all gets put together. Synthesis has always been my particular art form. But writing has this additional perk—it's an educational process, to the point where the ideas that I work with will often end up changing my thinking, or even my life. I don't think I could ever have had such an extended conversation with the world through painting. I'd say this book has put me precisely in the place of dialogue that I wish to be.

LZ: In your introduction you wrote about the challenges and attacks to your role as a critic that then caused you to reevaluate your methods and open up the process to include dialogue. Has that changed your definition of your role? Do you still think of yourself as a critic?

SG: I'm not sure I ever saw myself, strictly speaking, as an art critic, because I hardly ever write catalogue essays or art reviews. Now I would have to say that the importance and validity of dialogic practice has pervaded my whole life: it has helped me to understand how important it is not to be rigidly locked into one perspective, or vision, of things. Whatever view we hold to personally, we need to keep in mind that it is only one view among many others, and to include in our sense of things other positions and views. The truth is in the totality of views, it isn't in any one picture of reality. This is not quite the same thing as pluralism, though, which simply posits a multiplicity of coexisting views. What I'm talking about is feeling your way into the whole picture through experiencing the multiple perspectives and positions that everybody holds. I think the meaning of pluralism doesn't include this sense of a totality. What I'm trying to say is that these multiple views actually form a coherent picture, in some sense, if we can encompass them all. They constitute an on-going group process of understanding.

LZ: After all these conversations, would you say you feel any renewed optimism? Are you encouraged that the paradigm shift has become more entrenched?

SG: I very much share Thomas Moore's view about optimism versus pessimism—one needs to go down both paths at the same time, so that one can arrive at some other coherent place as a result. If it is unrealistic to be optimistic at this point, it would also do a disservice to our problems to maintain a paralyzing state of despair, such that one felt totally unable to participate in any kind of reconstruction or revisioning. The only path is the Yogi Berra path of "when you come to the fork in the road, take it." I've been trying to do just that in all spheres of my life.

A Farewell to Modernism

LEO CASTELLI

When I was a young artist growing up in New York City, there was always an eddy of excitement that rippled out from the Leo Castelli Gallery on East Seventy-seventh Street; I remember riding the claustrophobic little elevator up to the fourth floor, which was a regular Saturday afternoon ritual. Usually one encountered friends and fellow artists, and sometimes even Leo Castelli himself, impeccably suited and always ready with a warm smile and a suave *handshake. Anchored to the walls would be comic strip paintings by Roy Lichtenstein, silkscreened cow wallpaper by Andy Warhol, a Jasper Johns flag, or stationed in the middle of the room, a stuffed goat with a rubber tire looped around its waist, by Robert Rauschenberg. For many artists in the 1960s, this modest meeting place became their natural habitat. Not without reason has Leo Castelli been credited with being "largely responsible for the art world, and art market, as we know it today." Long considered the most influential purveyor of contemporary art in the world, Castelli is the only art dealer to have had a coffee-table monograph published about him in his lifetime. As well known as any of his artists, in 1980 he appeared twice on the Dick Cavett Show, and was profiled by Calvin Tomkins for the* New Yorker.

Castelli was born in Trieste, and studied law at the University of Milan before arriving in New York in 1941 as a refugee from Nazi-occupied France, where he had briefly run an art gallery in Paris with René Drouin. By the time he opened his gallery on Seventy-seventh Street in 1957, he was already a strong presence on the scene, familiar to those who frequented the Artists' Club meetings on Eighth Street, and the Cedar Tavern, where the "in" crowd hung out most nights to drink, smoke and debate. I must have seen him there in my many forays downtown, although I can't re-member it.

"In the early days when I showed Johns, Rauschenberg, Twombly, and Stella," says Castelli, "I was totally convinced that I had discovered the most important artists of the day. I do not want to seem arrogant, but I feel that during the first fifteen years of my activity, I hardly missed a major upcoming American artist." In those days, it was the dream of every ambitious artist to become part of Castelli's stable. "I'm very grateful," Johns has said, "that I haven't had to work with any other dealer." Although hugely successful as a dealer, Castelli claims that commercial success has never been his main concern: the artist has always come before the money. And indeed, making large amounts of money developed very slowly, and only really came about twenty years later. William Rubin, formerly the director of painting and sculpture at the Museum of Modern Art, has described Castelli as a "model art dealer," in the tradition of Ambroise Vollard, who was totally devoted to the Impressionist painters he handled.

When Castelli first began to show art in his fourth-floor apartment in 1957, he was nearly fifty years old. When I conversed with him last month in the office of his Soho gallery (which opened in 1971), he was eighty-seven, heartily alert and effervescent as ever. Having been a kind of magistrate, or doge, of the scene for more than thirty years, and its Great Khan for some fifteen of those years, his seemed the most appropriate voice with which to end these dialogues. Given the exhilarating exploration of aesthetic frontiers that had occupied his life for so long, and his great investment in the modern tradition, I was eager to find out how he felt about these unsettled times. What did he think, for instance, about the shift into overtly social and political art that was now disturbing the detached and idealistic image of modern aesthetics to which he had so unabashedly devoted himself? How did he feel about the challenge to his canonical favorites resulting from the wholesale rethinking that was going on? At age eighty-seven, was he watching all these messy and contradictory reassessments from the sidelines, or was he taking an active part in the debates himself? Did he believe—like so many critics of the democratization of culture, which has brought previously excluded groups into the aesthetic citadel—that serious high art was dead? I also found myself wondering, as well, if he had suffered personally from the collapse of the art market during the 1990s.

As Castelli's responses to my various questions show, truly creative individuals have an openness to experience and are willing to put their own beliefs and assumptions into question to a far greater degree than people who respond by dismissing new developments with sneers and ridicule, thereby closing themselves off from new ways of thinking. The destabilizing of existing concepts and assump-

tions demands a greater complexity of outlook, which Castelli promptly evidenced. He took the first step in dealing productively with today's conflicts: he recognized their legitimacy, and acknowledged that they can no longer be evaded or shut out. The sensitivity of his responses make one understand why Rubin described him as "enlightened."

The following conversation was taped at the Leo Castelli Gallery on February 19, 1994.

SUZI GABLIK: A little while ago at lunch, Leo, you told me that you thought the 1993 Whitney Biennial was a turning point, not only in the affairs of the art world, but also personally for you, in your thinking. I'd be very interested—since I didn't allow you to discuss it over lunch—if you'd be willing to share your feelings about all this now.

LEO CASTELLI: The Biennial didn't come as a total surprise. We all knew—at least, some of us knew—that there were lots of younger artists around whom we saw casually at one or another show in the smaller galleries in Soho, and elsewhere. But we didn't pay much attention to them. And then they suddenly appeared, massively—some that we knew and quite a number that we didn't know about at all—at the Whitney a year ago. The first impression that I had was pretty negative: it was a sort of mishmash of all kinds of work done in various media, but predominantly using video. I've never been terribly interested in video, although there probably are some artists who express themselves in an interesting way in that field. Now you'll want to say, "What about Bruce Nauman?", but he handles video in a very different way from most video artists. I think he probably was the first artist who did a work in video, when I first showed him back in '68 or '69. Anyway, I found all the video work pretty boring at the Whitney, and then, generally speaking, the extreme harshness of the content in the various works to be found there was hard to take. Some we only knew a little bit but were uncomfortable with, such as Kiki Smith, for instance, but others, such as the piece by Charles Ray called *The Family,* I found fairly interesting. But then there were all kinds of other works by artists that one hardly knew, or didn't know at all, which maybe had good intentions about describing racial tensions, sexual discontent, et cetera, that had perhaps some merit as far as content was concerned, but most of them had absolutely no aesthetic qualities—which a work of art must, after all, have. It can't just be purely based on some kind of idea that the artist may have about the present times and world.

SG: That literalism is what seems to have colored most people's view of the Whitney show—who thought that it lacked aesthetic merit. But you intimated earlier that even though you started out with a negative response, nevertheless the show was in some way a turning point for you, and it changed your thinking.

LC: Because I had to accept the fact that the wonderful days of the era that I participated in, and in which I had played a substantial role, were over. It was over well before that, actually. Already at the end of the seventies, there was the influx of the German Neo-Expressionists like Baselitz and Penck, Immendorf and Polke, and some of the Italian artists like Chia and Clemente.

SG: But surely they were all still painters—in a heavy-duty way.

LC: But they had a great influence on the scene here. Suddenly the dominance of American art, or New York art, if you wish—largely represented by what I was doing here at the gallery, where movement followed movement—seemed over. All that I had been doing for fifteen years, and they were very much my fifteen years, that I was so proud of because there was nobody who could come close to doing things that were so basic and important— well, to come back to the Whitney show: what was shown there was entirely different from what I'd done. I realized then that I was not there to dictate what should be considered interesting and that all this had changed completely. Of course, I'd had inklings of this before, and I'd tried to participate in some of the changes. For instance, when the Italians came along, I did show some of them, but I never showed any of the Germans. I tried to live with the times, but without conviction. I still had that nostalgia for the past, which started with the Abstract Expressionists.

SG: So did the Whitney experience wipe out that nostalgia once and for all? I mean, what emotions did you feel when you finally realized that life and history had moved on, and they hadn't really asked your permission, so to speak, to do so?

LC: Well, I must say that especially with the Whitney show, I came to exactly that realization. Before that, everything was a bit confused. There were, in addition to the Germans and the Italians, some other phenomena like Jeff Koons and others, all things that I had rejected, up to a point, of course. I felt that what had been there before, during the great era of the sixties, was just unbeatable, and that nothing of that kind could succeed the heroic times that we had had here in New York after the end of the war, which also included the painters I admired: Pollock, de Kooning, Kline, Still, that group. I just felt that that was all gone forever.

SG: How did that make you personally feel?

LC: It made me feel bad, but then after all, I realized that those changes had been very rapid during a brief period of time and that I couldn't expect things to go on in the same way forever. There was a certain sadness that I felt about it, but well, with the Whitney show, I realized that I had to change my attitude, and not be rejecting—as people generally are, as you know. Someone like Kahnweiler, for instance, after Picasso and the Cubists, felt that there was no good art anymore. I would say that there is a span, a relatively short span, in which somebody really lives seriously with a period of art and after that, all those people—whether it be dealers or art historians or museum directors—after that, they don't see what's going on anymore. They reject whatever comes after that. I didn't want to be one of those. I had been sort of spoiled by the fact that so many things occurred in my gallery, one after the other, that were considered of the first importance, and I would have liked to go on that way, but I felt a little bit powerless in front of new developments, although I did participate to some extent, as I said. I showed the American equivalents of the Germans, like Schnabel and Salle, even Robert Longo. And I tried to find some younger artists who would be fresh and interesting, like Mike and Doug Starn. But nothing occurred that was of the magnitude of those various movements that I'd been involved with.

SG: Did the experience of what you saw at the Whitney feel like a real diminishment of art, then, or was it more like an unexpected change in the name of the game?

LC: It was a sea change, not just any change.

SG: How would you define the nature of this sea change?

LC: I would say that there is a clear and evident involvement with social problems of all kinds, and they're not filtered. They're there, brutally.

SG: Are these changes also affecting the institutional structures, like museums and galleries? Are you being affected in your gallery by these changes?

LC: Well, up to a point one *is* affected. Museums, myself, and other galleries that handle important artists are affected, but only up to a point, because certain artists that had been, let's say, neglected have now become more acceptable, as a reaction to the fact that there were new things that were considered unacceptable. So there have been some advantages to all that. But the collecting public these days is very, very small, and what I keep saying is that there are hardly any collectors left. Those who are considered to be serious collectors, like the Tremaines and the Sculls, or Count Panza or Dr. Ludwig, hardly any of those are left. They have become dealers themselves.

SG: Or small institutions with their own museums.

LC: And then, Charles Saatchi, who was a tremendous, voracious buyer of things, just buys and sells thousands of pieces at the same time; then he drops an artist that he was involved with, like Chia, completely. So the market is flooded by Chias and it ruins his reputation completely.

SG: You've said somewhere that your policy was to have works by all the key artists of any new movement that appeared on the scene.

LC: I did have them, practically all, except of the Minimalist movement—Carl Andre and Sol LeWitt.

SG: So if your role has been to ferret out, as far as possible, the key artists in each new phase of art, how do you feel about that role now, in this new situation? Would you still wish to play that kind of role in relation to the present scene, or not?

LC: Well, I couldn't play that role anymore, because the key players are no longer so evident. I could have devoted myself—as Ileana [Sonnabend] did for a period of time—to the German artists, but I had no feeling for them, and I felt, quite frankly, that they didn't contribute anything that was as new as those artists that I had been dealing with. It was just a rehash of things that we knew about. You see, my basic involvement was with Duchamp, and whatever related to Duchamp was of interest to me. There, at the Whitney—

SG: Would you say that Duchamp was dead?

LC: I'd say that in the case of certain artists, Duchamp was still there. I think that whatever strays from the basic idea of Duchamp is not something that's interesting historically. Anything that relates to Duchamp is of interest and is in the mainstream, for me, of art history. In the Germans, I didn't find any connection with Duchamp, except perhaps for Joseph Beuys, who, you could say, was a pupil of Duchamp, too. But he was not as original as it was pretended here and in Europe. They made a great hero out of him in Europe, especially in Germany. But I would say that Johns and Rauschenberg were infinitely more interesting than Beuys at any time. Maybe that's being, well, overpatriotic.

sg: You've said recently, "I see a lot of things and they are all fascinating and searching, but there is nothing that I would say seems to me groundbreaking." Is that something you still feel? Because you've said that the Whitney show was groundbreaking in a sense.

lc: What we have there is a very important figure: Bruce Nauman. Everybody seems to agree that he was the greatest influence on what's interesting in the new generation. And the younger generation acknowledges its debt to Nauman. So for me, Nauman was really the last groundbreaking artist.

sg: Does it seem to you as if there are underlying social reasons for this absence of groundbreaking art at this time of the kind that was around when you were doing your most important work?

lc: Social reasons are always there, lurking under the surface, but I would say they seemed to be less important in my time, during the sixties, although the times themselves were very troubled with the Vietnam war and the student rebellions. So one would say that at that time there should have been quite a bit of social thinking underlying the work of the artists. Now, was there? I don't think so. In the case of Jasper, it's quite evident that he lives in an ivory tower. Perhaps the outside world is always present in Rauschenberg's art, but I don't think it's there in a consciously political way. Twombly, obviously, is pure, personal sensibility. Of course, if you take the Pop artists, it's a bit different in their case; they deal with the social phenomenon of the consumer society, but I think they probably were not very conscious of the fact that that's what they were doing.

SG: As a dealer, how do you feel about the changes that are taking art away from being a totally individualized expression and toward something that is more social, communal and enacted in spheres that are outside the art world?

LC: Can we break that question down a bit?

SG: Because you run a gallery, Leo, you are pretty dependent on an object-oriented form of artmaking. There is a lot of art being made today—I'm thinking of the community-based projects from Mary Jane Jacob's "Culture in Action" program in Chicago— that bypasses the gallery structure by its very nature. There's just a direct interaction within a community.

LC: I think this means that the times for dealers who are mainly interested in dealing with art as business— well, it's a difficult time for them. The dealers who are really successful are the ones who are involved in the secondary market—those who buy and sell works by the artists who are considered important —and who have little to do with presenting art because it's interesting, or groundbreaking. I'm in the category, myself, of having always dealt with art because of its groundbreaking importance, and the devil take the hindmost as far as the selling of that art is concerned. I went on showing people like, say, Flavin or Judd, who for a long time were totally unsuccessful, and whom I had to support, because I thought they were important. Some became successful, but others didn't. Judd died recently, but he had become very successful and went from gallery to gallery—he didn't behave very well in that sense. But I no longer had any connection with him. I had shown him, taken care of him, for nineteen years, and then one day, for simple financial reasons— because I couldn't come up with enough money for his extravagant desires—he left just like that, brutally, as he then left Paula Cooper to go to Pace, who is evidently more affluent and can afford to pay more money.

SG: Have you had many experiences of artists leaving like that?

LC: Well, it's sort of more complex than you think. One accuses the dealers like Pace or Gagosian, or others, of taking artists away from other galleries and of doing it from the profit motive, but the fact is that the artist, at one point or another, feels the gallery he's working with doesn't have enough fresh clients any longer, or doesn't do enough of that commercial work that I don't do. I mean, I just give my shows, and try to make everybody aware that they are there, through publications and so on, but then if people don't come—well, it's too bad. I can't really be on the phone all the time to find clients. Sometimes I feel very frustrated about it, but it's not in my nature to be somebody who runs after people.

SG: Leo, having run a very successful gallery for so long, and having had so many major artists under your wing all these years, would you say that there is a subtle way in which the reputation of the gallery contributes to the enormous success of those artists?

LC: The gallery does create the artist to a certain extent, but there is a close collaboration, I would say, between artist and gallery. The gallery obviously has to make the artist know that the most important thing that the gallery can do is to organize shows.

SG: But if an unknown artist is given an exhibition in a not well-known gallery, his or her destiny as an artist is likely to unfold quite differently than if he or she is given a show in your gallery, wouldn't you say?

LC: The gallery certainly plays an important role. But then there is a strange consensus that also occurs.

Let's say that I show Jasper for the first time when he is totally unknown, but immediately there are two or three other people who catch on, critics like Bob Rosenblum, or collectors like the Tremaines. So whether they're at my gallery or at an unknown little gallery, they will develop. They will develop better, of course, in a gallery that takes good care of them. But the gallery only takes the initial step—then immediately a consensus develops around any artist who is really important. That's been my experience with all the artists that I had.

SG: You've also said that "the simplicity and the loyalty of earlier times is gone." Does it seem to you that the world itself has undergone dramatic changes in your lifetime?

LC: The world is certainly undergoing dramatic changes, and probably has been doing that all along, but it's at a much faster clip now, and since the means of communication are so rapid these days, the changes are infinitely more visible right away.

SG: Do you feel any anxiety about these changes?

LC: No, I don't have any special anxieties. There are lots of people who foresee total disasters, and probably we are heading toward immensely more important changes than have occurred, let's say, during the past century. Now we are beginning to realize, perhaps, that all these inventions, the wars, and the political and geographical changes are coming to a head. All this has been brewing for many, many decades, and it's becoming more evident that all these changes will have results that we can hardly foresee. For instance, America will be an entirely different country in ten, twenty, thirty years from now with all these multicultures that we have.

SG: Suppose that you were starting your life's work now, instead of when you did; what do you think would happen? How would you proceed in today's world?

LC: It seems to me now that I was very naive. Everything seemed to be natural to me: there was no doubt that the artists I had chosen were the best. There was just no question about it. But I was naive because I didn't see that there were fantastic undercurrents threatening this sort of earthly paradise in which I was living. It was quite fantastic how confident I was about myself, about people who were my friends in museums, and so on—it seemed to be a perfect world. The age of the sixties, in spite of all the troubles we had, seemed to me just a wonderful world. We were doing the right thing, and people recognized that we were doing the right thing.

SG: And now that wonderful world is gone.

LC: The confidence is gone.

SG: Do you think humility has replaced the confidence? Or something else?

LC: Not humility, I would say. The useful arrogance of those years is gone. But I wouldn't say it's humility; it's being more realistic about the complexities of the present world than I used to be, than we all used to be. I think I share this with many people.

SG: I guess my question was whether you would even want to undertake the work you did, if this was the world you had to do it in.

LC: I undertook the work because it seemed to be there, lying in front of me, and it had to be done. There was no choice. Today, of course, I would be more historically minded. I would probably do the same thing, but perhaps eliminating the present and the future, as many people do, and I would reexamine the past. But it would be difficult to say what I would do because that whole venture started with great enthusiasm and, I would say, great naiveté. I just admired certain artists enormously; for me they were real heroes and I was full of admiration for them.

SG: Is it your sense that there aren't heroes like that now, that people aren't functioning in this heroic mode anymore in relation to art?

LC: I just feel that they don't, yes.

SG: Do you think it's because some former level of genius is failing to show up, or is something else going on?

LC: That level of genius—well, it doesn't seem to show up now. What shows up is enormous ambition, but perhaps not enough thinking or feeling, as we found in those artists of my era. It's become infinitely more mundane, and money has become the measure-all, which it wasn't in the early days. Money plays a role now that it didn't do before.

SG: Would you say that the careerist orientation of today plays a part in all this, too, by turning the life of the artist into a series of predetermined steps to be followed?

LC: Very important here, I think, is that the artists—and myself—have discovered the media world. The media do play an enormous role. Artists have become very media-conscious; they want to be, and some of them have become, celebrities. That includes me, which is something that I didn't even think of in the early days.

SG: What's the nicest thing about being a celebrity?

LC: It's satisfying. I wouldn't deny it. And I think somebody who's been chiefly responsible for that attitude has been our good friend Andy Warhol.

SG: So you feel you've had your fifteen minutes of fame in this lifetime!

LC: Well, it's been a long fifteen minutes. [Laughter] But certainly Andy played a tremendous role in making artists into stars. Although his art is good—he was a real artist. I don't say it was just pure pretense.

SG: Is there any connection, do you think, between this careerist world of art celebrities and what went on at the Whitney?

LC: I think that those people there—and that's again something that's very laudable—were very sincere. They didn't want to make a career, they wanted to make a point about social conditions. In that sense, it's a return to honesty. But there is also that sense that a new era has begun, and if we want to find a turning point—which is, of course, something that's a bit artificial—the Whitney show certainly was one. It made us conscious that not only the world around us has changed, but the attitudes of the artists about the world have changed. There was still that ivory-tower feeling that started with the Abstract Expressionists—God knows, they didn't really expect ever to be successful at all. But then, that went on, and strangely enough, the Pop artists were quite realistic about what they were doing—even Andy Warhol. But after that, the decadence set in. And now we are, I think, out of it, and art is struggling again to do something meaningful.

Selected Bibliography

BOOKS BY CONTRIBUTORS

Becker, Carol. *The Invisible Drama: Women and the Anxiety of Change.* New York: Macmillan, 1987.

———, ed. *The Subversive Imagination: Artists, Society, and Social Responsibility.* New York: Routledge, 1994.

Danto, Arthur C. *Beyond the Brillo Box: The Visual Arts in Post-Historical Perspectives.* New York: Farrar, Straus and Giroux, 1992.

———. *Embodied Meanings: Critical Essays and Aesthetic Meditations.* New York: Farrar, Straus and Giroux, 1994.

————. *Encounters and Reflections: Art in the Historical Present.* New York: Farrar, Straus and Giroux, 1991.

————. *The Philosophical Disenfranchisement of Art.* New York: Columbia University Press, 1988.

Dissanayake, Ellen. *Homo Aestheticus: Where Art Comes From and Why.* New York: The Free Press, 1992.

————. *What Is Art For?* Seattle: University of Washington Press, 1988.

Gablik, Suzi. *The Reenchantment of Art.* New York: Thames and Hudson, 1991.

Hillman, James. *Archetypal Psychology: A Brief Account.* Dallas: Spring Publications, 1983.

————. *A Blue Fire: Selected Writings.* Ed. by Thomas Moore. New York: Harper Perennial Books, 1991.

————. *The Thought of the Heart and the Soul of the World.* Dallas: Spring Publications, 1992.

———— and Michael Ventura. *We've Had a Hundred Years of Psychotherapy—And the World's Getting Worse.* San Francisco: HarperCollins, 1992.

Kramer, Hilton. *Abstract Art: A Cultural History.* New York: The Free Press, 1994.

————, ed. *The New Criterion Reader: The First Five Years.* New York: The Free Press, 1988.

————. *The Revenge of the Philistines: Art and Culture 1972–1984.* New York: The Free Press, 1985.

Kumar, Satish. *No Destination: An Autobiography.* Pant Mawr, Wales: Black Pig Press, 1978. Rev. ed., Totnes: Greenbooks, 1992.

Manes, Christopher. *Green Rage: Radical Environmentalism and the Unmaking of Civilization.* Boston: Little Brown, 1990.

Merchant, Carolyn. *The Death of Nature.* San Francisco: Harper, 1990.

———. *Ecological Revolutions: Nature, Gender, and Science in New England.* Chapel Hill: University of North Carolina Press, 1989.

———. *Radical Ecology: The Search for a Livable World.* New York: Routledge, 1992.

Moore, Thomas. *Care of the Soul: A Guide for Cultivating Depth and Sacredness in Everyday Life.* New York: HarperCollins, 1992.

———. *Dark Eros: The Imagination of Sadism.* Dallas: Spring Publications, 1990.

———. *Soul Mates: Honoring the Mysteries of Love and Relationship.* New York: HarperCollins, 1994.

Plante, David. *The Accident.* New York: Ticknor & Fields, 1991.

———. *Annunciation.* New York: Ticknor & Fields, 1994.

———. *The Francoeur Novels: The Family, The Woods, The Country.* New York: E. P. Dutton, 1983.

Roszak, Theodore. *The Cult of Information: The Folklore of Computers and the True Art of Thinking.* New York: Pantheon, 1986.

———. *Person/Planet: The Creative Disintegration of Industrial Society.* Garden City: Doubleday Anchor, 1979.

———. *The Voice of the Earth.* New York: Simon & Schuster, 1992.

———. *Where the Wasteland Ends: Politics and Transcendence in Post-Industrial Society.* Garden City: Doubleday Anchor, 1973.

Shusterman, Richard. *Analytic Aesthetics.* Cambridge: Blackwell, 1992.

———. *Pragmatist Aesthetics: Living Beauty, Rethinking Art.* Cambridge: Blackwell, 1992.

Andrews, Valerie, Robert Bosnak and Karen Walter Goodwin. *Facing Apocalypse*. Dallas: Spring Publications, 1987.

Aufderheide, Patricia. *Beyond PC: Toward a Politics of Understanding*. St. Paul: Graywolf, 1992.

Bishop, Peter. *The Greening of Psychology: The Vegetable World in Myth, Dream, and Healing*. Dallas: Spring Publications, 1990.

Bohm, David. *On Dialogue*. Ojai: David Bohm Seminars, 1990.

Brown, Tom, Jr. *The Vision*. New York: Berkeley Books, 1988.

Felshin, Nina, ed. *But Is It Art? The Spirit of Art as Activism*. Seattle: Bay Press, 1995.

Gates, Henry Louis, Jr. *Loose Canons: Notes on the Culture Wars*. New York: Oxford University Press, 1992.

Graeff, Gerald. *Beyond the Culture Wars: How Teaching the Conflicts Can Revitalize American Education*. New York: W. W. Norton, 1992.

Hughes, Robert. *Culture of Complaint: The Fraying of America*. New York: Oxford University Press, 1993.

Hunter, James Davison. *The Struggle to Define America*. New York: Basic Books, 1991.

Lacy, Suzanne, ed. *Mapping the Terrain: New Genre Public Art*. Seattle: Bay Press, 1995.

Levin, David Michael, ed. *Modernity and the Hegemony of Vision*. Berkeley: University of California Press, 1993.

Mindell, Arnold. *The Leader as Martial Artist: Techniques and Strategies for Resolving Conflict and Creating Community*. San Francisco: HarperCollins, 1992.

Morrison, Toni. *Playing in the Dark: Whiteness and the Literary Imagination.* New York: Random House/Vintage, 1993.

Partisan Review. Special Issue, "The Politics of Political Correctness." Fall 1993 (no. 4).

Slater, Philip. *A Dream Deferred: America's Discontent and the Search for a New Democratic Ideal.* Boston: Beacon Press, 1991.

Snyder, Gary. *The Real Work: Interviews and Talks 1964–1979.* New York: New Directions, 1993.

1993 Biennial Exhibition. Catalogue. New York: Whitney Museum of American Art and Harry N. Abrams, 1993.